Band on the Run

Band on the Run

A History of
Paul McCartney and Wings

Garry McGee

TAYLOR TRADE PUBLISHING
Lanham • New York • Oxford

First Taylor Trade Publishing edition 2003

This Taylor Trade Publishing softcover edition of *Band on the Run* is an original publication. It is published by arrangement with the author.

Advertisements: courtesy the McMarr collection
Photographs: courtesy PJ! Archives
Sheet music: courtesy Marald/Geran
Records and collectibles: courtesy the GCMII collection; LJM ltd.

Every effort has been made to trace the ownership of all copyrighted material and to secure permission from copyright holders. In the event of any questions arising as to the use of any material, we will be pleased to make necessary corrections in future pressings.

Published by Taylor Trade Publishing
An Imprint of Rowman & Littlefield Publishing Group
200 Park Avenue South, Suite 1109
New York, New York 10003

Distributed by National Book Network

Library of Congress Cataloging-in-Publication Data

McGee, Garry, 1966–
    Band on the run : a history of Paul McCartney and Wings / Garry
McGee.—1st Taylor Trade Pub. ed.
      p. cm.
    Includes bibliographical references and index.
    Discography: p.
    ISBN 0-87833-304-5 (pbk. : alk. paper)
    1. McCartney, Paul. 2. Rock musicians—England—Biography. 3. Wings
(Musical group) I. Title.
ML410.M115 M3   2003
782.42166'092'2—dc21   2002151274

∞ ™ The paper used in this publication meets the minimum requirements of American National Standard for Information Sciences—Permanence of Paper for Printed Library Materials, ANSI/NISO Z39.48–1992. Manufactured in the United States of America.

Contents

Acknowledgments

A book is the work of not one person, but many people: Henry McCullough for sharing his recollections of Wings; Michael Dorr, Ross Plotkin, and the staff at Taylor Trade Publishing for their work and efforts in publishing this book; Nigel Martyn for his connections; Jean Larson, Kathy Martin, Joan Kufrin, and Rosemarie Larson for their suggestions, research, and comments to persevere. A special thank you goes to my parents, family, and friends for their much help and confidence while I was writing this book; and to everyone else who either supported me or the work, I thank all of you. And, of course, thank you to all the members of Wings for the music . . .

"I think, looking at (Wings) overall, I don't regret it and I don't think it was that much of a mess. My feeling all the time was 'hanging in there' rather than 'doing very well.' But look at it—there's 'Mull of Kintyre,' the biggest record ever in Britain since the gramophone. So that's not bad if you're looking for that kind of thing. Then there's stuff like 'Junior's Farm' and then sorta stuff like 'My Love.' When I break it down like that, I really don't think it was a mess. But in my mind I was going through a bit of a mess."

—PAUL McCARTNEY, 2001

Prologue

On April 9, 1970, Paul McCartney announced that he was leaving the most successful musical group of the rock and roll era. In the previous six years, the Beatles—Paul McCartney, John Lennon, George Harrison, and Ringo Starr—helped change the face of popular music and were an undeniable force in the turbulent 1960s. But now the end had come, and Mr. McCartney was declaring his independence. The Beatles had grown up—and apart.

Fans were shocked and angered. Many blamed the Beatles' wives for the breakup. Lennon had married Yoko Ono on March 20, 1969; eight days earlier, McCartney had wed Linda Eastman. (Harrison had married a few years earlier, as had Starr.) Both Linda and Yoko came from wealthy families and were strong, independent women. Both were divorcees and mothers before entering the Beatles' circle. Fans believed that Linda and Yoko had swayed their respective husbands away from each other, urging them to branch out on their own as solo artists.

At the time, the public did not entirely understand the tremendous personal pressures and legal hassles the Beatles had been involved in, primarily with their company, Apple. The group was not seeing nearly the amount of money they were earning, as much of it was tied up with the company. Apple was also in mismanagement, with petty thefts and inadequate bookkeeping that furthered the existing problems among the band.

In addition, the Beatles' longtime manager, Brian Epstein, had died of an accidental drug overdose in 1967. The group decided to manage themselves and had formed Apple in 1968. Almost immediately, it became all too clear that they still needed a manager. In early 1969, Lennon, Harrison, and Starr wanted to sign Allen Klein to represent the group. Klein had represented the Rolling Stones, Herman's Hermits, and the Dave Clark Five. At first, Paul agreed to this; however, after looking into Klein's background and questionable business practices, he changed his mind. Linda suggested her father and brother's business, Eastman and Eastman, to sort out the Beatles' financial difficulties. Paul contacted Lee Eastman, and the firm became Apple's legal advisors and acting managers on February 4, 1969. But the firm headed Apple for only a month. The other three Beatles still wanted Allen Klein, and they, without Paul, signed with him. The trio, however, agreed to keep Eastman and Eastman on as legal advisors.

Rolling Stone called Klein the embodiment of "much that's wrong with old-style American business." So great was the magazine's dislike of the Beatles' association with Klein, it printed an editorial about the announcement. "We have come to expect innovation, new perspectives, and honesty—especially honesty—from the Beatles and especially John, and this is what made (Klein's) signing so shocking."

Paul absolutely did not want any involvement with Allen Klein. His only recourse was to remove himself from the group. Under the advice of the Eastmans, Paul sued the other Beatles in order to clear his ties to Apple and Klein. This act allowed Paul to be a free agent and choose his own manager and enabled him to have better control of his earnings and where the money was being spent, and finally allowed him to gain artistic control of his work. John Lennon had threatened to quit the Beatles several times, George had contemplated moving on, and Ringo had once left the group for a week before returning. But in the end, it was Paul who made it official.

But his doing so meant the end of the Beatles as a group, and for a while as personal friends as well. No one knew at the time, however, that the lawsuit would also mean a loss of reputation for Paul, whose solo work at times rivaled and even surpassed his success with the Beatles. Fans eventually accepted Paul and his music in the 1970s, but the press was harsher and less forgiving.

The lawsuit also meant a decade's worth of legal entanglements with Allen Klein and almost twenty years of additional record company and royalty litigation before everything was finally sorted out. And out of the ashes of the most successful band of the 1960s arose one of the most successful bands of the 1970s. It was a group that accomplished almost as much as the Beatles had, from gold records and Grammy Awards to sold-out concerts and successes on the music charts.

Wings won a legion of new fans, including some who never knew its leader had been in another group.

1

Children, Children

James Paul McCartney was born in Liverpool, England on 18 June 1942, the first son of James (Jim) and Mary McCartney. Paul was born at Walton Hospital, where Mary had worked as midwife. He was delivered in a state of white asphyxia (a lack of oxygen) and had to be resuscitated.

Music filled the McCartney household, as Jim was an accomplished musician, having been a trumpet player. Jim also had a musical group called Jim Mac's Band that played several musical styles, including ragtime. Young Paul began trumpet lessons and then piano. He also sang with the St. Chad's church choir. Paul decided, however, that he really wanted to play guitar. His father purchased one for fifteen pounds.

In October 1956, Mary suddenly died of cancer. Paul, his father, and his younger brother were struck not only with an emotional loss, but an economic one as well, as Mary's income as a nurse had been the family's main source of money. While Jim took additional work to support his sons, the boys were left much on their own.

In 1957, Paul had met John Lennon when Lennon's band, the Quarrymen, played at the Woolton Parish Church Youth Club. The two had quickly become friends, and Lennon, two years older than Paul, asked him to join the band. Paul did, and he also eventually asked George Harrison, a younger guitarist, to join. Slowly, the group emerged not only as a talented band, but also as a popular band. By 1962, they evolved into the Beatles and secured a recording contract. With drummer Ringo Starr, the quartet conquered the music world by 1964 and eventually changed the face of popular music.

Paul wrote several songs with and without John Lennon, but both made a pact that their songs would be credited as Lennon–McCartney. Among the many Beatles songs Paul wrote without Lennon's help were "Hey Jude," "Let It Be," "Birthday," "Penny Lane," "Lady Madonna," "The Long and Winding Road," "Get Back," "Helter Skelter," and "Yesterday."

Linda Eastman was born 24 September 1941 into a successful and powerful family of attorneys. The second of four children, Linda grew up in Scarsdale, a posh suburb in New York's Westchester County. Linda's father, Lee Eastman, was Harvard-educated and a well-known entertainment lawyer. Linda's mother, Louise, was a department store heiress. After she graduated from Scarsdale High School, Linda attended the University of Arizona. When Linda was nineteen, her mother died in a plane crash. In 1962 Linda married Joseph Melvin See, a geologist who had gone to Princeton. "He was sort of a Hemingway fellow," she recalled. The couple had a daughter, Heather, but the marriage did not last. After their breakup three years later, Linda went back to Tucson with Heather. "I loved it," Linda said. "I was living again."

Through the encouragement of friend Nina Hill, Linda decided to take a course in photography. "It was a night course, a history of photography sort of course, about the artists' lives," Linda recalled. "But each student would take pictures and then we'd critique them in class."

Shortly after, Linda moved to New York City and landed a job as a receptionist at *Town & Country* magazine. When she came across an invitation to a press party for the Rolling Stones in 1966, Linda seized the moment and attended. The band saw Linda there and selected her to photograph them. When she got the pictures back from the lab, Linda realized they were special, and thus began her career in photography.

"She was a real rock and roller," recalls Danny Fields, a freelance music writer who became friends with Linda. Fields recalls Linda

THE BEATLES

APPLE RECORDS, INC.
ABKCO INDUSTRIES, INC.
1700 BROADWAY
NEW YORK, N.Y. 10017

APPLE CORPS., LTD.
3 SAVILLE ROW
LONDON W.1
ENGLAND

George, Paul, John, and Ringo circa 1969. The end of the Beatles and the end of an era.

photographing the royalty of rock, including Jimi Hendrix, Janis Joplin, and Jim Morrison. She also shot the 1968 Eric Clapton cover for *Rolling Stone*, and several of her other photographs were published by the magazine. "And with all that going on," Fields says, "she maintained a household suitable to raise a child."

Linda's first recollection of meeting Paul McCartney was in 1966, when the Beatles performed at Shea Stadium in New York. It was John Lennon who first caught Linda's eye, but her interest later transferred to the unmarried Paul McCartney.

Linda met Paul again, quite by accident, at the Bag O' Nails bar in 1967 when she was in London. Each was with a group of friends when their eyes met; Paul walked over to Linda and introduced himself. Their paths crossed yet again two days later at a press conference for the Beatles' *Sgt. Pepper's Lonely Hearts Club Band* album, when Linda was there to photograph the group. Paul was instantly attracted to the strawberry blonde. "A lot of the girls I had met were just girls," he later told *Vanity Fair*; "(Linda) was a real woman."

Linda slipped Paul her telephone number, and when he and John Lennon arrived in New York to announce the formation of Apple in May 1968, Paul stayed with Linda. Meanwhile, Paul had been engaged to actress Jane Asher. The wedding plans were called off after she discovered he had been unfaithful to her.

Later in the year, Linda returned to England. By the end of 1968, Linda was pregnant with Paul's child. He proposed marriage, but Linda turned him down. "I wanted to be me and not have men tell me what I should be," Linda later said. It took Paul several weeks, but he convinced Linda to marry him. The couple married at London's Marylebone Register Office on 12 March 1969. The weather was rainy, but hundreds of news reporters and weeping female Beatle fans crowded the building to witness the newlyweds.

The couple, along with Linda's daughter Heather (whom Paul later adopted), retreated to Paul's Scottish farm, where they lived a reclusive existence away from the legal and emotional problems of the Beatles. The couple stayed out of the spotlight for such a long period that a rumor of Paul's death began circulating. Physically, Paul McCartney was very much alive. Emotionally, however, he was a broken man.

Daughter Mary's birth in August did not completely heal Paul. He was torn apart over the breakup of the Beatles and the financial mess and litigation that loomed as a result. Linda continually encouraged Paul, telling him all would be well, but it took many months before he was able to return to being the man he once was.

To bide his time, Paul began work on a solo album he simply called *McCartney*, on which he played all of the instruments and sang all of the lyrics. (Linda provided backing vocals when required.) All of the other Beatles had previously recorded solo projects, and Ringo Starr had his *Sentimental Journey* LP set for release in the spring of 1970. The 9 April announcement of Paul's leaving the Beatles was shortly followed by the release of *McCartney*. The album was met with huge sales but dismal reviews. Critics expected more from the man who had spearheaded *Sgt. Pepper's Lonely Hearts Club Band* and *Abbey Road*. The reviews did not do much to boost Paul's already fragile confidence.

When Paul wasn't involved in litigation with the other Beatles, he spent the remainder of the year writing songs. By the end of 1970, he was ready to return to the recording studio. Although *McCartney* had been made under primitive conditions and was basically a homespun production, Paul set his sights high for his next album. The new album would feature studio musicians, the New York Philharmonic Orchestra, and the hope that it would be the best album Paul had ever made.

The McCartneys went to New York in January 1971, taking the Isle de France Cruiseliner. They visited Linda's family, then went to Manhattan to audition local musicians to play on the new album. "I had a beard, looked fairly anonymous anyway," Paul recalled of the trip. "I used to wear a combat jacket and jeans, and in New York you just look like any junkie on the street. So you don't get noticed.

"(It) was talent contest night at the Apollo. So we went up there and we were late but Linda persuaded the (man at) the door to let us in. And I think we might have been the only two white people there. It was still Black Panther time, but we just trusted that it wasn't going to be a bad vibe.

"So that was the flavour that we did *Ram* under, and we just worked at it."

A handful of musicians were called and asked to audition, although they did not know it was for Paul McCartney. Denny Seiwell was one of the drummers invited to attend the auditions. The six-foot-two-inch Seiwell hailed from Leighton, Pennsylvania and had been a drummer in the U.S. Army before moving to New York. There, he worked in several recording sessions and in jazz clubs.

Seiwell appeared at the audition, which was held at a "burned-out" building in New York that did not have a studio. He discovered that the audition was being held in a dingy basement room, with beat-up equipment and the worst drum kit he had ever seen. "Paul just asked me to play, he didn't have a guitar, so I just sat and played. He had a certain look in his eye . . ." A lot of the musicians were put off by being asked to audition, but Seiwell felt McCartney had done this because he was looking for "a certain attitude. I just played . . . I always say that if you can't get it on by yourself, you can't get it on with anyone."

Eight other drummers were tested, with Seiwell chosen in the end. The deciding factor was Seiwell's "tom toms," Paul divulged. "That

U.S. Ad for Ram, *1971.*

may not sound like (much) to anyone who is not a musician . . . but if you see a drummer playing tom toms, you learn a lot about him."

McCartney picked Ron Carter and Richard Davis to play bass on several tracks on the album, and David Spinoza was selected to play guitars. Spinoza was New York's premiere session guitarist; he commanded fifteen hundred dollars for a three-hour session, when the going rate in 1971 was ninety dollars.

It was Linda who had telephoned Spinoza earlier and introduced herself as Mrs. McCartney. "Who?" Spinoza had asked her. Linda had replied that her husband would like to meet him. Spinoza still had no idea who she or her husband was. He had asked if he had worked with Mr. McCartney before. Finally, Linda had told him her husband was Paul McCartney. "(L)ike I was supposed to know Paul McCartney was calling my house," he thought.

Spinoza arrived for the meeting at an unkempt Forty-Fifth Street loft and was surprised to learn that not only was he expected to audition, but that others were also invited and had been trying out for the previous three days.

Spinoza did his bit, said his goodbyes, and then went home. He wasn't there very long before he received another call from Linda. She informed Spinoza that he had gotten the job and asked him to do sessions in the following weeks. However, Spinoza was in demand and told Linda he was unable to keep every week open for them. Linda asked for five days. He replied that he could keep two of the days open, but not all five. She pleaded with him to reconsider. "She really speaks for (Paul) and handles all the business," Spinoza recalled of the time, adding that he was not allowed to talk directly to Paul regarding the schedule.

Much of the recording of *Ram* took place at Phil Ramone's A&R Studios. Paul laid down around two dozen tracks, twelve of which made it onto the album. The album was constructed with Paul singing his parts while the musicians played along, developing the tune as they went along. "It was that simple," Seiwell later recalled. "It was really a nice procedure because there were only three of us there (not including Linda)."

For David Spinoza, however, this was difficult, as he felt relegated to being merely a "second-class citizen" rather than a creative source. There was no challenge. He simply played what he was told to play. However, Spinoza found that Paul was very prompt and businesslike, beginning at nine o'clock in the morning and listening to what was recorded the previous day. This was usually followed by eight hours of playing and recording. There was "no smoking pot, no drinks or carrying on, nothing," he recalled. "Just straight ahead."

One other item that Spinoza found difficult to swallow was the constant presence of Linda in the studio—and the children. Even at four o'clock in the morning, the children were there, sleeping from either exhaustion or boredom, which Spinoza and others at the session felt was not right.

In addition, Paul was constantly persuading Linda to involve herself in the recordings. "I worked her so hard in New York because I thought it's all well having Linda on harmonies," Paul later recalled,

Paul's first post-Beatles single, 1971.

"but I'm not havin' her do bum harmonies. So I worked her like mad. She had never done it before.

"But if you listen to *Ram*, all those harmonies on there are just me and Linda. Pretty good, some of them. It was pretty good, but it was quite hard work on that album. There was a bit of 'You're flat. You're singing flat,' but in the end it was just get it on and we did it."

As for Linda's contributions on the album, Spinoza felt she didn't do much, other than making "comments on what she thought was good and bad." He also felt Linda sang "fine—like any girl that worked in a high school glee club." Still, he wondered, "What on earth is she doing singing with Paul McCartney?"

After Spinoza completed work on a few tracks, Linda telephoned him at home and politely told him not to bother coming into the session the next day, as they were doing some other work on the project. He somewhat expected to be called back in a few days, but the call never came. Possibly, his private disapproval of Linda was not so quiet. Denny Seiwell recommended guitarist Hugh McCracken, who was hired and who completed the remaining guitar work on the album.

Paul enlisted the New York Philharmonic orchestra on three of *Ram*'s tracks, "Uncle Albert/Admiral Halsey," "Long Haired Lady," and "The Back Seat of My Car." The recordings were refined at Columbia Studios, and the final mix was done at Los Angeles Sound Recording.

While recording *Ram*, Paul released the pure pop song "Another Day," backed with the harder, driving "Oh Woman, Oh Why" (complete with the sound of an actual gun going off in the studio) in late February. Credited as a solo, "Another Day" featured Linda's backing vocals and was a certifiable top five hit on both sides of the Atlantic.

Ram was released in May 1971 and was credited to both Paul and Linda McCartney. Its cover featured a photo by Linda of Paul holding a ram by its horns, bordered with artwork designed by Paul and Linda. The letters "L.I.L.Y." written on the side were widely assumed to stand for "Linda, I love you." The back cover featured a blown-up photo of two beetles fornicating, an obvious statement by Paul on how he felt about his former band mates.

Paul was shocked to discover that most critics slammed the album.

Rolling Stone called *Ram* "the nadir in the decomposition of Sixties rock thus far." When he came across the beginning of one review that read, "How do you tell an ex-Beatle that he has made a lousy album?" Paul threw the paper to the floor in disgust. He refused to read that particular publication for several weeks afterward.

Although most reviewers dismissed the album itself, several also personally attacked Paul and Linda. In retrospect, the album was not as bad as the reviewers felt, and it is arguable that the critical attacks were in vengeance for Paul's having "broken up" the Beatles.

John Lennon disliked *Ram*, too, finding personal offense in the songs "Dear Boy" and "Too Many People," which decried hypocrites who voice one opinion in public while following another lead in private. Lennon retaliated with the song "How Do You Sleep?" on his masterpiece *Imagine* album later that year. In the song, Lennon shot barbs at Paul, claiming all he had done was the song "Yesterday," even though Paul had been the driving force of the Beatles' final four years, spearheading the *Sgt. Pepper* and *Abbey Road* albums and most of the group's singles. To add further insult, Lennon also included in the album's packaging a postcard of himself holding a pig by its ears, a parody of Paul's *Ram* cover.

"He says the only thing I did was 'Yesterday,'" Paul later told *Melody Maker*. "He knows that's wrong. He knows and I know it's not true."

Ringo disliked the album as well, commenting that Paul was a brilliant artist but that this album revealed only a shadow of the real person. He felt that *Ram* contained not one worthwhile song. George Harrison had no comment, and the Beatles' record producer, George Martin, simply said: "I don't think Linda is any substitute for John Lennon."

To promote the album, the McCartneys concocted a little-heard record entitled *Brung to Ewe by Hal Smith*, which was sent to radio stations and various rock journalists. It included bits of dialogue, the bleating of sheep, and Paul and Linda singing portions of "Now Hear This Song of Mine." Those who heard the promo were dumbfounded and felt it was made by two bored people sitting in an isolated farm smoking dope. But no one would tell Paul it was a bad idea, or one that wasn't thought out well enough.

Ad for the U.K.-only released single "The Back Seat of My Car," 1971.

On the positive side, *Record Mirror* remarked that Paul and Linda sounded as close together as the Everly Brothers ever were. In addition, the public liked the album. It shot to the top of the charts on both sides of the Atlantic, reaching number one in Britain but stalling at number two behind Carole King's *Tapestry* in America.

Ram included the song "Uncle Albert/Admiral Halsey," which Paul said was about his Uncle Albert, with Admiral Halsey added because he liked the name. It was released in the United States as a single in late summer 1971 and became Paul's first post-Beatles number one single. It also held the distinction of jumping to number one from outside the top ten on *Billboard*, a record it held for more than twenty years until Whitney Houston did the same with her version of "I Will Always Love You." "Uncle Albert/Admiral Halsey" was not issued as a single in Britain. "The Back Seat of My Car" was released instead, but it charted on only one of the three main music charts.

Both "Uncle Albert" and *Ram* went gold in the United States. One person who noticed the commercial success of *Ram* was Sir Lew Grade of ATV and Northern Songs: Although Paul still had a contract with Northern Songs (left over from his Beatles years), Linda did not. As half of the cuts on *Ram* were co-written with Linda, and as she was not part of Northern Songs, 50 percent of the royalties on these compositions would now be going to Linda and the newly formed McCartney Music, an early incarnation of Paul's MPL company (McCartney Productions Ltd.). (Grade had also noticed that Paul's first post-Beatles single, "Another Day," from early 1971, carried the songwriting credit of Mr. and Mrs. McCartney.)

"As I wasn't collaborating with John anymore, I looked for someone to collaborate with," Paul reasoned. "I assumed there wouldn't be any sweat.

"If my wife is actually saying, 'change that' or 'I like that better than that,' then I'm using her as a collaborator."

Grade filed a lawsuit against Paul, claiming that the songwriting credits were a sham and that Linda did not and could not compose songs with Paul McCartney. Paul was embittered. "They were so wonderful to me after all the successes I'd brought them with me and John—more than they ever dreamed of earning anyway—they immediately slapped a million-dollar lawsuit on (Linda and me). So they were charming pals who shall be remembered ever thus . . ."

The lawsuit further deepened Paul's money woes. Most of his cash flow was diminished by the Apple/EMI/Beatles lawsuits that had been flying around since the Beatles disbanded (and that would not be completely cleared until the early 1990s). "The joke at the time was that Linda was the only one getting paid in our household," Paul later said, " 'cause we were all held up with Apple being subject to litigation. I wasn't seeing any money."

In late summer 1971, George Harrison organized two concerts held at New York's Madison Square Garden to benefit the starving people of Bangladesh, with the proceeds being given to UNICEF. It was—up to that time—the largest collection of rock superstars performing onstage to benefit a cause, a sort of precursor to Live Aid. In addition to Harrison himself and Ravi Shankar (who had originally introduced the idea to George), also featured were Bob Dylan, Eric Clapton, the Apple Records group Badfinger, and Ringo Starr. George had approached both John Lennon and Paul McCartney to participate. Although John initially agreed, he backed out when the invitation was not extended to Yoko Ono.

Paul, on the other hand, considered it inappropriate to appear onstage with Harrison and Starr at the same time as he and the three other Beatles were tied up in lawsuits. It didn't help when Paul also learned that Allen Klein was involved, as was Phil Spector, who'd produced the Beatles' swan song album, *Let It Be*. Paul felt that Spector had destroyed the *Let It Be* album with his overproducing, especially Paul's songs, including the title track and "The Long and Winding Road." Perhaps it was best Paul did not become involved.

The concerts were successful, and the album produced from recordings of the event became a best-seller and won the Album of the Year Grammy Award. Unfortunately, legal problems between George and the United States Internal Revenue Service prevented a majority of the money generated from the event from going to Bangladesh for several years.

The three other Beatles had individually achieved both critical and commercial successes after the group broke up: Lennon with his *Imag-*

"Mary Had a Little Lamb" U.K. ad, 1972.

ine and *Plastic Ono Band* albums; Harrison with the *All Things Must Pass* album and the Concerts for Bangladesh; and Starr with his single "It Don't Come Easy." Paul McCartney was, arguably, the least successful or popular of the four.

"I felt like I didn't have a use anymore," Paul later said. "I'd been a bass player, and I'd been a co-writer with John and suddenly all of that was taken away. And I just thought, 'Am I any good on my own?'

"I think the most difficult thing was not so much the writing as playing with a band. Because I decided early on that I wanted to carry on being a singer working with a band. And I had no band. So I thought if I don't sing for a year, it's going to get a bit croaky. And if I don't sing for two years, I'm going to suddenly think I'm not a singer anymore. You can get really rusty very quickly. So I decided to get a band together, just to give me something to do, keep me off the streets, and to practice and rehearse."

But Paul ran into a problem: he realized he had never put a band together. He had, after all, joined John Lennon's band. Paul knew he had to do something creative. He was a songwriter and a musician, after all, and that was his job. With much of his money and royalties tied up in litigation with lawsuits, he also had a family to support. In addition, Linda was pregnant again.

By the time "Uncle Albert/Admiral Halsey" was racing to the top of the American charts, Paul announced the formation of a new band. To the public's surprise, Paul included his wife as a member of the group.

2

Get on the Right Thing

Paul was inspired by country singer Johnny Cash, who hired different musicians to play various concerts and albums. Paul thought he'd do a similar thing with his new group. "I'll just get a band and it'll really just be for the playing and the singing," he thought, "just so I don't forget how to do it."

"I had a talk with Linda (about joining the group)," Paul told writer Tim White. "She said, 'If it's gonna be kinda casual and we're not gonna sweat it, we could maybe do something together.' So we started it on that basis . . . That was the kind of spirit we approached it all in and it was the only way we could have done it, we wouldn't have even dared stay in the business."

" 'Want to be in a group?' " Linda recalled when Paul asked her to join. "Well, of course I did: I was a 'sixties rock 'n' roller, and I pictured the Shangri-Las or the Dells . . . But tell me I've really got to learn how to play the piano; that I've got to sing in *tune* . . . *what?* We did have fun at first, but then I had every single critic on my back, and I realized what Paul had been through all those years."

Paul first began by teaching his wife the keyboards. Linda was a gifted artist in photography; however, her talent did not transfer as quickly to musical instruments. This led to her frustration and Paul's impatience as she was unable to grasp the technique of playing keyboards. "We had a few rows as he tried to teach me," Linda said. "He really put me through it. When everything went wrong I used to say,

'I thought you knew how to make a group.' I never realized how hard it all was."

Paul decided his band would play small venues and hold jam session rehearsals in order for the group to develop their own style. "I wanted . . . *our* sound. I wanted the amateur approach, something we could make ourselves and then work on."

The first musician recruited for the nameless band was Denny Seiwell. Paul admired his work on the *Ram* album and felt he would fit in. Seiwell accepted Paul's offer and flew with his wife, Monique, from New York and moved into an outbuilding on the McCartneys' High Park Farm near Campbeltown, Scotland.

Despite David Spinoza's respectable guitar work on *Ram*, he was not asked to join. Paul instead recruited an old acquaintance, guitarist and songwriter Denny Laine. "It's one of those things when you're starting a band," Paul said. "Several ideas go through your head, different names are suggested to you, and then I remembered 'Go Now.' That was the single Denny made with the Moody Blues, and it has always been one of my favorite records."

Born Brian Hines in Birmingham, England, Laine had been a member of the Moody Blues and sung lead vocals on the group's first major hit, "Go Now." But Denny had left the group before they achieved continued successes with albums and singles. He played in a variety of bands and spent a year in Spain to learn flamenco guitar. Denny was living in his manager's London office when Paul called offering him a job with his new band.

"When Paul called me up," Denny Laine recalled, "I just thought, 'Thank Christ for that. Now I have somebody to work with whom I don't have to explain everything to.' So that was the decider, really . . . just one of those things of fate." He immediately went to Paul's farm.

Joining the group in Scotland was guitarist Hugh McCracken, who had worked with Paul on *Ram*. He nearly joined the group, but bowed out after a few days. Paul felt that McCracken simply did not want to "go that far out with his life" with a band.

Paul told the two Dennys his idea of going into the recording studio to capture the immediacy of the group rather than rehearsing until the freshness disappeared. Paul had had the same idea for the Beatles and their *Get Back* sessions, which proved disastrous. Rather than capturing the creative forces of the Beatles, the sessions resulted in few completed songs but plenty of animosity among arguing band members—and miles of tape recordings from the sessions. The project was later renamed and reproduced as the album *Let It Be*. Still, Paul felt the concept could work, especially taking a cue from Bob Dylan, who had been returning to the simplicity of recording without overdubbing.

The band went into the studio, rehearsed, and recorded an album in less than two weeks. Five of the eight songs were each recorded in one take, which Bob Dylan was also doing at the time. "If it's good enough for Bob," Paul said, "that's cool."

Alan Parsons engineered the recordings and noticed that Denny Laine was "very much manipulated by Paul, being told what notes to play" during these sessions. "He hadn't got a lot of freedom, musically," Parsons said. "I think Denny had a lot of respect for Paul, but he was like a puppet on a string at that time." Paul and Denny Laine's working relationship changed dramatically as the group evolved.

"I think I've got some idea of the way (Paul) feels about things," Denny Laine once said, "and I know the kind of pressure he's under because I've been through a lot of the same stuff myself. The longer you go on the tougher it is in a lot of ways. People expect more and more of you. For Paul, having been part of the best rock 'n' roll band in history, it must be very heavy."

Rolling Stone, 2 September 1971:
Paul McCartney Forms a Band

LONDON—Paul McCartney has formed a band behind him, with both records and live performances in mind. The group includes wife Linda on piano and vocals, Denny Laine on guitar and Denny Seiwell on drums. The group has spent two weeks recording at EMI studios on Abbey Road, but live performances are not in the offering for several months.

Laine has played with the Moody Blues and Airforce, and made an album with a group called Balls that was never released, presumably because there would never have been any airplay on BBC. Seiwell, a studio musician, was on *Ram*, and Linda (nee Eastman) is a photographer.

On 13 September 1971, Linda was in London's Kings College Hospital awaiting the birth of her third daughter. It was a difficult labor, and Paul moved into Linda's room, sleeping on a cot. After the Cesarean birth, she and Paul debated over what to name their girl. They eventually decided on Stella. Paul mentioned names for the new band as well. "How about Wings of Angels?" he asked Linda. "Or Wings of Eagles?"

"How about just Wings?" Linda suggested. "It's got a nice sound to it." She felt that the single-word groups were easier to remember and could have many meanings, as with the Beatles. Thus, Wings was born. The only question was, after Paul's extraordinary success with the Beatles, would the public be willing to accept him and his new group?

The arrival of the album and Wings was previewed at a gala held on 8 November at the Mecca Ballroom in Leicester Square. Among the 1,000 guests attending were Paul's protégé Mary Hopkin (the Apple artist who, with Paul's help, had several hits including "Those Were the Days" and "Goodbye"), as well as Elton John, Keith Moon, Jimmy Page, Deep Purple, and Gilbert O'Sullivan. While the partygoers danced to the big band sounds of Ray McVay's Orchestra, drinks were provided on a Dutch treat basis, and the party lasted until 3:00 A.M.

Wild Life was released in early December 1971. It was credited to only Wings, and as Paul's name did not appear on the cover, several people had no idea who Wings were. The cover photo of the group was a faraway pose, and Paul wasn't readily recognizable. In addition, the work was sparse, containing only eight listed cuts.

Although the Beatles had shied away from liner notes on their albums, feeling that liner notes cheapened the product, *Wild Life* included them. Slapped on the back cover with a caricature of Wings jamming, the notes were written by a Clint Harrigan—who many suspected of being Paul:

> "They rehearsed for a while, sang some old songs, wrote some new ones and in time headed for the big city studios.
> "In three days they had laid down most of the tracks and at the end of a couple weeks the album was finished.
> "In this wrapper is the music they made. Can you dig it?"

Much of the record buying public could not "dig it." Shortly after the LP's release, a sticker reading "Wings Wild Life" was affixed to the cover to help gain some public recognition and increase sales. It did not help. The work was not the type of McCartney production to which the public had grown accustomed. Reviews for the album were worse than those for *Ram*. "McCartney is a spent force," one critic wrote of the album. "Third-rate suburban pop."

"I don't care if people don't like [it]," Paul said shortly after the dismal reviews came in. "I like it. I've got an awful lot to live up to, that's the problem."

"I must admit, you must like me to like the album," he said twenty years later. Paul acknowledged that he made mistakes with the album, and especially by including the song "Bip Bop." "It just goes nowhere. I still cringe every time I hear it."

With *Wild Life*, "Paul wanted to give the world a real honest, true

From top, clockwise: Denny Seiwell, Paul, Linda, Denny Laine,
and Henry McCullough circa 1972.

look at a new band," Seiwell says. "I think Paul was trying to shake the whole Beatles thing. 'OK, I'm gonna give you something you can't compare to the Beatles' records.' There was some really neat stuff on the record."

The album commenced with "Mumbo," which, although some critics dismissed it as junk, was a rocking jam session. Seiwell recalled that it was made up at the studio and that Paul yelled "Take it, Tony!" as the piece was taking shape while the band played. Tony Clarke, the album's engineer, had already pushed the "record" button and was drinking a cup of tea before Paul cued him. The command stayed on the released track. Paul called "Tomorrow" a "real big song," and "Dear Friend" was created for John Lennon as a gesture of peace, a letter Paul could not write himself.

"With the business pressures of the Beatles breaking up, it's like a marriage. One minute you're in love, next minute you hate each other's guts," Paul later said. "I don't think any of us really ever got to the point where we actually hated each other's guts, but the business people involved were pitting us against each other, saying, 'Paul's not much good, is he?' or 'John's not all that good, heh, heh, heh.' What can you do? You can't write a letter saying, 'Dear Pal of mine, I love you.' It's all a bit too much. So you do what we all seemed to do, which was write it in songs."

The album's sole non-McCartney-penned tune, "Love Is Strange" (which, Seiwell remarked, was the first reggae track recorded by a Caucasian group) had been a hit for Mickey and Sylvia in the 1950s. Plans were to release the song as a single with "I Am Your Singer" on the B-side, and promotional copies of the single had been issued in Britain. But after the lackluster reviews of *Wild Life*, the proposed commercial single release was scrapped.

Oblivious to the critical reactions of Wings' debut, Paul decided to take his new band on the road. He had pleaded with the Beatles to continue touring, but only two short years after their 1964 breakthrough in the United States, the Beatles had stopped touring altogether. The other members found it exhausting, as did Paul, but he also found it exhilarating. Additionally, Paul felt it important to keep in touch with his audience.

Now he was with a group who agreed to perform in front of live audiences. Denny Laine suggested that another guitarist would help the live sound of Wings, so Irishman Henry McCullough was recruited. McCullough was an old mate of Denny Laine's and had already established himself as a member of Sweeny's Men and the Grease Band.

Although each member of Wings agreed to tour, one member was reluctant: Linda. She knew she wasn't a professional musician, and she felt that playing in front of an audience would only add fuel to the contempt a majority of the press and public held against her. But Paul convinced her she was a good keyboard player. More importantly, he wanted her with him onstage, as a support. Linda gave in.

On 3 January 1972, the animosities in Ireland between the Republicans and the IRA erupted into open warfare. The result was thirteen civilians being killed on 30 January by paratroopers after a banned civil rights march in Londonderry's Bogside. The massacre was named Bloody Sunday. A bitter Paul read of the events and watched them unfold. Paul's hometown, Liverpool, had been jokingly referred to as the capitol of Ireland. As the name suggests, the McCartneys are of Irish decent. Paul poured his feelings about Bloody Sunday into a song called "Give Ireland Back to the Irish," which Wings immediately recorded before setting out on tour.

After packing equipment; three dogs; daughters Heather, Mary, and Stella; road managers Ian and Trevor Jones; Denny Seiwell's wife Monique; and themselves into a rented Avis van, Wings began a series of unscheduled concerts throughout Great Britain, a series that became known as the University Tour because most of the concerts were held at universities and colleges. With each stop, Trevor Jones asked permission for the band to play a short concert. The first concert was held at Nottingham University on 9 February 1972. During lunchtime, 800 curious students paid fifty pence each to watch and listen to Paul and his new band.

After each show, Paul divvied up the money evenly. Actually seeing one hundred or two hundred dollars in cash for their efforts meant more to him than the alleged huge checks that stumbled onto the desks of the Beatles' accountants and lawyers.

The informality of the tour baffled industry insiders. Paul McCart-

"Give Ireland Back to the Irish" single, Holland, 1972.

ney and Denny Laine were established names with their previous bands, and Seiwell and McCullough were respected musicians; their formation of Wings could have ensured massive crowds. But Paul knew exactly what he was doing. He did not want the media attention—and scrutiny—that would judge Wings as concert performers before they had time to hone their style. Paul wanted Wings to start out like a new band, beginning at the bottom and working its way up.

"Once you get up there and start rehearsing, the chemistry starts going," Paul later remarked. "I suppose everyone was wondering 'Is he going to make it?'"

The tour had its moments, including one day when Wings rolled into a town only to find that it didn't have a college or university; at another town, the group was turned away because the students were busy studying for their final exams. When the group played at a small theater in Salford, near Manchester, a play was currently running, and the management was worried that the pounding of the groups' instruments would cause the scenery to topple over. It didn't.

On 11 February after playing Hull University, the group booked themselves into a local bed and breakfast where the owner did not recognize the famous McCartney. "(It was) a third-rate hotel there,"

Linda recalled. "The manager was a real Hitchcock—thought we were the lowest."

After eating fish and chips, some of the group left their trash on the bar. The next morning the owner was shouting to one of the roadies about the mess. Although he was angry about the tirade, Paul did not say anything. Instead, he nudged the man in the nose with his elbow. The man threatened to call the police. Heather ran to gather the rest of the group and roadies, knocking on their doors and saying, "Get up! Get up! Get dressed now! We gotta move! The cops are on the way!" Soon after, the group immediately departed as if nothing had happened.

Publicly, Linda said she was enjoying herself on the tour. "So far, audience response has been good," she initially told *Melody Maker.* "Surprisingly, perhaps, I am enjoying these one-night appearances— it's like a touring holiday. If we wake up one morning and decide we don't want to go to, say, Hull, we don't have to! With an organized tour, your freedom is limited. Eric Clapton once said that he would like to play from the back of a caravan, but he never got around to it. Well, we have. We've no managers or agents, just we five and the roadies. We're just a gang of musicians touring around."

After the first week, however, Linda's confidence diminished, and she was still unsure of herself as a musician. When the band stepped onto the small stage at Leeds University on 16 February in front of an audience numbering 1,500, Paul greeted the crowd and began the concert with a countdown to the song "Wild Life." "One, two, three . . ." he said. Nothing happened. He counted a second time. Still nothing. Paul turned to Linda, who was supposed to play the introduction on her electric piano. He saw that she was experiencing stage fright.

"I've forgotten the chords," she mouthed to Paul. The audience began chuckling nervously and sympathetically.

"OK, Linda, just put this finger on C, that one on F-sharp, like this," Paul calmly explained. "That's right, and then you'll remember the rest . . ." The audience began to laugh out loud, believing it was an act.

"OK, this time we're really going to it. One, two, three . . ." Linda played, and the concert went smoothly. But later that night, Linda broke down to her husband. "I feel totally out of place," she wept. "Everyone is so down on me."

Denny Laine accepted Linda in the band; however, both Henry McCullough and Denny Seiwell tried hard to disguise their feelings. Although they had worked their way up in the music business, it was clear to them that Linda was only in the band because she was the leader's wife. Plus, they found it difficult to work with an untrained musician, although they both liked Linda as a person.

Paul encouraged Linda and managed to bring her spirits up. He remembered when the Beatles' record producer, George Martin, hadn't felt that Ringo was a strong enough drummer at the group's first recording session. Although Ringo did play drums on the "Love Me Do" session, Martin had brought in another drummer who was also recorded. Although Ringo had felt slighted, he had pressed on to become one of the greatest drummers of the 1960s.

"Everyone has to start somewhere," Paul told Linda. "Anyway, I like the innocence that your playing brings to the band. It stops us from becoming the Beatles—too slick and clever." Linda was encouraged by Paul's philosophy, and although she never evolved into an accomplished musician, with Wings she became a capable one and established herself as the band's "raw edge."

The university concert series lasted for two weeks and was a success. As small and intimate as it was, the tour brought a new confidence to Paul and furthered his belief that the public not only still accepted him, but Wings as well. Paul later said he could have gone on touring for two months but that after listening to Ian Jones' recordings of the concerts, it became painfully obvious the band had a long way to go in refining their act.

The critics, however, were still barking from the *Wild Life* album, and they continued when "Give Ireland Back to the Irish" was released as a single after the University Tour. The BBC instantly banned the song from its airwaves for being too political. According to BBC press officer Rodney Collins, the reason for the ban was because the disc made a political point rather than telling listeners that there was a good deal of suffering and sadness resulting from the political situation. (The BBC is not an independent commercial station whose revenues come from independent advertisers; rather, it is funded by the government.) Regardless of the ban, "Give Ireland Back to the Irish" still hit the top twenty on the British charts. In the United States, the single received limited airplay but still managed to hit the top forty. The song did reach number one in Ireland—and in Spain, of all places.

"I figure I'm a (tax) payer. So that entitles me to an opinion," Paul explained. "I'm living in the West, so we're allowed to talk over here, right? So when the English paratroopers, *my* army who I'm paying (taxes) for, go into Ireland and shoot down some innocent bystanders . . . I'm moved to make some kind of protest. So I did 'Give Ireland Back to the Irish.'

"A lot of people said, 'Please don't release this. We don't need this right now.' And I said, 'Yes we do. Gotta have it.' "

Denny Laine was one who did not want the song put out. He felt that Paul was quite naive to write a song with the title 'Give Ireland Back to the Irish,' and he anticipated that there would be problems. It certainly did not help Paul's image.

In late May 1972, Wings released their second single, a reworking of the nursery rhyme "Mary Had a Little Lamb." By this time, the McCartneys had become vegetarians, although it was rumored that Paul had fallen off the wagon at times and had snuck in a hamburger here and there when Linda was not near. Nevertheless, the animals on their farm were allowed to live their lives out naturally.

Perhaps "Mary Had a Little Lamb" had an indirect connection with their lifestyle. Directly, however, daughter Mary loved the song whenever Paul sang it. This was not known to most of the public, and so at the time, some critics thought that as "Give Ireland Back to the Irish" was considered political and was banned, Paul had decided to release something completely opposite and apolitical.

The record-buying public on both sides of the Atlantic saw that the single charted, but with varying results. It hit a high of number six on two of the British charts, and in the United States, it hit the top forty on two of the national charts. Pete Townshend of The Who told Paul his daughter loved the song.

But the critics, once again, dismissed Wings. "So the once-great Paul McCartney has fallen to tripe like this?" one critic sniffed. Others followed suit. When John Lennon was asked to comment on the song, he replied, "Why should I? What could I possibly have added? The fact that he put it out was comment enough, I rather thought." Denny Laine later said he would not have released the song as a single, had he a say in the matter.

What many detractors failed to realize was that Paul had written—or rather rewritten—the song mainly for an audience of children, not the pop fans or hard rockers who were accustomed to his music. Paul and Wings were simply branching out into various types of music for different audiences. They would not be labeled a band who made one style of music exclusively for one set group of people.

After almost one year together, critics felt that Wings was not working well as a musical group. In fact, one American magazine wished Wings "a crash landing." Whether critics were angered that Paul had broken up the Beatles, or whether they expected better of him, or whether they were unwilling to listen objectively to the direction Paul and Wings were aiming their recordings is a matter of debate. Regardless, *Wild Life*, "Give Ireland Back to the Irish," and "Mary Had a Little Lamb"—the first three official Wings recordings—were strikes.

Paul later said that in the early days of Wings, none of the members dared to disagree with him. "(N)o one would say, 'No, Paul, that's a mistake' and that those first records were sort of a dip for me and my writing. There were a couple years when I had sort of an illness. I was a little dry."

Paul decided to tour once again. Rehearsals took place at the Manticore studios owned by the group Emerson, Lake, and Palmer, in Fulham, West London. For the 1972 summer tour, Paul rented an open-topped double-decker bus (which went only thirty-five miles per hour), painted it with a modified Wings emblem in shades of yellow and blue, and set off on a relaxed tour of Europe. The summer concert series was not widely promoted, in order to keep the still-vehement press away, but the news media found out anyway and descended on Wings.

The first concert was held in an open-air amphitheater at the Centre Culturel at Chateau Vallon near Toulon in the south of France on 9 July 1972. "We were scared shitless," Denny Seiwell later said. "The world press was out there. Linda was even scared shitless." Linda cried to Seiwell about her insecurities and put her head on his shoulder. "I don't want to go out there," she said. "Come on, baby, we're going," Seiwell replied, and the group put on a respectable show.

The song selection included Wings' recent singles, their new songs, and some old rock classics. Paul did not include any of his Beatles songs. Paul later admitted to the *Sunday Times* that he intentionally stayed away from playing any of his Beatles songs in public, for fear that they would take away from his Wings compositions. "(The Beatles) were too big for us. I knew the audience would be thinking: 'Oh, not as good as the Beatles.'" Denny Seiwell later said Wings was trying to be a "real, true and honest rock 'n roll band. The hardest part was that everyone was trying to compare us to the Beatles. Try to live up to that!"

Backstage after the show, Paul and Linda were questioned by some reporters who happened to see the show:

Reporter: "Why did you choose to start your tour here?"
Paul: "Actually we wanted to start it at a sort of smallish place to play in, so this is a small, out-of-the-way place, but still get quite a reasonable audience."
Reporter: "Linda, did you feel very nervous before tonight?"
Linda: "The first half. Second half I had a great time. I was nervous the first half. Definitely. We had no sound check, no rehearsal, no nothing. We had to go on cold. So I had to warm up a bit. We were very hot the second half."
Reporter: "Do you find it a great strain working with someone, you know, like Paul? I know he's your husband."
Linda: "Easy. Really, I find it very easy. Totally. You know, I'm still learning. It's fun. It's like life. It's just another thing in life."

Joe Stevens, a New Yorker who was working in London for the underground press, was hired as a photographer to document the tour. Because of difficulties in obtaining work permits, Stevens operated under the name "Captain Snaps." A company was formed by Stevens and the McCartneys to divide the profits from the sales of his pictures, with Linda suggesting the name "Women's Tango Lessons Ltd."

A few days into the tour, Stevens was talking with Paul and Linda while the bus took them to another concert. Linda asked him if he was having a good time. He answered that he was, and that it was "really great working for the Beatles." A few minutes later, Linda started preparing some food and called Stevens over to her. "Listen," she quietly suggested, "don't ever do that again. Paul doesn't like to talk about the Beatles, and he certainly didn't appreciate that remark at all—it's not very funny. If you want to continue working with us, you'd better cool it."

Stevens was sent off to ride with the road crew for a week before being allowed back on the main tour bus. He learned his lesson. "I think he'd been almost brain damaged for awhile having been Paul of the Beatles," Stevens later said.

During the last ten days of July, the band took a break. Paul and Linda flew to New York to attend a surprise birthday party being thrown for Mick Jagger after a Rolling Stones concert at Madison Square Garden. The couple returned to Europe, and, when Wings began the second leg of the tour on 1 August, they appeared more confident and relaxed as a band.

At Juan les Pines, the crowd was enthusiastic. In the audience that night was American model Joanne Petrie, who was then doing runway modeling in various European countries. JoJo, as she preferred to be called, watched the band members leave the stage after the show. She knew Paul was married to Linda, but she wondered which of the three other members were single. JoJo became attached to one of the group's roadies and joined Wings as they traveled on the German and Swiss legs of the tour. She eventually became involved with Denny Laine.

It was not long after that when Paul asked Denny to tell JoJo to leave. Denny carefully told his new girlfriend that his boss and boss's wife were uptight having her around, and that Linda felt that she was after Paul. Although JoJo admitted she was a fan of the Beatles, she denied having any interest in Paul. Denny Laine, however, was another story. Denny explained the situation to Paul, and JoJo was able to stay on the tour.

JoJo was a minor sideline compared to the other situations arising during the tour. Linda's keyboard playing hadn't improved quickly enough to satisfy Henry McCullough or Denny Seiwell. When the pair either commented about this or gave Linda a certain look, Paul quickly silenced them. Both felt that if Wings had a professional keyboard player—someone like Billy Preston—the group could become a prominent force in the music field. In fact, Paul once lashed out at Linda and threatened his sobbing wife that he was going to replace her with Preston. But he soon apologized for his momentary lapse and kept Linda in the group.

Paul himself was changing during this tour, partially because Linda was not completely accepted by the audiences, the critics, or the band in total. Another reason was the largely bad press he'd personally received since leaving the Beatles. He seemed to speak more infrequently to the news media.

The press continued to write mostly negative stories, concentrating on Paul's "arrogance" and "unfriendliness." Reports began surfacing that summer of Paul becoming short-tempered and, at times, unkind. He refused to sign autographs for enthusiastic fans who asked during inconvenient times, and he berated hotel staff who failed to provide him with a double bed or late-night meals.

"I was always very well-mannered and polite," Paul retorted. "My dad brought me up to always tip my cap to my elders and I used to do it until I was about fourteen and I didn't wear a cap anymore. Now I force myself not to tolerate people I don't like. If people do something which irritates me, I let them know about it.

"You can so easily lose your identity in this sort of business. You confuse the myth with the person you really are. Like Marilyn Monroe must have got to the point where she didn't know who she was anymore. She was a walking legend, not a person. And because she was a legend, she had to be kind and patient to every little creep who ever pestered her. I make sure that being well known doesn't stop me being an ordinary bloke who won't tolerate people he doesn't like."

Touring throughout various European countries did pose one problem with the band—namely, where to hide their marijuana. While with the Beatles, Paul had carried his supply in carry-on luggage, which was jokingly dubbed "diplomatic bags" because the customs officials were usually too busy asking them for autographs to look inside the bags.

Wings, however, were not the Beatles, and they would be going in and out of many customs posts. If caught with the illegal drug, chances were they would be jailed. To avoid this, a friend in London was secured to mail marijuana to the hotels where they would be staying. They'd smoke the dope in the country where they were playing, then dispose of any leftover amounts before arriving in another country. By having the pot mailed to them, the band wouldn't be caught in possession of it when going through customs, and if the postal customs ever intercepted it, they could deny having any knowledge that the package contained marijuana.

When Wings arrived in Copenhagen, Denmark, the group was spotted visiting a club where smoking hash was legal. But when the band was in Göteborg, Sweden, police intercepted nearly one-half pound of cannabis that had been sent from London in an envelope addressed to Denny Seiwell at the hotel where he was staying. When Wings were finishing their encore, "Long Tall Sally," at the Scandinavium Hall on 10 August, they were met by police officers. The band was taken backstage to a dressing room.

Joe "Captain Snaps" Stevens was told to go to the dressing room and start clicking away at the scene unfolding. He started taking photos of Linda being mauled by an officer. When Stevens asked her what was happening, Linda replied, "Just get the pictures."

Paul, Linda, Denny Seiwell, and Wings' traveling secretary Rebecca Hinds were escorted to the police station. There they were detained by police for several hours, being interrogated regarding the grass. In addition to the illegal substance, the police had obtained a transcript of a taped telephone call Linda had made to MPL in London. The tape revealed Linda asking for two cassette boxes (plastic containers made to hold cassette tapes) of marijuana to be sent to a hotel: "Where shall they send it? Do you have a copy of the itinerary?" Linda called out to Paul on the recording. "Send it to Göteborg," Paul replied, "to the hotel."

"We told them we had found marijuana in the letter. At first they said they knew nothing about it," said a police spokesperson. "But after we had questioned them for about three hours, they confessed and told us the truth. McCartney, his wife, and Seiwell told us they smoked hash every day. They said they were almost addicted to it.

They said they had made arrangements to have drugs posted to them every day they played in different countries so they wouldn't have to take any drugs through the customs themselves."

John Morris, the group's local promoter, had a different story of the event. He said: "Paul, Linda and Denny did admit to the Swedish police that they used hash. At first they denied it, but the police gave them a rough time and started threatening all sorts of things. The police said they would bar the group from leaving the country unless they confessed."

Although possession of marijuana is illegal in Sweden, the Swedes, like the Danes, have a more liberal standing on the matter. Paul, Linda, and Seiwell were fined $1,000, $200, and $600 respectively. They were then freed, as the pot was intended for their personal use and they clearly were not going to sell it.

The next day, photos taken by Stevens of the bust made the cover of Britain's *Daily Express*. The night after the bust, Paul complained to reporters: "We smoke grass and we like it, and that's why someone sent it to us in an envelope. . . . At the end of the day most people go home and have a whiskey. . . . Well, we play a gig and we're exhausted, and Linda and I prefer to put our kids to bed, sit down together and smoke a joint. . . . That doesn't mean we're heavily into drugs or anything. Neither Linda nor I have gone further than grass. You simply couldn't if you want to get out there and entertain people. But you can't expect us to pretend we don't smoke for the sake of our fans . . .

"But now that I've been caught I'll say, 'Yeah, it's true . . .' People will be looking at us and wondering what we've got with us. And we're not the kind of people who can't go on without it. We wouldn't go on tour if we were. We're just easy people who like to smoke if we can, but now that's out of the question and I'm sorry."

But they continued to smoke, and the tour continued with more caution. When they neared another border, the dope was thrown out before going through customs. Their supplies were later replenished after they entered the new country.

Drugs were not the only problem the McCartneys faced during the tour. Once when the band was in Sweden, Paul and Linda were visiting a basement nightclub when a young man walked up to them. He calmly told Paul that he had a revolver hidden under his coat and that he was going to kill Paul.

The guy walked to the other side of the bar while Paul and Linda sat frozen with fear. A few minutes later, Denny Laine and Henry McCullough walked inside and joined the couple. Paul relayed to the band members the threat he had received. McCullough pulled out a long, thin knife he had hidden in his boot and placed it on his lap. Paul described the man to them, and the two slipped across the room and stood on either side of the man. They pulled the guy down to the floor and searched for the gun. None was found, and the man said he was only joking. Denny yelled angry profanities at the guy, then let him go. He ran out of the nightclub, never to be seen again. The group left the club and returned to their hotel to settle their nerves.

The Wings European tour ended in late August and was a quiet triumph for the group. With the events that had transpired in previous weeks, Henry McCullough called the travels the true "Magical Mystery Tour—it was everything the Beatles' film wasn't."

Because of Paul's celebrity, the incident of the drug bust in Sweden had spread throughout the world press. Among those who read of it was police constable Norman McPhee, who was in a special drugs identification course at Glasgow. Since Paul's High Park estate was in McPhee's jurisdiction, the constable decided to take a look around the McCartney grounds on 20 September. In the greenhouse, he discovered marijuana plants growing among several tomato plants. McPhee left, but returned shortly after with seven policemen and searched the farm, finding nothing more. Paul was later charged on three counts of growing and possessing marijuana. He said that he had received seeds in the mail, but did not know what they were. Being an avid gardener, Paul had planted them to see what kind of plants they were. The court found Paul guilty and fined him close to $150 for possession.

Paul was angered not only that his privacy had been invaded, but with the uproar over marijuana use. "I don't think it is as dangerous as drink," he remarked. "It should be like homosexuality—legal among consenting adults. I don't even think cannabis is associated with hard drugs. There is as much danger of a man who drinks ending up an alcoholic as there is of a cannabis taker graduating to hard drugs."

That summer, the band also shot footage for an uncompleted film entitled *Bruce McMouse*, about a family of mice traveling with Wings. Seiwell recalls it as one of the most embarrassing moments in his life. He was asked to stand in front of this room filled with people and speak to an imaginary mouse. Seiwell had to repeat scenes several times, so much that he had become self-conscious. "I'm not an actor," he says. "That was one of the hardest things I had to do in Wings."

In the autumn of 1972, the group returned to the studio to record songs for their new album. (At this time, they also recorded Linda's "Seaside Woman," which would not be released until 1977.) Two songs from that period, however, were released that same year. The "Hi, Hi, Hi"/"C Moon" single came out in early December 1972 and did much to restore the public's confidence in Paul and Wings and to further the group's reputation. Denny Laine and Henry McCullough both played lead guitar on the song, and critics were warmer to the group with this record than with their previous attempts. Although "Hi, Hi, Hi" was an all-out rocker, "C Moon" had a bouncy pop/reggae mixture.

But for the second time that year, the BBC banned a Wings single. The organization felt that the song's title, "Hi, Hi, Hi," promoted drug use, and they erroneously believed that the cut contained sexual references. Thus, the song was deemed unsuitable for airplay. The British disc jockeys, however, discovered "C Moon" and played that side on the airwaves. It became a top five hit on all three U.K. charts. The Americans weren't so concerned with "Hi, Hi, Hi's" lyrics (both implied and explicit); on the three U.S. charts, that side peaked in the top ten in early 1973.

Eighteen months after their formation, Wings finally had a bona fide hit.

Shortly after, Paul and Linda quietly went on vacation to Morocco, away from everyone to relax and clear their minds. Although "Hi, Hi, Hi"/"C Moon" was a hit, as had been the tours, neither they nor Wings were up to the caliber Paul felt the group was capable of reaching. In addition, Paul was still trying to resolve the numerous lingering Beatles entanglements, waiting for Lennon, Harrison, and Starr—and their lawyers—to consent to some sort of agreement so that he could be free of the Beatles.

"Simon" ("C Moon") EP, Mexico, 1972.

Although enjoying being away from the pressures back home, Paul was more than surprised when he received a telephone call from London. Sir Lew Grade, Paul's foe in the battle over the publishing company that owned the rights to many of the Lennon/McCartney songs, wanted Paul to star in a television special for Grade's company, ATV. A producer flew to Morocco to discuss the details. Paul agreed to the program, and the case that Grade argued regarding the Paul and Linda McCartney songwriting partnership was settled. Linda was allowed to keep her share of the royalties.

On 18 March 1973, Wings performed a live set before a specially invited audience at Boreham Studios which was filmed for inclusion in the *James Paul McCartney* special. In the evening, Wings played a surprise show at London's Hard Rock Café to help raise money for Release, a British charity devoted to helping people with drug problems.

In April, Paul and Linda lent their background vocals and the song "Six O'Clock" to Ringo Starr for his album *Ringo*. Both George Harrison and John Lennon had donated either songs or musical contributions to the album as well. It was a sort of Beatles reunion, even though all four Beatles were never in the recording studio at the same time. It didn't matter to fans. When released later in the year, *Ringo* became a huge success, going platinum and spawning three top five singles in the United States—a feat none of the other ex-Beatles had accomplished up to that time.

Also in the spring of 1973, Wings completed the *Red Rose Speedway* album. The record was not composed of entirely new songs, as a snip of "Big Barn Bed" had been heard on the *Ram* album, and "Get on the Right Thing" was left over from the *Ram* sessions. Although Paul felt his vocals on the latter were not up to par, Denny Laine told him they were and convinced Paul to include it on the new album. It was perhaps the first time Paul did not dismiss a band member's suggestion.

"I think I've been accused of treating people just like sidemen, which I never meant to do. But if you're in a session, and you want a song to go a particular kind of way and you start ordering people around, they can get a bit shirty about it—'Oh you're treating me like sidemen,'" Paul recalled years later. "With Wings I was a bit conscious about that. I tried to let people be themselves. It worked out on a few occasions."

McCullough and Seiwell also felt that the band was becoming a stronger unit. "The band has really progressed as a team," McCullough said in early 1973. "Everybody wants to make it as a band, whereas before it was just Paul. Wings has all the makings of a great group, but our battle is to keep it as a band and not let it fall apart as it could so easily do. It's worth going at it. I'm there 100 percent, I know I've got a lot to offer."

While recording the album's cut "My Love," which Paul dedicated to Linda, McCullough was allowed to show what he had to offer. Paul recalled: "With 'My Love,' we rehearsed it and had full orchestra. It

"My Love" sheet music, 1973.

was recorded live, and the whole orchestra waiting for the down-beat—we're ready to go. Henry McCullough came up to me and said, 'Just a minute. Do you mind if I change the solo?' 'Not at all. Go ahead.' And actually it was one of the best solos he ever did."

In fact, McCullough's sensitive and brilliant guitar work on the song helped make the song Wings' biggest hit to date. "My Love" went gold and spent a month at number one in the United States while resting in the top ten in Britain. Its success did much to restore Paul's confidence. The single was backed by "The Mess," which was recorded live during their 1972 concert at the Concertgebouw, the Hague, in the Netherlands.

Red Rose Speedway was planned as a two-record set ("we had about 30 finished songs," Linda recalled), but EMI asked Paul to trim it down to a strong, single disc. But even as a single record, the album did little to fully redeem Wings. "I thought *Red Rose* was a disaster and so did everyone connected with it," remarked Joe Stevens. "Except Paul."

Denny Laine recalled that Paul and secondary producer Glyn Johns did not get along at all while making the album. Apparently, Paul had wanted to experiment with new sounds and ideas, but Johns wasn't readily flexible to Paul's ideas. Denny felt, however, that this "competition" between the two actually helped the album.

In 1977, Paul admitted, "Every time I make a record it takes me about three months before I can listen to it . . . after *Wild Life* . . . I thought, 'Hell. We really have blown it here.' And the next one after that, *Red Rose Speedway*, I couldn't stand." Although she was in Wings, Linda McCartney was able to view each piece optimistically and conclude the reasons for its success or failure. *Red Rose Speedway*, she felt, "was such a non-confident record. There were some beautiful songs . . . there was 'My Love,' but something was missing. We needed a heavier sound. It was a terribly unsure period."

Red Rose Speedway was released in spring 1973, and it shot to the top of the charts, buoyed by the massive success of "My Love." After knocking *The Beatles 1967–1970* (a compilation album) from the top of the U.S. album charts, *Red Rose Speedway* spent a month at number one. In turn, it was displaced by George Harrison's latest album offering, *Living in the Material World*.

Some fans assumed that the title was a homage to Paul and Linda's devoted housekeeper Rose Martin, but Paul later verified that wasn't the case. The disc was contained in a gatefold sleeve that included a twelve-page booklet featuring drawings by Eduard Paolozzi and photographs by Linda McCartney and Joe Stevens. On the back cover was a message in Braille: "We Love You," which was intended for Stevie Wonder.

The album featured Paul alone on the cover and was credited to "Paul McCartney and Wings." Although Paul initially vetoed the idea of putting his name before the group's, it's been said that Linda suggested that the group's releases should be credited as such. Other sources believe it was the heads at EMI who made the suggestion. The reasoning was that the record-buying public didn't know who Wings were, but they did know Paul McCartney. Regardless, the sales of the LP demonstrated the public's growing acceptance of Paul and Wings.

Although an improvement over *Wild Life*, Wings' second album failed with most critics, some of whom wrote Paul off as nothing more than an ex-Beatle who produced a few good singles. Lenny Kaye wrote in *Rolling Stone* that Paul's music "tends to crumble under prolonged examination. He is not an especially intense lyricist, preferring instead to choose his words according to sound and feel alone and his melodies—particularly on more up-temp material—appear to be fostered through basic reliance on a rotating riff."

The critic's attacks against Linda were more vehement: she was an embarrassment; she sang off-key; she had hair on her legs. One cruel joke that circulated at the time was "What do you call a dog with wings? Linda McCartney." Mick Jagger publicly said he would never let "his old lady" play in his band. "The British media (were) worse than any of them," Denny Seiwell remembered. "They treated Linda very poorly."

The criticism continued to mount, and nothing Linda did with Wings seemed right to a majority of the public. She had, after all, married the last eligible Beatle. And it was less than a year after their marriage that Paul filed suit to dissolve the Beatles. Linda received a lot of the blame for that. Interestingly, only one other celebrity's wife in the twentieth century had been so vilified by the press and the public: Yoko Ono.

But all of the ex-Beatles said Linda was not the cause of the breakup, nor was Yoko. In fact, John Lennon once said if Linda and Yoko had been the cause, they should be given credit rather than blame. After all, four solo Beatles churned out more music in the 1970s than one group of Beatles had in the 1960s.

Within Wings, too, McCullough and Seiwell also asked Paul why Linda was in the group. "I don't know," he answered. "I can't put it into words, but I know there's a good reason for her being here." Years later, Seiwell understood why Linda was in Wings: "(T)hey were in love. And she was a safety blanket. And that's the way he wanted it—that was his choice."

The *James Paul McCartney* television special was aired on 16 April (10 May in Great Britain) and featured Paul with Wings singing fifty minutes' worth of music, including "Big Barn Bed," "Maybe I'm Amazed," "My Love," a medley of "Little Woman Love" with "C Moon," and "Mary Had a Little Lamb." Paul's rendition of "Gotta Sing, Gotta Dance" was originally written for Twiggy. The segment, complete with Paul in a pink tuxedo with tails, and with women dancers dressed as half-males, half-females, was reminiscent of the "Your Mother Should Know" scene from the Beatles' television special *Magical Mystery Tour*.

"I suppose you could say it's fulfilling an old ambition," Paul said of the Bugsy Berkeley-styled segment. "Right at the start I fancied myself in a musical comedy. But that was before the Beatles." Paul admitted he was no Gene Kelly or Fred Astaire, nor was he branching out into too many different areas. "I'm sticking to what I am."

For the first time since the disbanding, Paul sang Beatles songs in public. His compositions "Blackbird" and "Michelle" were part of a medley, and "Yesterday" closed the show. Although the special accomplished much in establishing McCartney's versatility, critics once again picked. "It was a showcase," one wrote, "for Paul's amazing ability to be all things to all men, women, and little lambs."

Melody Maker commented that McCartney "always had an eye and ear for full-blown romanticism, and nothing wrong with that but here . . . he too often lets it get out of hand and it becomes overblown and silly." One segment it called "particularly sickening" was one in

A bootlegged soundtrack from the 1973 TV special James Paul McCartney. *Even the TV Guide cover is a fake, as Paul did not appear on the magazine the week the special aired.*

which Linda photographs Paul while he sings alone. "The effect is ... marred a little by Linda joining in with a decidedly flat voice. On the face of it, she does seem to be forever frustrating the best-laid plans of mice and men."

One American critic found the program entertaining, just as Americans were embracing Wings more so than Britons. The critic applauded the program as a celebration of "Paul's various talents. In a visual and musical context the show was an adequate piece of programming and quite an ambitious project."

"There was a lot more things we would have liked to put into it and couldn't," Paul said shortly after the broadcast. "It was sponsored in the States by a firm that makes nice family cars, so they want nice family films. What's more, a lot of people liked it. Elton John had it showing on his last plane trip."

Although Henry McCullough called the special "just another gig," Denny Seiwell recalls the segment in which the band and an orchestra performed the group's upcoming single "Live and Let Die" for the special. The piano on which Paul played the song was rigged to explode as a finale in keeping with the theme of James Bond.

"The lid from the piano was made of balsa wood," Seiwell says. "But when this thing went off, it was *much* bigger than anybody had anticipated. And this lid of the piano just went into a ball of flames and went flying up over these old violin players! They were clutching their Stradivariuses shouting, 'Oh my God! What was that!' I thought they were going to have heart attacks."

3

Don't Let It Bring You Down

"I don't suppose we'll be together forever," Henry McCullough told *Melody Maker* in 1973. "I'm sure Paul's got more of a tie to the Beatles than to Wings." Denny Seiwell felt that the Beatles would reunite. "I should think there's a strong possibility that they will all get together again," he said.

In May 1973, Wings embarked on a formal seventeen-day, twelve-city tour of Britain. Announced in advance, the tour allowed fans to purchase tickets ahead of time, rather than needing to chance into it as with the 1972 University Tour. The pre-announced dates also allowed critics to know where and when Wings were performing. Although Paul believed the group was strong enough to withstand the critics, he felt the audience was the real critic. "Publicity alone can never do it," Paul said in a pretour statement. "The nitty-gritty is the performer clicking. That only happens when the performer has direct contact with his audience."

Despite many brutal attacks from the British press, there were a few critics who applauded the group. After the May 12 show at Oxford, one critic wrote, "If the second night is anything to go by, Paul McCartney's Wings have got off to a tremendous start. The group gave an extremely tight performance and were able to dramatically raise the pulse-rate of an already enthusiastic audience." *Rolling Stone* reporter Paul Gambaccini, who saw the Oxford concert, felt that it was "respectable. Wings don't rate raves yet, but the time for snickering is over."

The audience at the Oxford concert was quiet and reserved in the beginning but gave the group a standing ovation at the end of the show, calling for an encore. Paul apologized that they could not perform an encore. The band had exhausted its repertoire.

Of course, many in the audience were Beatle fans who were there mainly to see Paul, a fact not unknown to Linda. "I hope the (audience) goes away digging it," she said. "Paul really digs being in a band. He really loves performing, he loves it to be good and loves things to end up well. He's not into that Beatle trip, none of us are."

In the end, audiences not only went to see Paul, but Wings as well. After two triumphant appearances at Hammersmith Odeon at the end of May, a third concert was hastily added to accommodate the overwhelming demand for tickets. Four additional dates in Newcastle, Leicester, Stoke, and Sheffield were also added. Linda was playing better, and Wings looked like a tight-knit group. Appearances, however, were deceiving.

"I felt (Paul) should have shared more with the rest of the band," Henry McCullough later said in regard to singing leads, playing instruments, and brainstorming ideas. "He shared it, but he didn't share it, if you know what I mean. It was not a real sharing, and he was afraid to rely on other people to do anything about it."

Throughout the tour and the summer of 1973, the band was coming apart. Denny Seiwell missed doing session work and was disturbed that business matters had not been resolved. "It was the Seventies. We were doing everything on a handshake," Seiwell said. Seiwell and McCullough both felt Paul listened to Denny Laine's ideas, but not to theirs.

Nick Lowe, who played with Brinsley Schwartz, the group that was the opening act for Wings during this tour, recalled that Paul was very supportive and encouraging of his music, and that Linda was a charmer. "Both of them," Lowe said, "have been much-maligned people."

Lowe said McCullough was at times rude to Linda in public. Another strike against McCullough was when Wings were taping a promotional film of "My Love" for *Top of the Pops*. He vomited onstage as the cameras rolled, much to the horror of his ever-professional boss. It seemed that McCullough's days were numbered.

Temporarily, however, the internal strife within the band calmed in June 1973 when Wings' next single exploded onto the music charts. It was the theme song for the James Bond film *Live and Let Die.*

"If you're a writer, there's these kind of work jobs that you imagine," Paul recalled when he was asked to write the song. "One of John and my ambitions were to write a song for Frank Sinatra. I don't think writers today think of, but things were such, that the pinnacle . . . were to write a song for Sinatra. Another pinnacle was to write a Bond song. It's like an Oscar, to write a Bond song." Paul shared the writing credits on the song with Linda. Her contribution was the four-line lyric about doing a job well and giving the other people hell who get in the way. Linda also suggested that part should sound a bit reggae, one of her favorite music styles.

Paul asked George Martin, who had produced a vast majority of the Beatles' recordings, to produce Wings' "Live and Let Die." Afterwards, Martin took a copy of it to Jamaica and played it for Harry Saltzmann, one of the film's producers. "Very nice record," Saltzmann replied. "Who should we get to sing it? What do you think of Thelma Houston?" After Martin realized the film producer was not joking, he told them the song was finished as it stood. If they wanted it, they could take it as it is or not at all.

Roger Moore was making his debut as Bond in the film, and he heard the theme song. He wrote about it in a diary that was later published as *Roger Moore as James Bond*: "Paul McCartney has written the song and I had lunch with the man who is arranging the music, George Martin, who was responsible for so many of the Beatles' hits. It is a tremendous piece of music and I will stick my neck out and say that three weeks from its release it will be number one in the charts. It's not last year's music, it's not even this year's music, it's next year's."

Fortunately for Wings, their version was used in the film and became one of the group's biggest sellers. It went on to become the most successful of all James Bond themes, won a Grammy Award, and received an Academy Award nomination for Best Song. In addition, the "Paul McCartney and Wings" credit was dropped and the single was released with credit simply given to "Wings." (The credit change was only temporary. The next single reverted back to the "Paul McCartney and Wings" credit, which remained on all future releases until 1975.) Also, by having the Denny Laine lead vocal on "I Lie Around," the B-side of "Live and Let Die," Wings was becoming more and more of a group effort.

The single sold more than a million copies in the United States and made it to number one in both *Record World* and *Cash Box* magazines. Oddly, "Live and Let Die" stalled at number two on *Billboard*'s charts for three weeks while three different songs (Maureen McGovern's "The Morning After"; Diana Ross' "Touch Me in the Morning"; and "Brother Louie" by Stories) topped the charts. The film's soundtrack album, containing the score by George Martin and the title song by Wings, peaked at number seventeen in the United States, mainly on the strength of Wings' growing popularity at the time.

Paul decided to return to the recording studio to begin the next Wings album in the summer of 1973. He envisioned recording outside of Britain, hoping to create a new sound for a different type of album. He asked EMI for a list of studios they owned outside of London. Looking at the list of exotic places including Peking, Bombay, and Rio de Janeiro, it was Lagos, Nigeria that caught his eye. He thought about the African rhythms and envisioned lying on the beach during the day and recording at night. Paul decided on going to Africa.

Before the group departed for Nigeria, they spent a few days rehearsing in July 1973. There, matters came to a head between Paul and Henry McCullough. Paul began to tell McCullough how to play, not unlike the way he had with George Harrison (which was captured in the Beatles' film *Let It Be*). "Look," Paul once growled when McCullough did not play a part the way he wanted. "Don't tell me it can't be played. I know it can be played."

"It's impossible," McCullough replied. "You're wrong."

"OK—give me the guitar and I'll show you."

McCullough stood up in a quiet fury, packed his guitar and walked out. That evening he called Paul and told him he was leaving the band. He was sick and tired of not being able to branch out more musically with the group. Although his solo guitar work on "My Love" gave a

By the summer of 1973, Wings were in flight with a number one album and single, but the best was yet to come.

hint as to what he could have done with Wings, his creative suggestions fell on deaf ears.

McCullough also held Linda in contempt as a musician. "I wouldn't have Linda in a band," he later told *Melody Maker*. "She doesn't have a musical head on her." Another British newspaper reported him as saying, "Trying to get things together with a learner in the group didn't work as far as I was concerned."

Linda was not blind to McCullough's feelings toward her. "I could feel this," she later admitted. "(He) thought I was getting the best bits without being any good."

Although disappointed to a degree, Paul could not have been entirely surprised when McCullough decided to leave Wings. "Henry preferred to lead a more bluesy way of life," Paul later said, "and he left over musical differences. He was very good at the other stuff but more into blues."

Before the band was to leave for Africa, Denny Laine's girlfriend JoJo gave birth to a son in Campbeltown Hospital, Scotland that August. She had been with Denny as he and Wings were rehearsing at Paul's farm, and she gave birth in the nearby small, country hospital. Denny decided to drive several hours to Birmingham to bring his parents up to the hospital to see their grandson. Although he was reluctant to leave JoJo and his son alone, JoJo told Denny to go ahead. Paul and Linda were only a couple of miles away in case she needed anything. JoJo was sure they would stop to look in on her.

But the McCartneys did not visit. Instead, Heather drew a picture of horses with a handwritten message. That was all she and Denny received from Paul and Linda. Although JoJo was deeply hurt, Denny did not feel the gesture was atypical.

Denny Seiwell tried to convince Paul to replace Henry McCullough before recording the new album, but Paul vetoed the idea. Paul suggested that the group record, then do overdubs in the studio as had been done on *Ram*. "That's when I got a little bugged," Seiwell says. "After all this work, we're gonna go back to a bunch of overdubs on a record rather than the true live sound that we accomplished."

The night before Wings were to depart to Africa for sessions on what was to be *Band on the Run*, Seiwell called and told Paul he did not want to go to Nigeria to record, thus terminating his standing with the band. "There were many things," Seiwell said, referring to his departure. "I was starting to miss my session world where you are playing with great musicians and you are playing different stuff every day. I had been doing the same material (with Wings) for three years."

As for Linda, Seiwell said years later, "she wasn't a great piano player. She wasn't a great singer. But she had a great attitude. She gave it her best shot. I think she did a helluva job." As for Paul and leaving the group abruptly, Seiwell says: "I was mad. I was angry. There was a lot of stuff going on. So for years, Paul and I had no contact. I thought he hated me—which he probably did for awhile. But, you know, time heals all." Several years after leaving Wings, Seiwell made an effort to contact Paul and apologize for his actions. "We became friends again," he says today.

After McCullough and Seiwell departed, Paul and Linda were worried that Denny Laine wouldn't show up at Gatwick Airport, where they were to depart from—economy class, no less. Denny did arrive, and he, Paul, and Linda remained the core of Wings until the end.

"I liked the (original Wings line-up) just before it broke up," Denny Laine recalled. "I found the faith I'd been looking for a long time. I had the faith that we could get a good group on the road. The way things were going in the early days—it was too chaotic because we were starting again but we were very aware that we were being looked at, stared at. And we were nervous. We were all to blame if (Wings) didn't make it in the early days because we did take our time and do it right."

The desertion of McCullough and Seiwell brought back memories of the Beatles' breakup to Paul. He experienced guilt feelings in how he had handled the two members, but they were the ones who decided to leave, and Paul was not going to ask them to return.

"I don't think there was anything wrong with them as musicians," Paul simply said. "They were both good, but they just didn't fit in."

Although Nigeria was a member of the British Commonwealth, the government had been taken over by a coup seven years earlier, and the country was now run by a military government. At the airport, the group saw men carrying machine guns. When they arrived in the city, they discovered that Lagos was overrun with poverty and angry natives.

None of the depressing aspects of the excursion were known to fans or the press at the time. When people asked why Wings chose Africa of all places to record, Apple simply said: "Well, the sun was shining out there. After all," Apple's release read, "as one of the roadies put it: 'One EMI studio is very much like the next.' It could have been Rio, it could have been Communist China. But in Lagos, the sun was shining. It's as simple as that."

The sun may have been shining, but it was only on occasion, as it was the end of the monsoon season. "Red mud," Paul recalled, "pouring out of the skies." The unpaved streets were muddy from the rains, and the oppressive heat was almost unbearable, even for the insects and bugs, who sought refuge inside the buildings. Geoff Emerick, who had engineered some of the Beatles' works, including the *Revolver, Sgt. Pepper's Lonely Hearts Club Band,* and *Abbey Road* albums, was hired to engineer *Band on the Run.* He, too, disliked the weather and primitive conditions in Africa. But it was the abundance of spiders that caused the arachnophobic Emerick to "freak out" on many occasions when he saw them.

While Emerick was sharing a rented house with others in the entourage, Denny Laine put a spider in his bed as a prank. Emerick decided to move to a hotel to be safer from the bugs—and Denny. Another rented house held the McCartney clan including daughters Heather, Mary, and Stella.

Another blow was delivered when the band arrived at the recording studio, located in the Lagos suburb of Apapa. There they found that the studio was still under construction. "Here we were, the three of us in the studio. No facilities," Denny Laine remembered, "things were hanging out of the wall and no one knew where to hang them." The microphones were still in their boxes, stuffed away in a cupboard. Also, the sole recording machine was an outdated 8-track Studer.

"They didn't use booths or separation barriers, so they were constructing booths just for us and the guy was saying, 'Do you want glass in them?'" Paul recalled. "They were just gonna make big wooden things with holes in them!"

In exchange for an autograph, Paul obtained a temporary member-

Wings, 1973.

ship at a local country club so he could swim in the daytime. By late afternoons, the group gathered to work on the project. Most nights lasted until just before midnight, but some sessions went on until five in the morning—the coolest temperatures of the day. Weekends were spent touring the city and countryside, with no recording.

One evening when Paul and Linda were taking a walk, an old, beat-up car was slowly following them. Paul simply thought he had been recognized, as there were few places on Earth where he wasn't known. But this gang of six were not fans.

The group bolted from their car with knives and surrounded Paul and Linda. They demanded money, their watches, and their cameras. "Don't kill us!" Linda pleaded. "We're musicians—he's Beatle Paul!" One of the men laughed arrogantly while another grabbed the loot and also the demo tapes of the recordings Paul had from the sessions. The group ran back into their car and sped off. They were never found.

The shaken couple reported the incident to the police. "You're very lucky," an officer told them. "If you'd been black, they would have killed you. But they know that you won't identify them because to white folks, all us blacks look alike."

More mishaps followed, including one day while recording, when Paul experienced trouble breathing. He then began gasping for air and staggered outside onto the dirty street. A sharp pain ripped through his right side, and he began trembling. He could not fill his lungs with air. Paul felt he was having, at the age of thirty-one, a heart attack. He thought he was dying as he passed out.

A doctor was immediately called. After examining Paul, the doctor diagnosed him with an acute bronchial spasm, probably brought on by heavy smoking. Paul stayed in bed for several days before feeling strong enough to return to the studio.

One night while in Lagos, Paul, Linda, and Denny went to a nightclub where musician Fela Ransome-Kuti performed. Paul especially enjoyed hearing Ransome-Kuti's music and its throbbing jungle beats. He described the performance of Ransome-Kuti and his group as "the best band I've ever seen live."

"We saw him one night," Paul told *Musician*, "and I was *crying*." More than a spiritual experience, Paul's breaking down was the result of many things that had happened since their arrival in Nigeria. "A lot of it was just relief. There were a lot of crazy circumstances and weird things happening."

But the evening ended on a sour note when the musician accused Paul of exploiting Nigerian musicians and stealing the culture's music for his own gain. Ransome-Kuti had not heard one note of the Wings sessions, but that did not stop him from going on Lagos radio where he publicly charged the band of stealing African music.

Ransome-Kuti did not stop there. With a group of people, he visited Wings at the studio. He once again accused Paul in person.

"Look," Paul shot back, "we've done all right without Africa so far. Nobody's going to swipe your music." He played Ransome-Kuti some tracks to prove his point. Paul felt compelled to avoid having any of the songs sound anything close to the Nigerian music.

"Obviously we were influenced (by Nigeria)," Denny Laine later told author Geoffrey Giuliano. "We were influenced everywhere we went in the world. If you like a piece of music and you go and sing it, that doesn't mean you're stealing it."

One of the few humorous moments while the band was in Nigeria was when some locals appeared on the band's front lawn with a traveling flea market. Everything they had to offer was for sale to the wealthy Britons who were visiting their country. In fact, one local had wanted to go back to London with Denny as his assistant.

Nevertheless, Paul later referred to the fall of 1973 as "one of the most frightening periods of my life." Wings had not become the success he envisioned, his band had fallen apart, and the critics were claiming that his best years of songwriting were behind him.

In retrospect, the loss of McCullough and Seiwell was not crucial, as the band was recording. Paul could have hired a local drummer for the sessions, but when "it would have taken hours to tell him exactly what I wanted, I knew basically that I could do most of it (myself)." Being versatile musicians, Paul and Denny took the place of the pair, while Linda added her keyboards. The three worked well together, and from a vocal standpoint reached near perfection for a rock group. Denny Seiwell, however, later commented that Paul had used all of his drum parts in the album "because we had done all the rehearsals. The album was ready and we were ready to go (and record it)."

"Paul didn't change much of what we played when he recorded it," he told *Goldmine* in 2001. "I thought the two-track demo we made was better than the (final) record, to tell you the truth."

After three weeks in Africa, the trio returned home in late September. There Paul discovered a letter dated prior to his leaving: it said, "do not under any conditions go to Lagos. Cancel—there's been an outbreak of cholera."

In England, the group went into the studio to finish the album. The recordings were completed, and despite the concern over the African's mistrust of him, there was one direct African connection with the album. "The only guy from Africa we used was someone we met in London (drummer Remi Kabaka), then we discovered he came from Lagos," Paul recalled. "But that was purely coincidental!"

Although the vocal tracks were mainly recorded in Africa, the recordings had very little African influence. In fact, it is perhaps Wings' most British-flavored collection, from "registered charities" and a "pint a day" in "Band on the Run," to "suffragettes" in "Jet" and the "M6 south down to Liverpool" in "Helen Wheels." "Down in the jungle, living in a tent" in "Mrs. Vandebilt" was taken from a quote by Charlie Chester, a British comic. "Mamunia" came from the name of a house Paul saw while on holiday in Marrakech earlier that year. It means "safe haven" in Arabic.

In London, Geoff Emerick took on the task of mixing the recordings. Howie Casey played sax solos on "Bluebird" and "Mrs. Vandebilt," and Tony Visconti wrote the score for many of the songs, contributing some of the most memorable arrangements ever composed on a rock album. (Visconti was then married to Mary Hopkin, the former Apple artist whose recording career Paul had launched.)

During the mixing, Paul felt that the album was coming together into something special. After a three-day marathon mixing session at Kingsway Studios, *Band on the Run* was ready.

The album cover was Paul's idea. Along with the three Wings, it featured a group of prisoners escaping a jail, but stopping in their tracks as a spotlight shines on them. On closer scrutiny, one sees that the others in the photo are noted personalities—particularly noted in the United Kingdom—including actors Christopher Lee and James Coburn, TV talk show host Michael Parkinson, singer Kenny Lynch, Parliament member Clement Freud, and boxer John Conteh. They had been invited to appear "just for a lark," Paul said. He added that there was no detailed plan as to who would be included, unlike the Beatles' *Sgt. Pepper's Lonely Hearts Club Band* cover, for which it took several weeks to decide which personalities were to crowd the band on the cover.

To show his gratitude to Denny Laine for staying with the group, Paul told him he'd receive a percentage of the royalties from *Band on the Run*. This act of kindness would allow the Wing years of royalty checks, especially if the album was a hit. Denny moved from a houseboat on the Thames to a mansion. Up to then, Denny had been making a meager salary of thirty-five pounds per week. Despite the royalties, the money was nothing like what Paul had promised, according to Denny. And as there were no contracts drawn up and signed, Denny could take only whatever amount his boss deemed appropriate.

Not quite number one, but "Jet" was a worldwide top ten hit and critical favorite. Ad, 1974.

While in England, the three Wings cut "Oriental Nightfish" with Linda on lead vocal. The trio then took a van to Paris in late November 1973 and recorded a few songs at EMI studios, including the backing track for Linda's song "I Got Up," although her vocal wasn't added until 1998. Also recorded was Linda's country-flavored "Wide Prairie." "I always thought of this song as Linda's fantasy," Paul later recalled. "Her tongue-in-cheek attitude and her . . . 'twangy' voice combined to make this joyful little rocker." All three songs were eventually released on Linda's *Wide Prairie* CD.

Around this time, guitarist Jimmy McCulloch just happened upon a guy he had worked with earlier. He was told that Paul was now looking for another guitarist to work on some recordings. (Paul hadn't wanted to immediately replace the two lost band members when the band was preparing to record; now however, he was ready to find someone new.) "I've been in the business a long time, but it never occurred to me I'd ever play with McCartney," McCulloch later said. "I went along to chat about (working with Paul) but it was like some kind of dream. Paul was there chatting happily and I just kept staring at him, thinking to myself, 'Christ! He used to be a Beatle. And here he is talking to me like I matter.'" Paul asked McCulloch to join them in recording.

Joining McCulloch in the session was drummer Davy Lutton. There was speculation that Lutton and McCulloch would soon be joining Wings, but Paul said he'd simply asked a few people to join him in the studio "just to see how it'd feel playing with musicians on a loose, no-string-attached basis." Jimmy McCulloch later reemerged, however, as a nemesis to the band.

Band on the Run was released in early December 1973 to near unanimous glowing reviews. Many critics felt it was the best 'Beatles' product since the group's two masterpieces, *Sgt. Pepper* and *Abbey Road*. A few hinted that it equaled those albums.

It was a time for the critics to feast. Those few who still believed in Paul's talent called the album a banquet, a masterpiece. Critics who had previously dismissed Paul and Wings could not overlook this powerful work. *Melody Maker* cheered, "It now stands as the best by any Beatle since their 'divorce.' It's done wonders for McCartney's confidence . . ."

A lot of critics wrote that McCartney "came of age" after the Beatles with *Band on the Run.* Paul disagreed. "I know what they mean," he said, "looking at it very black and white, I think it's true . . . Maybe if what they were talking about is that it was an album, more complete as an album.

"But again, some people say that's what makes good albums—all that slogging and suffering for art. I hate to think that myself, actually."

The U.S. version of *Band on the Run* contained "Helen Wheels," which had been originally issued strictly as a non-album single in mid-November, a couple of weeks before *Band on the Run* was released. But the EMI-owned Capitol Records convinced Paul to include the song on the album in order to help the company promote the album, as "Helen Wheels" had proved a hit. Paul agreed, but only for the American pressings.

The song fit in well with the other tracks and enhanced the theme of flight and freedom found throughout the package. By Christmas, "Helen Wheels" had entered the U.S. top twenty and was on its way into the top ten.

Although the album went gold in the United States twelve days after its release, it settled comfortably in the bottom half of the top ten, where it then stalled. It was not the hit it could or should have been. Once again, Capitol Records took charge. A promotional record was made for *Band on the Run,* which consisted of an open-ended interview. Radio dee-jays simply had to read questions from a prepared script, then play Wings' prerecorded replies on the disc, giving the illusion the band was in the control booth of the local radio station. Ads were placed in industry magazines, and promotional stickers were pressed and distributed to push the album. But such gimmicks did not make *Band on the Run* a success. The strength was in the music itself.

In early January 1974, Capitol Records' promotion man Al Coury confronted Paul to allow him to pull a single from the album, as a hit song would lead to increased album sales. "You gotta let me work on this record!" Coury pleaded to Paul. "I've got a real feeling about it!" Although he had been reluctant to have "Helen Wheels" added to the

U.S. version of *Band on the Run*, Paul did not want singles released from the LP. Finally, he relented.

"Al released 'Jet,' which I wasn't even thinking of releasing as a single, and 'Band on the Run,' too," Paul remembered. "He single-handedly turned that album around."

"Jet" was released in the United States in late January 1974 with "Mamunia" on the B-side. Then it was reissued in late February, replacing "Mamunia" with "Let Me Roll It," EMI's choice for the rest of the world. "Jet" hit the top ten on both sides of the Atlantic. The title cut was finally released in the spring; it hit number one in the United States and got near the top of the U.K. charts.

Coury's strategy worked—perhaps better than anyone expected. The album became the first LP in the history of the *Billboard* charts to hit number one on three different occasions. *Rolling Stone* named *Band on the Run* the best album of the year. By 1976, *Band on the Run* had sold more than five million copies in the United States and was still on the charts, one of the decade's most consistent and best-selling albums. It was also Wings' first album to be issued in the Soviet Union.

The album also spent ten weeks at number one in Britain, albeit seven months after its release. Better late than never: *Band on the Run* was Britain's best-selling album of 1974 and the seventh biggest of the decade. It also became the first platinum LP in the United Kingdom, an honor it shared with Pink Floyd's *Dark Side of the Moon*.

Throughout the first months of 1974, Paul worked intermittently on his brother's album. Having been a member of the successful recording group The Scaffold, Mike McCartney had adopted the surname McGear so as not to appear to be cashing in on the family's famous last name. Paul produced the album *McGear*, which featured two songs he wrote by himself, five with his brother, and one with poet Roger McGough.

Jimmy McCulloch also played on the album, as did Linda McCartney and Denny Laine. Denny felt the album was more of a Wings effort than a true solo album—and that it was very good. But the album failed to sell anywhere close to expectations when released.

Paul also spent the first part of 1974 working with legendary singer Peggy Lee. "Paul and Linda McCartney are two people I sincerely like," Lee said. "I remember once when I was playing London I invited them up to the Dorchester for dinner when Paul said to me, 'Instead of bringing you a gift or a bottle of champagne, I'm bringing you a song.' It was called 'Let's Love,' and I was very thrilled about it. Anyway, when I got back to the United States, he and Linda came over to help record it with me, which was lovely. Later in the studio he played on the song and even conducted it; that whole side was all his. Unfortunately, due to an unexpected merger between my label, Atlantic, and Electra Asylum, the tune never quite made it out as a single, but one thing's for sure, that man has loads of class and we had a wonderful time working together."

With the unqualified success of *Band on the Run*, Paul's confidence was restored, and Denny and Linda were relieved that Wings had finally arrived. Paul now had his sights set on touring again. He decided to hire two musicians to replace the long gone Henry McCullough and Denny Seiwell.

Paul knew Jimmy McCulloch's talents and felt he would fit in with the band. McCulloch was short, dark, and a partier. Although only twenty-one, McCulloch was an established guitarist whose playing was at times compared to Eric Clapton's. He had achieved a huge U.K. hit with Thunderclap Newman's "Something in the Air" (which was a minor hit in the United States), then moved on and joined John Mayall's Bluesbreakers and Stone the Crows. "I'm sick and tired of being in and out of bands," McCulloch said. "I want to get something down on record that's going to be appreciated instead of always being in new bands that so few people hear."

The person Paul chose for Wings' drummer was the complete opposite of Jimmy McCulloch. Geoff Britton was tall, blond, and soft-spoken. He was also a black belt karate expert and was invited to represent England in an international karate competition with Japan. As a drummer, Britton had played with Wild Angels and East of Eden.

"(East of Eden) was a great band who never made it and should have," he later recalled. "It must have been mismanagement . . . because so many of the bands like Yes and Free who were on that circuit at the same time as us *did* make it."

Unlike McCulloch, Britton auditioned to become a Wing. Auditions

In Los Angeles in March 1974 for the Academy Awards. Paul and Linda were nominated for the Best Song Oscar for "Live and Let Die." The victor was "The Way We Were."

for drummers were held April 1974 at the Albery Theater in London. Britton arrived to discover that there were fifty other drummers vying for the same spot. "You should have seen the people there," Britton said. "It was like a Who's Who of the music industry." Among those was Mitch Miller, a former drummer for Jimi Hendrix.

Rather than turn around and leave, the undaunted Britton decided to go ahead and play. "I wasn't really nervous. I'm never nervous," Britton recalled, "although I might be a bit apprehensive. We had to play about four numbers—some of it quite advanced stuff for an ordinary rock & roll drummer. Anyway I got up there and did my stuff.

"I was a bit disappointed actually because I thought it would be a chance to play with McCartney, but they'd hired session men instead," he later told *Disc*. The members of Wings sat in the audience and watched—and listened.

"(T)he one guy that shone at the end of the day was Geoff," Denny

Laine later said, "and that's the truth of it." A few days later, Britton was telephoned, informing him he was among the top five who were being invited to audition again, this time with Wings.

"I met Paul and the group and they were really nice," Britton said of the meeting. Shortly after he played with the group, he received another telephone call. The list had been narrowed down to him and one other drummer. After Britton was invited to spend a day with Wings and have dinner with the group, Paul phoned him. "Well," Paul said, "we've decided."

"(H)e was mucking about, geeing me up," Britton said of the call. "In the end I said, 'Well, who's it gonna be?' and he said, 'You got the job.'"

Paul was careful not to make a formal announcement about the newly reformed Wings until after he was convinced that McCulloch and Britton would work with the group. Although the core members welcomed the two new members, the new pair of Wings disliked each other from day one.

The newly reformed Wings flew to Nashville on 6 June 1974 to privately acquaint themselves with each other and to record without fanfare. Although there was no advance publicity about the trip, word leaked out shortly before their arrival. Fifty-some fans and reporters arrived to greet the band as their flight landed in Nashville in the early evening. While he and Wings breezed through the terminal, Paul answered a few questions from the reporters about topics ranging from the question of a possible reuniting of the Beatles (which he dismissed) to Geoff Britton's inclusion in the band. "(He) has a black belt. I feel with those credentials he'll be able to whip the band in shape," Paul laughed.

A few of the younger fans were intrigued by Paul's accent. "Say 'elevator,'" one boy asked him. Paul told reporters that he might record there in Nashville. When singer Jerry Reed heard that Wings were in Nashville to possibly record and go on the road with a tour, he joked, "Man, if I was Paul McCartney, I'd *buy* the road!"

On 16 June, Paul, Linda, and their daughters went to the Grand Ole Opry to attend the third annual Grand Masters Fiddling Contest. The intermission act was Porter Wagoner and Dolly Parton. It was at this event that Parton played with Wagoner for the last time (after that, she left the duo in order to pursue her solo career).

When asked if the performers knew about the McCartneys' being in the audience, Opry radio station WSM's president, Irving Waugh, replied, "I doubt Grant Turner (the Opry emcee) even knows who he is." For about forty-five minutes, most of the audience did not know Paul was there, until a young man yelled from a few seats behind the McCartneys, "Hey, Mr. McCartney!" in order to take a picture of Paul. Then the word spread like a brush fire. "He (was) very cordial to the fans," Waugh said, "always stopping for autographs and pictures with the girls and babies."

Linda left her seat twice to go to the side of the stage to photograph Parton and Wagoner, and she and the family went backstage to meet the performers after the show.

Opryland hostess Ann Burns was amazed that Paul was at the Opry. After Paul left, Ann, a lifelong fan of his, ran to where he had been sitting and "picked up a little plastic sword that held the orange in his drink" for a souvenir. She was even offered fifteen dollars for it from another fan.

Wings spent several weeks in Nashville during the summer, rehearsing and getting to know each other. The band did record, taping several unreleased songs including "Hey Diddle," "Send Me the Heart," "One Hand Clapping," and "Proud Mum." Paul also employed other musicians in sessions, including Lloyd Greene, Vassar Clements, the Cate Sisters, and Bobby Thompson.

"We had a lot of tracks that were going to be wasted and just thrown away," Paul said. "But I thought there was some good stuff on them so we just cleaned them up, and then I did the stuff here so we could make them up into a record." But those sessions were never released. Four songs, however, were later released as singles.

One disc contained the instrumental pairing of "Bridge on the River Suite" and "Walking in the Park with Eloise," which was written by Paul's father. "When Paul was a little boy, about ten," Linda told *Sounds*, "he remembers sitting at the foot of the piano while his dad was playing this song. We were having dinner with Chet Atkins one night in Nashville, and Paul had been playing a lot of his music for

Chet and he said, 'Here's one that my dad wrote a long time ago'—
and he started playing it.

"Chet got talking to Paul, saying that the song should be recorded
and that it would be nice for his dad . . . So we got Chet playing on it
and Floyd Cramer the piano player . . . (and) lots of other Nashville
people."

Paul's father was touched by his son's gesture. "He loved having a
record out—but he's very shy," Paul told *Disc*, "and he didn't like all
the publicity. I remember him being very emotional about it when I
first played it to him—he said I really shouldn't have bothered, but I
know he enjoyed it."

As the disc was credited to the group "the Country Hams" and not
to Wings, few people knew it was a McCartney recording. It did not
receive any airplay or sales, but it quickly became a collector's item.

While in Tennessee, Wings stayed at the home of songwriter Curly
("D-I-V-O-R-C-E") Putnam, whose sprawling country estate was
located outside of Nashville. Paul rented the farm for two thousand
dollars per week and later paid homage to his host with the song
"Junior's Farm." Paul also bought a Honda motorcycle and drove it
around the farm and on nearby country roads. A security guard hired
to protect the McCartneys remarked, "The next headline he makes
will be about a motorcycle wreck. He doesn't know how to drive that
thing."

Paul composed the country- and western-influenced song "Sally
G." while at a Nashville bar. Skull Schullman, owner of Printer's Alley
Club in Nashville, recalled Paul visiting his bar and the fact that "Sally
G." was composed in Skull's Rainbow Room. Paul was going to call
the song "Diane," after singer Diane Gaffney, but he changed his
mind after learning that Gaffney was suing a newspaper reporter for
writing a story about her without her permission.

Paul completed the song and left the place after consuming, but not
paying for, $4.75 worth of drinks. Schullman did not hold a grudge,
and he placed Paul's name at the top of a list of famous musicians
who'd passed through his doors. As for the tab, a fan saw to it that
Paul's name was erased from the "delinquent payments" book.

As the band was staying in a remote area, a publishing company
that handled some of the Beatles' recordings decided to send some

NO. 2. 1974

P.O. Box 4 UP
LONDON W1A 4UP.

wings

OFFICIAL FUN CLUB

An early Wings Fun Club issue from 1974 reporting Wings' tenure in Nashville.

liquor to them as a gift. Catherine Darnell, a secretary at the company and a fan of Paul's, was asked to make the delivery. Darnell called Paul's people to inform them that she was coming, and she drove there with a friend who was also a Beatles fan. A pickup truck met the pair at the end of the long driveway.

Determined to get into the house, Darnell explained that she needed to use the bathroom, as there wasn't one for miles around. The security men allowed her to go to the house. As she walked indoors, Darnell noticed Paul shooting basketball baskets with one of his daughters. Inside, Linda was stuffing a turkey (?!) and waved Darnell toward the bathroom. She went in, followed by Stella, who stayed with her the whole time she was in the bathroom.

After she went outside, Paul came around and introduced himself to the starry-eyed fan. "You've got the phone number here, don't you?" he asked. She nodded. "Well, if you can think of anything interesting for us to do, let us know and we'll all go together." Darnell couldn't think of anything they could do without being mobbed, so she didn't telephone them.

With little to do, the group rehearsed. In this confinement, Geoff Britton recalled a controversy during rehearsals one day when "everyone was a bit stoned." Jimmy McCulloch had apparently berated Linda, and Britton told him off before storming out. Britton wanted to leave Tennessee for a while, but he did not have enough money. He asked one of Paul's management team for some money so that he could travel around the United States before returning to Great Britain. The next afternoon, Paul and Linda convinced him to stay.

The day before Wings left Tennessee, Paul and Linda met with reporters at the Putnam estate. They spoke of how they had enjoyed visiting the state, meeting the local people, and staying on the Putnam farm. "I've got a farm in Scotland," Paul said. "You're not the only people who have farms, you know. Back in Scotland, we're country people in our own way." Paul refuted rumors that he and Linda were moving to Nashville permanently. "No thank you. I'm British to the core. We're always being advised to move out of England because (of the taxes)."

Although the McCartney girls were supposed to remain indoors throughout the outdoor interview, Stella and Mary slipped outside to play. "They're always running around naked," Linda laughed.

Although Paul and Linda were lenient with their children, there was always a point at which they did not accept certain behaviors. Stella, who was three at the time and not yet toilet trained, had a habit of discarding her soiled panties wherever she was. Once, it occurred in a business office. Paul scolded his daughter firmly.

Still, the couple found joy in their daughters. "Remember that night they went over to Johnny Cash's house? Heather was playing with Johnny's son and some of the animals in the barn. When Heather came back to us, she was talking Southern. 'Those chickens are really beautiful,'" Paul mocked in a drawl. Linda added that Heather liked to cook and made "great eggs and chips." Linda also divulged that during their vacation, Heather burned her chin when she examined a baking fudge cake too closely.

Although the reporters at the McCartneys' predeparture press conference enjoyed hearing about the McCartney girls, the meeting with the press took place in ninety-degree heat and high humidity. One reporter commented afterward, "Reckon why they didn't invite us into the air conditioned house or serve us a cold drink or two . . . at least Kool Aid?"

Apparently the group was in a hurry to leave. Jimmy McCulloch had had a run-in with the law shortly before leaving Nashville. Although the details of the incident were not revealed, it was rumored to have been so severe that authorities had asked the guitarist to leave the country.

Upon the band's return to Britain on 17 July after seven weeks in Nashville, they were met with outrageous rumors. "The existing lineup of Paul McCartney's Wings appeared this week to have broken up," claimed the *New Musical Express*, "following what is understood to have been a major internal policy disagreement. Sources close to the band suggest that Denny Laine and the two 'unofficial' members, guitarist Jimmy McCulloch and drummer Geoff Britten [*sic*], are no longer working with Wings. A spokesman for Laine confirmed that there had been 'personal difficulties,' while another contact stated emphatically: 'Wings have split—the old band doesn't exist anymore.'"

The rumors were furthered when a "Wings spokesman" issued a statement that read, "Wings members are free to pursue their own musical careers. This will enable them to develop working relationships free of contractual ties. In (the) future Wings will have a fluid concept, which will be adapted to suit current and future projects."

The British newspapers scampered to find the truth of the rumor. *Sounds* manipulated Denny Laine into admitting that there were problems while in Nashville, a "showdown," Denny said. "No that's a bit dramatic because it's not that these things hadn't been said before. Various things were said like they're said in any group—you can't deny that. You know how it is . . . you say something and if someone else doesn't respond to what you're saying then you're walking out, but the next minute you can be walking back. People have been thinking that finally I've said my piece, but that's not true—I just said my piece about what was happening at this time."

"It's all right if a band has come up together and they are all millionaires," Geoff Britton remarked of this time. "They can talk to each other as equals. But with Wings there were these incredible imbalances which manifested themselves in so many ways. For example, we were offered a gig to play a festival with Stevie Wonder for half an hour. The money being offered was a fortune. I instinctively said, 'Let's do it!' My cut alone would have bought me a house! I said, 'Fucking great!' But Paul didn't want to do it. So as a result I didn't do any live gigs with the band."

Although Britton did not tour with Wings, he did appear in an interesting hour-long documentary about the band recording in London after their Nashville trip. Produced by MPL and directed by David Litchfield, *One Hand Clapping* was never officially released, although bootleg video copies have been circulating on the underground market.

Britton also appeared in a 1974 thirty-two-minute documentary called *Empty Hand*, which was about him at a karate competition. Paul produced the piece and also provided the percussion background on the soundtrack. *Empty Hand* was quietly released in 1977.

4

Rock Show

1974 had been a quiet year for Wings in terms of recording and touring, but the group was heard constantly on the radio while *Band on the Run* continued its chart run through the year. The group spent much of the year on the singles charts with the releases of "Jet" in January, "Band on the Run" in April, and the double-sided hit "Junior's Farm"/"Sally G." in November. The hard-rocking "Junior's Farm" prompted some of the still-doubting critics to comment that Paul was no longer a Beatle and that Wings was a real band.

Wings performed "Junior's Farm" on Britain's *Top of the Pops* on 20 November to promote the single, and shortly after, a formal announcement about Jimmy McCulloch and Geoff Britton joining Wings was made. There were two items of business that needed to be resolved before the announcement, though. First, McCulloch was tied to a contract with Robert Stigwood, which he needed to honor before joining Wings as a permanent member. Second, a decision had to be made on whether or not the new Wings members should have formal contracts with the group. "There was a lot of talk of contracts in the beginning," Britton said, "but we decided it was better if nothing was contracted. If you're a real pro and you've got a tour booked, you don't phone up and say, 'I'm not coming.' That's just not on."

Also that month, Paul and Linda sang backing vocals on Rod Stewart's rendition of the McCartney-penned "Mine for Me" during Stewart's live performance at the Odeon Cinema near South London. The couple also began work on the next Wings album, cutting the basic tracks of "Love in Song," "Medicine Jar," and "Letting Go" with the band.

Although he was nowhere near completing an entire album of new songs, Paul had planned to release another Wings album at the end of 1974 entitled *Cold Cuts*. The album was to include Wings hits like the recent "Junior's Farm" and non-album singles like "Hi, Hi, Hi," as well as previously unreleased recordings, including "Mama's Little Girl" and "I Don't Want to Smile." Paul also planned for *Cold Cuts* to retail for less than the standard rate that companies were charging for albums.

"The new album (*Venus and Mars*) wasn't ready," Paul recalled, "so *Cold Cuts* was to fill in. I mean, I have a few tunes from *Ram* which I wrote and which never found their way onto plastic. What it really was meant for, in England that is, was a kind of budget album. People in America think if you're bringing out a budget album, you're not selling well. (T)he record executives over in America would say, 'You're big, what do you want to do that for?' If I answered, 'For the people'—and believe me, I would mean it—they would reply, 'Oh man, screw the people. They can afford it,' 'cause that's the way they look at business over there."

Paul inexplicably scrapped his plans, and *Cold Cuts* was never officially released, although many unauthorized bootleg versions cropped up throughout the years.

In the second week of January 1975, Wings flew to Louisiana to continue recording the long-awaited follow-up to *Band on the Run*. Paul chose Louisiana because the drum sound on LaBelle's hit "Lady Marmalade" had caught his ear. He learned it was recorded at the Sea-Saint Studios in New Orleans by Allen Toussaint, a co-owner of the studio.

Although New Orleans was well known for its abundance of marijuana, Paul said Wings went there simply because he and the group wanted to record in the United States and in a musical city. "There's not that many," he explained. "Only New York, Nashville and LA and I'd never been to New Orleans, except on tour (with the Beatles) when we never saw anything except the inside of a trailer. The only thing I remembered about New Orleans was a vibrator bed in the motel. And it was sweating hot."

Geoff Britton, however, did not want to go to New Orleans. He had grown depressed and miserable, and he hated being in the band at that time. He felt there was "no sincerity in the band, and every day was a fight for survival. It was very fragile," Britton recalled. "Words would be said and Linda inevitably got upset. Jimmy would say something about the chords being wrong, and the worst thing you can do to a musician who is struggling is to put them under pressure." (When *Rolling Stone* "misquoted" Britton, he called *Melody Maker* to vent his anger. "They said I hate Jimmy McCulloch's guts. What I really said is that he's a nasty little cunt.")

Jimmy McCulloch did not defend himself. He knew he was not an angel. "I am a bit weird," he told *Sounds* magazine. "Immaturity, I suppose. I've had a lot of experience in music, but experience of life— knowing how to treat people, when to say something and when not to and when you've put your foot in it—I'm still a bit green that way . . . Sometimes there's a Jeckyll and Hyde within me. Sometimes I really blow it and get on people's nerves."

Linda was not the only member singled out by McCulloch, Britton claimed. "Jimmy would be short with Denny, too, about his tuning. If he came in wrecked and hungover everything about him would be negative."

Britton did not care for Denny Laine, either. "He tried to get Jimmy shafted out with a knife in the back. He's a bastard," Britton said. Looking back, he regarded both Laine and McCulloch as "ignorant," guys who were good musicians "and that was it." Interestingly, the only member of the band about whom Britton had nothing bad to comment on was Linda.

Britton regularly wore a karate suit to rehearsals, which brought snickering from the other band members. Denny was snide with Britton, asking him, "What are you gonna do? Play the drums or chop them in two?"

Britton left the group after completing only three songs for the new album the previous November. Linda later said that the New Orleans sessions with Britton "just didn't jell. It was horrible because we really wanted it to work . . . it was another depressing period. We had just started *Venus and Mars* and it just wasn't working."

"We were in the States and my wife started talking separation and divorce. I came home to sort it out," Britton recalled. "In retrospect, it would have been better to try and keep both things going, but I had to consider that Wings would one day be over and my marriage was a lifelong thing."

Denny, however, felt that Britton was an opportunist and was in the band for only the money. "He was always talking about, 'When I get my big house. . . '" When Wings members spoke like that, Denny said, it did not sit well with the boss.

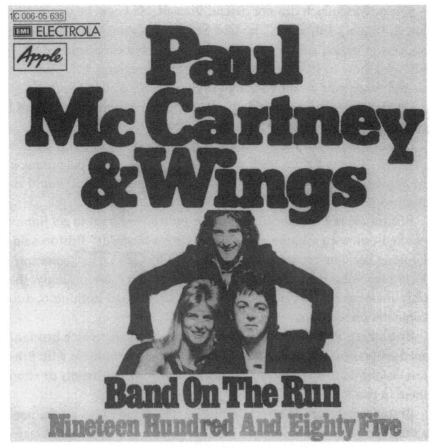

"Band on the Run" single, Germany, 1974.

Denny's girlfriend and future wife, JoJo, however, believes Britton was "a lovely guy" but was too straight for Wings. Unlike the other band members, Britton did not smoke marijuana and seldom partied, which was a common occurrence for the band after rehearsing or giving a concert. When he did go to a party with the group, Britton was more or less the designated driver. He said there'd be alcohol, pot, and tables "laid out with coke and anything you wanted . . . So everybody got absolutely legless, on the knowledge that I would drive them all home."

Not long after, Geoff Britton was out of Wings. Rumors surrounded his dismissal, with some concluding that he was forced out of the group. Britton later admitted it was he who decided to leave Wings. He also said it took him a year to get over losing the role.

"It's a funny band, Wings," Britton said at the time. "From a musician's point of view, it's a privilege to do it. From a career point of view, it's madness. No matter how good you are, you're always in the shadow of Paul."

Britton told the British press that when he joined the group he was promised royalties in "telephone numbers" (seven figures), but all that he saw was a scale wage with session fees and bonuses. Britton's blatant confessions to the press about Wings added fuel to the fire that a majority of the press already had against Linda, even though Britton had little to say about his former boss's wife. The press, however, felt that she was the main problem with the internal rifts inside Wings. Why was she in Paul McCartney's band? Linda continued to explain that she was simply "part of the frosting for this band. The four lads are the nucleus of the band."

The press also wanted to know why Denny Laine continued to stay with the McCartneys despite the number of personnel changes. "Wings is a challenge for me more than anything. People tend to forget, but it's the same for me: the challenge to get back up there after the Moodies," Denny replied, referring to Paul after the Beatles.

Tony Dorsey, the arranger of the brass section for *Venus and Mars*, introduced Paul to drummer Joe English. Impressed with him and his drumming, Paul invited English to play with the group—but he was not immediately asked to join Wings.

Joe English hailed from Rochester, New York and had joined Jam

Factory in 1968 when he was eighteen. He toured with Jimi Hendrix, the Grateful Dead, and the Allman Brothers Band. He had also played with Delaney and Bonnie before Wings. English, however, had fallen on hard times in the previous two years. "Everything was working against me," he recalled. "My old lady and two kids left me. I had no gigs, no money. I was on the bottom. But (my girlfriend) Dayle stuck with me, kept my spirits up, and helped me through."

With Geoff Britton out and Joe English in, the *Venus and Mars* sessions progressed. English was having the time of his life, like a number one fan hanging out with his idol. "Paul made it so if you wanted to come in every day and be part of the recording, mixing, ideas, and putting it all together, you could. He really gave everyone a lot of freedom," English said. "Of course, if he thought something should be played a certain way, he'd tell you to do it, and ninety-nine percent of the time I'd go along because it was usually the right thing. But if I came up with something better, I'd tell him and he'd go for it."

Also recorded during the *Venus and Mars* sessions in New Orleans was Linda's "New Orleans," but it wasn't included on the album. Neither were Paul's "Karate Chaos," his "Sea Dance," nor a live version of "Baby Face" recorded with the Tuxedo Jazz Band. The instrumental "Lunch Box/Odd Sox" wasn't released until 1980, as a B-side to the single "Coming Up." The New Orleans-influenced "My Carnival" remained shelved until ten years later, when it was finally released as a B-side to Paul's "Spies Like Us" single.

The group went to Los Angeles in February to complete the recording of the album. While on the way to Wally Heider's studio for mixing sessions, Paul asked Joe English to permanently join Wings. He was impressed by English's musical ability, but perhaps it was the drummer's lifestyle that swayed Paul into choosing him. English admitted he was "from the New York ghetto" and found fulfillment in the southern Georgia countryside. "We have three dogs, twenty-five chickens, a goat, six horses, and a cat, Amos, who we brought back from near death after he'd been thrown out of a car. I like to run a Massey Ferguson tractor, fish and plough the farm. It gets me away from the business." He sounded like Paul McCartney.

When Paul asked English to join Wings, "I said yes, and that was it!" English recalled. "Who wasn't a Beatles fan? You flash back to those first days and it's fun! What shocks me is to realize how many tunes he's written." English confessed that he, like the others, had no contract with Wings. "Paul's gone through that whole bit about being tied up with contracts and he doesn't want to get involved with that."

On the evening of 3 March 1975, Paul was driving a rented Lincoln Continental with Linda next to him in the front. He ran a red light on Santa Monica Boulevard and was pulled over by a policeman. The officer smelled a strange odor as he approached the driver's window, and then saw a smoldering marijuana joint on the floor. A plastic bag containing eighteen grams of marijuana was discovered in Linda's purse. Linda said the pot was hers, as was the joint on the floor, and that she was smoking it—not Paul. The officer looked and saw the three frightened McCartney girls cowering in the back seat.

Linda was taken to the police station and held until a five-hundred-dollar bail was posted. Paul had only two hundred dollars cash on him. After making several telephone calls, he came up with the remaining three hundred dollars from former Apple executive Peter Brown, who was staying at the Beverly Hills Hotel. Charges against Linda were later dropped when she agreed to attend six sessions with a psychiatrist. To make the arrangements more convenient, the judge allowed Linda to see a doctor in London. Some felt that because she was Paul's wife, she received a light punishment; however, drug counseling was not an uncommon sentence in Los Angeles for first-time offenders, which Linda was.

There is no denying that marijuana played a major part in the McCartneys' lives. Paul and Linda "did smoke a fantastic amount" of marijuana, Denny Laine recalled. "They smoked joints the way ordinary people smoke cigarettes." Laine felt that Paul's habit was the reason Wings' albums took so long to make, as the drug made Paul feel indecisive. In 1979, Paul alluded to this: "Sometimes I worry about the recording because you can just record things a little bit to the left of what you intended and the song doesn't sound as good as it could. That's why I spend so much time mixing. I know I worry too much, but it's impossible not to. And obviously when things get criticized by the press it still gets to me, although I try not to read it. It's impossible not (to) be sensitive to criticism."

Paul, Linda, and Denny with some recent gold, silver, and platinum. Band on the Run broke many industry records, including hitting number one on three separate occasions in Billboard magazine. Ad, United States, 1974.

The annual Grammy Awards, given for excellence in the recording field, were held in March 1975 while Wings were still in Los Angeles. *Band on the Run* was nominated for three awards, including Album of the Year. Although the album lost the top prize to Stevie Wonder's *Fulfillingness' First Finale*, it won two others: one for best-engineered recording (by Geoff Emerick), and one for best pop vocal group. The group celebrated by staying at the Beverly Wilshire Hotel and partying with an extravaganza that was unusual for the usually frugal McCartneys. In fact, Joe English said his new Porsche was stolen from the hotel's parking lot during their stay.

As a preview to *Venus and Mars*, "Listen to What the Man Said" was released as a single in May 1975. While recording the album, Paul enlisted saxophonist Tom Scott, whose solo on the cut was recorded live in one take while he was leaning over the control board. The song hit number one on the U.S. charts—Wings' eighth consecutive trip to the top ten singles charts, and one of the longest streaks of consecutive top ten hits by any performer in the 1970s.

"Listen to What the Man Said" was the first record by an ex-Beatle not to appear on the group's Apple label. By 1976, the ex-Beatles' contract with EMI had come up for renewal. George decided to form Dark Horse Records and signed with A&M (and eventually with Warner Brothers). Ringo, despite having the most success of all the ex-Beatles as a singles artist (from 1971 through 1975, all but two of his Apple singles hit the U.S. top ten), was not asked by EMI to renew. He secured contracts elsewhere. John, on the other hand, announced his retirement with no plans to record. Only Paul agreed to stay with EMI/Capitol—for a reported eight million dollars.

The Beatles "and Company" partnership was formally dissolved in 1975 at a private hearing in London High Court, more than four years after Paul's original request. The Apple company, however, continued to exist, primarily collecting record royalties and protecting Apple and the Beatles' name and likeness from copyright infringers.

On 2 May 1975, Apple Records closed. Save for most of the Beatles' records and the four Beatles' solo records (which were reissued by EMI/Capitol), after 1975 the Apple catalog was deleted for almost twenty years due to the continuing legalities between the Beatles,

"Junior's Farm" sheet music, 1974, with Geoff Britton as the
poker man and short-term Wings drummer.

Apple, and EMI. Thus, songs like "Those Were the Days" by Mary Hopkin, and Badfinger's "No Matter What" and "Day After Day" could not be purchased in music stores. Only after all was finally resolved in the 1990s did the Apple catalog once again become available to the record buying public.

Eighteen months had passed since the release of *Band on the Run*. Wings celebrated the completion of the long-awaited *Venus and Mars* album with a huge party in Los Angeles. The Queen Mary was rented in Long Beach for a star-studded party that was attended by the likes of Bob Dylan, Cher, Michael Jackson, Dean Martin, and George Harrison, which marked the first time since the breakup of the Beatles that Paul and George were seen socializing in public.

The album's cover, photographed by Linda, was simple, with one red and one yellow billiard ball shining against a black background. "Turns out Mars is vaguely red and Venus is vaguely yellow. But it's just guesswork," Paul remarked. "We thought, 'billiard balls, yes that's nice.' We were going for a package that would be nice to get, and also something recognizable. There's no story like *Band on the Run*." The cover design and Linda's photography ultimately won Britain's *Music Week*'s "Album Cover of the Year" award.

If the public and press expected a full-fledged, Cajun-sounding collection, they were disappointed. "There's a couple tunes of tunes we've got brass on and it's New Orleans brass," Paul said, "but the album doesn't sound too New Orleansy to me. I don't know. It's your opinion. Everybody says something different about every track anyway."

Critical response was mainly respectable, although not as strong as for *Band on the Run*. One of the industry's most critical of all critics, Robert Christgau of the *Village Voice,* approved of the album. "Superficially, which counts for a lot with McCartney, his New Orleans venture is his most appealing post-Beatles album—straight rock and roll with a few pop detours and one excursion into 'When I'm Sixty-Four' nostalgia. So clear in its melodies, mix, and basic pulse that his whimsical juxtapositions—robots on main Street, Rudy Vallee cheek by jowl with Allen Toussaint—sound like they might make some sense. Don't get me wrong—they probably don't, because McCartney's a convinced fool. But when the music is coherent it doesn't matter so much."

"I love this album," a *Disc* reviewer commented. *"Band on the Run* was a great album but (it) took a little while to grow on one. This is far more immediate, and a fine piece of work." *Record Mirror*'s reviewer commented, "McCulloch and English have added new vitality to Wings as is proved (on this) excellent album."

English reviewers, however, were dismayed when a version of "Crossroads" appeared at the end of the album. *Crossroads* was a popular British television soap opera. Americans had no idea what *Crossroads* was, other than a slow, if not fitting, instrumental song that closed the LP.

"Quite why Paul put Tony Hatch's forthcoming theme from the TV series *Crossroads* on the end of a superb album I cannot be sure," one British critic wrote, "except that it's published by ATV Music and gives Jimmy a chance to sign off with some long drawn out blues lines. Just a little jape, I suspect, like Paul adding 'nice base player,' a brief comment which sneaks onto the last few millimeters of groove."

"The tune is Tony Hatch's. It is a bit of a British joke," Paul attempted to explain. "I thought it might be too much of a British joke, but I'd still like to put it out . . . If you don't get the joke on it, it sounds like a closing theme. Sort of like, 'Ladies and gentlemen! Miss Diana Ross!' and Diana walks off with the orchestra playing. It's like one of those closing themes, if you don't get the joke.

"But if you see the joke, it comes after 'Lonely Old People'—nobody asked us to play. Nobody gets involved with lonely old people. One of the big things for lonely old people in England is to watch *Crossroads* . . . so that was it, originally used as a joke at the end."

The British critics were not amused, and England's *New Musical Express* dismissed *Venus and Mars*. " 'Listen to What the Man Said' is about the only half-way decent track. It is, in fact, almost exactly half-way decent, and has been made into a single on account of this semi-decency that it possesses." Another British journalist wrote that *Venus and Mars* was "one of the worst albums I've ever heard from a so-called 'major artist.'" The reviewer continued that until *Band on the Run*, McCartney was the possessor "of a 'basically bourgeois talent'— which meant that he was essentially uncommitted to rock & roll, was (still) cutesy pie . . . wrote songs that begged for Andy Williams to cover them . . . allowed an overwhelming facility for pleasant melody and easy-going charm to degenerate into vacuous glibness, angled his music at the mums and dads, came off poorly in comparison to the gritty honesty and commitment of John Lennon."

Many critics harped that if McCartney had been more committed to rock music, "He could be so good." But Linda commented, "Paul isn't God. The Beatles were not Gods."

The album was a commercial success and had a prerelease order of 1.5 million copies; it sold more than two million copies in the United States. It was the first album to be credited to Wings since *Wild Life*. "'Paul McCartney and Wings' is an embarrassment to me," Paul said in a press release in 1975. "It was never Paul McCartney and the Beatles, Paul McCartney and the Quarrymen, or Paul McCartney and the Moondogs. Wings is quicker and easier to say and everybody knows I'm in the group anyway."

In the summer, Paul, Linda, and the three girls moved to a circular, two-bedroom cottage near Rye in Sussex. Paul had spotted the property in a real estate catalog and was immediately intrigued by it. Despite owning larger dwellings, including a spacious home in London and the large farm in Scotland, Paul and Linda chose this cramped and less-than-modern dwelling for their home. The McCartneys maintained that their reason for making the change was so that they could raise the children out of the public eye and have them go to a public school in a smaller community. Three years later, Paul purchased a 160-acre property nearby called East Gate Farm. There he built a five-bedroom house with a swimming pool and stables, and enclosed it with a high fence and a lookout tower for intruders. Paul named the new estate Waterfalls.

After the release of and the favorable public response to *Venus and Mars*, Paul felt that the Wings lineup was strong enough to begin a full-fledged tour. In fact, the song "Rock Show" on *Venus and Mars* hinted that Wings may tour again, with its lyrical references to Wings' past and future concerts: the Hollywood Bowl, which had been a historic concert stop for the Beatles; the Concertgebouw, which was a highlight of Wings' 1972 tour; and Madison Square Garden, where Wings would eventually play.

During the first part of Wings' world tour in 1975, the band was set to play Japan, but then at the last minute were denied admission into the country. All shows were canceled.

It was to be an enormous tour. Paul planned for it to have things the world had never seen before: state-of-the-art sound equipment, lights and lasers, twelve and one-half tons of equipment, semi-trucks, and a specially chartered jet with "Wings over America" emblazoned on its sides.

Tony Dorsey was recruited to lead and organize a brass section. He enlisted Steve Howard on trumpet and flugelhorn and Thaddeus Richard, who was proficient on saxophone, clarinet, and flute. Howie Casey, a Liverpudlian whom Paul knew and who had been with Derry and the Seniors in the early 1960s, was also added for the tour's horn section. Casey, a session saxophonist, had previously played on Wings' *Band on the Run* album.

Several dozen more people were added to help supplement Wings in putting each concert together. Thirty-seven guitars would be needed for the tour, and Linda's equipment alone included a Fender-Rhodes electric piano, a Mellotron (a type of keyboard instrument), a model C3 Hammond organ, an ARP brand synthesizer, a Hohner Clavinet (another type of keyboard instrument), and a mini-Moog synthesizer.

Paul and the rest of the band were very aware of the savage attacks George Harrison had received from the press during his 1974 tour. It was Harrison's first—and last—tour of the United States. Paul had attended George's concert at Madison Square Garden in disguise, wearing an Afro wig and a mustache. Although George's voice was not in top form, Paul had concluded that his main mistake was altering the lyrics and arrangements of songs the audience had grown to know and love. For his tour, Paul decided it would be a mistake not to acknowledge the past by performing a few Beatles (and Paul McCartney-penned) songs.

Paul also decided to put the band through a series of long rehearsals, perfecting every element of the show before appearing in public. The sessions took place in both a vacant movie theater in Rye and on the huge sound stage at the EMI film studios in London. Not only did the band rehearse, but so did the lighting crew (who incorporated lasers and strobe lights), sound men (who were responsible for "flying monitor speakers," which hung above the audience, enabling even those in the back rows to hear every word and chord played), and everyone who would take part in working on the road crew, which numbered nearly fifty people. Ever the perfectionist, Paul took control and sent the entourage through exhaustive rehearsals in order to iron out any problems beforehand.

On 6 September 1975, Paul and Wings held a dress rehearsal of the concert before twelve hundred EMI employees and some members of the U.K. Wings Fan Club. After considering the audience's opinions and making a few changes in the show, Paul and Wings were ready to officially soar over Britain three days later.

The first leg of the tour consisted of twelve British cities in a two-week spread, with the first concert at the Southampton Gaumont on 9 September 1975. The crowds and reviewers were largely ecstatic. *Melody Maker* (which rarely gave much praise to Wings), however, sent a critic who commented that a London concert he attended was "vapid . . . a lackluster performance . . . nothing will shake my conviction that (the audience) was applauding an ex-Beatle's appearance rather than the Wings concert. For there are equally good rock shows on in most cities all the time; but a real live Beatle? That's a rarity."

Fortunately, one of the magazine's staff also attended the concert and felt the concert "was excellent from all points of view," and commented kindly that Linda's keyboard playing "is more than adequate for the fills she (is) called up to produce."

Paul was undaunted by any negative comments or attempts to change his mind about the tour. "I like music and we are in very depressed times, so if the music cheers people up that must be good."

Meanwhile, in late September 1975 a second single was pulled from *Venus and Mars*, the slow rocker "Letting Go." Although the song was remixed to make it a tighter, hotter cut for the single release, it failed to catch on with the radio programmers and record buyers. "Letting Go" barely made the American top forty, and it did worse in Britain. It broke the group's string of top ten hits and holds the distinction of being Wings' worst chart outing. (Strangely, the song was a favorite among concertgoers during the Wings world tour.) Just a month later, Capitol rush-released another single, a remixed version of "Venus and Mars Rock Show," which did much better but fell short of the top ten in the United States.

Not that it mattered to Wings. The *Venus and Mars* and *Band on the*

Run albums were still selling well, and the first part of the world tour concerts were sellouts.

Wings planned to fly through Australia after Britain, and then to Japan, where Wings were so popular that they were selling more records than in any country in Europe—Britain included.

On 28 October 1975, when Wings were to fly to Australia to begin that leg of the world tour, Qantas Airlines received a telephone call informing them that the band would be delayed and to please hold the flight. The jumbo jet, filled with disgruntled passengers, sat on the runway at Heathrow Airport for an hour waiting for the group. There were angry protests that the airline consented to Paul's request to wait, and the London *Sun* ran an editorial cartoon of a jet in the air turning around with the caption "We regret having to turn back. Mr. McCartney has forgotten his toothbrush."

The Australian leg of the tour was another success, with scalpers selling tickets for several times their face value. Or, as Paul put it, "Sinatra prices." Paul and the band enjoyed the tour, and he commented that it wasn't like work, but "more like a holiday." Wings gave interviews, but most of the questions were directed to Paul, and many of them regarded the Beatles. He politely answered, but reminded the interviewers that he was a member of Wings, and that the tour was not Paul McCartney, ex-Beatle.

Linda, of course, was understandably nervous about the tour. Like any other person, she disliked the press and fans being downright nasty to her. Although she had, by this time, a growing group of supporters. "I could have done a smart bit of p.r. during the time she was being criticized," Paul told biographer Hunter Davies. "But I thought 'Sod 'em.' I don't have to explain her away. She's my wife and I want her to play with the group. She'll improve. She's an innocent talent. That's all rock 'n roll music is. Innocent music."

Paul later said he needed her onstage "for my confidence. I, like an idiot, asked her to do it. And like a wonderful person, she agreed. It was mad, really. And we did it. On the '76 tour she was there, by God, doin' it all."

The audience response to the tour was tremendous from the start. The concerts sold out and were well received by the critics. Paul included several cuts from Wings' previous two albums, several

Ad for the upcoming At the Speed of Sound *album, 1976*

Wings hits, and also five Beatles songs. Many critics felt that "Yesterday" was the high point of the concert.

"When we first went on tour in England we were worried that the audience would be enthusiastic for the Beatles song," Paul later said. "After all that was the big challenge: 'Follow the Beatles.' But when we started doing the shows we found that there were a lot of people in the audience who weren't actually that keen on the whole thing that went before. They were quite familiar with the new stuff.

"Some even say, 'Why do the old stuff?' which is kind of weird for me, but I love that because it means you don't have to live in the past. It means you can keep moving. That's what I want."

"Paul, with his reputation, could have come back and played all the old Beatle numbers associated with him," Denny said. "It would have been very easy.

"I just dig those songs Wings plays. I was very much into the early Moody stuff. Later it became all very serious and bored me a bit. I want more immediate music, something you can really get involved with. Paul has this running right through him."

While in Australia, the group, their families, and their roadies decided to take a coach trip of the sites, including a visit to a zoo. The McCartneys' longtime housekeeper, Rose Martin, who traveled with Paul and Linda to help care for their children on the tour, arrived as the group entered the bus. She was prepared for the day, sporting a new hairdo and equipped with a camera. In front of everyone, Linda announced that Rose wasn't invited. She had a list of things for the housekeeper to do. Like Cinderella not going to the ball, Rose timidly stepped off the bus, and most everyone was embarrassed for her—except Linda. Denny Laine's then-girlfriend, JoJo, witnessed the incident but wasn't entirely surprised. Rose had told JoJo how "gracious and ladylike" Paul's former fiancée, Jane Asher, was. "I wouldn't like to repeat what she used to say about Linda," JoJo said.

Everything was set for Wings to tour Japan, from the group's visas being stamped, to the tickets being sold to the fans. But while in Melbourne, Australia, the band received a call. Paul was informed that his visa had been canceled because of his earlier drug convictions. The tour was called off, and everyone in the band was disappointed, especially Denny, who had wanted to visit Japan for several years.

"It was the Minister of Justice's fault," Paul told *Melody Maker*. "I suppose he'd say it was my fault for having smoked some of the deadly weed. But we had our visas signed by the London Japanese Embassy. Everything had been cleared . . . and we were in Australia, just about a week from going to Japan when a little note arrived saying the Japanese Minister of Justice says 'No' . . . It was just one of those things but we felt a bit sick about it."

To console their Japanese fans and to show the government what they denied their citizens, Paul offered a film of the group performing, to be shown for public viewing on Japanese television. At first the Japanese broadcasters were skeptical. They feared that a public showing of the film might be viewed as an endorsement for Paul's drug use. In the end, though, the broadcasters decided to air the film, followed by a debate over the "evils" of marijuana. The latter bothered Paul. "In a way we became martyrs for the cause," he complained, "which is a drag."

In a filmed statement at the time, Paul said: "If the Minister of Justice says we can't come in, then we can't come in. So we'll see you next time. Don't worry. We'll see you when we come back to your beautiful country. Sayonara."

5

Hands across the Water

The cancellation of the Japanese leg of the tour allowed the group to vacation. The McCartneys flew to Hawaii, where Paul set down plans for a new studio album. In January and February 1976, Wings returned to the studio and recorded the *At the Speed of Sound* album.

Perhaps the most democratic of all of Wings' albums, *At the Speed of Sound* featured lead vocals from each group member. Denny Laine had Paul's "The Note You Never Wrote" and his own composition "Time to Hide." Jimmy McCulloch sang his own "Wino Junko," and Joe English led Paul's "Must Do Something About It." Getting the group's total participation was "always the object of anything I do," Paul said, "to try and get out of a rut and do something different."

Linda sang lead on Paul's "Cook of the House," which he called "the first British cooking on record." McCulloch publicly commented that he was pleased for Linda and that the song was a tribute to her talent of whipping up a meal in no time. When a journalist asked Linda about her place in the kitchen, she snapped, "My answer is always 'Fuck off!'"

A small controversy occurred shortly before the album's release. Radio station KHJ-FM in Los Angeles played *At the Speed of Sound* twenty-four hours before other stations in the area received their copies. Many Los Angeles radio stations claimed that KHJ-FM had received special treatment from Capitol Records, and, as a result, these other stations refused to play the album. Station K100 went one step further and removed all McCartney and Wings material from their library. But as the summer progressed and the album became a huge hit, the stations relented and lifted their ban.

Although *At the Speed of Sound* was an immediate hit with the public, it was unable to warm most critics. Although they gave Paul credit for trying to make Wings more of a total group, most felt it was a letdown after *Band on the Run* and *Venus and Mars*. American critic R. Meltzer (who never cared for Wings' music) carped that the LP was "homogeneously tinkle-tinkle" and that the group was more like Percy Faith or the Ray Charles Singers with an "intrusive dose of English accent." Another critic called the album "a major disappointment," a "predictable drone (featuring) rocking chair music."

Cream magazine also reviewed the album: "The only substantial talent in this group is . . . Paul McCartney, and he is at full singing and composing strength only on the impassioned 'Beware My Love.' (T)he supporting cast is disgracefully third rate. It's my feeling that the vocals of Denny Laine are even lamer than those of . . . Linda, who at

Performing "Magneto and Titanium Man" from the Venus and Mars *album during the world tour.*

least fits in nicely as a background singer. Then again, that may simply reflect McCartney's cunning as a producer. He certainly adds some tricky textures to otherwise forgettable songs, but that can't disguise their triviality. C + ."

"It's crazy to have other people sing your songs when you can sing them so much better yourself," another critic harped. "It's just about understandable letting the wife to sing a track . . . but to have drummer Joe English and Laine have a go is simply not on when they're so obviously inferior singers to Paul himself."

But one critic defended English: "(He) unleashes a really professional soul sound." Paul agreed: "He can sing well . . . but it's nothing to what he *could* do."

"Silly Love Songs" was the first single pulled from the album, and it became a huge summer hit. The song went gold and hit the top of the three American charts. It also spent five weeks at the top of *Billboard*'s charts and was named the number one single of 1976. Paul became the only artist to have the number one song of the year in three different years (with the Beatles' "I Want to Hold Your Hand" in 1964 and "Hey Jude" in 1968 being the other two).

"Silly Love Songs" became Wings' biggest single, which *Time* called "The sort of tune that comes at the unwary out of car radios and open windows, attaching itself like a particularly stubborn cat. It will probably never go away . . . It is a sort of refined disco tune, made for dancing and casual listening." (While in Berlin on the Wings tour, Paul and Linda painted the words "Silly Love Songs" on a bed sheet and paraded it along the Berlin Wall with the rest of the group. The walk ended at Checkpoint Charlie.) The song was allegedly written in reaction to the critics who complained that McCartney's music was lightweight (obviously they never heard "Hi, Hi, Hi," "Junior's Farm," or "Get on the Right Thing" from *Red Rose Speedway*, among others).

"Let 'Em In," the second single from the album, also went gold and raced to near the top of the charts in late summer. *At the Speed of Sound* placed as the year's third most successful album in the United States, after Peter Frampton's *Frampton Comes Alive* and Fleetwood Mac's self-titled LP.

In March 1976, Wings continued their European tour. While in Denmark on 20 March, Paul and Linda made an unannounced visit to the

Danish Queen. Although the Queen was not there, the visit was leaked to the press. The Danes did not look upon the act as pretentious, but appreciated the friendliness and respect Paul and Linda showed to their beloved monarch.

It was a strange act considering that only two days earlier, on 18 March, Paul's father Jim McCartney had passed away. Jim had spent several years suffering from arthritis, and he died at the small home in Heswell that Paul had bought for him. At his side were his stepdaughter, Ruth, and his second wife, Angela, whom Jim had married in 1964.

Jim was cremated, and a small funeral was held on 22 March. Although his brother Mike attended the ceremony, Paul did not. "It was no coincidence," Mike McGear/McCartney later wrote, "that Paul was on the Continent at the time of the funeral (as I'm sure he'll tell you). Like Dad, who'd apologize for not being able to hold our

Paul entering his chartered jet for the 1976 Wings over America tour.

stomachs when, as kids, we were being sick, Paul would never face that sort of thing. As Dad would say, 'It's just the way you're made, son.'"

Paul did not speak about his father's death to anyone outside of his family. On 26 March, while the band was being interviewed in Paris, Paul was asked if his parents were living. He replied that they were not, and Denny Laine, who was sitting close by, nearly fell off his chair when he heard the revelation.

Nor did Paul speak about his father's home life. His stepmother, the former Angela Williams, had married Jim McCartney when she was thirty-four and he was sixty-two. Paul was not particularly close to his stepmother or to his stepsister Ruth, who had been five at the time of the wedding. After Jim's death, Angela ran an entertainment agency to make ends meet, but Paul felt that she was simply exploiting the McCartney name.

Wings were set to play in the United States in April and May, but Jimmy McCulloch had gotten into a fist fight with an American television and recording star and had broken a finger on his left hand. This prevented Jimmy from playing guitar, so the American tour was rescheduled for May and June. A reporter later asked to inspect McCulloch's broken finger. "Look," he said, holding it up, "it's fine now." "Yeah," Paul replied, "we're gonna break his arm next week."

The delay actually worked in the group's favor, however, as *At the Speed of Sound* and "Silly Love Songs" were climbing the charts when Wings flew in to conquer the States. Paul's methodical planning of the world tour—first Britain, then Australia and Europe, and ultimately the United States—made sense, building the tour from small to large venues. "America *is* the . . . biggest place on earth that you can go to play, outside of China and Russia," he reasoned. "America is the biggie, there's no doubt about that.

"It would have been silly to do it the other way around, to come into your biggest halls . . . I mean, to play 20,000 people you've got to have it together. About 14,000 was the top we played in Australia. In England, you can play certain special halls, but the normal venues are like 3,000. So very naturally we started off with 3,000 people, and then we went to 5,000, 6,000, 14,000 in Australia, and then we played some bigger halls in Europe which were more towards 15,000 . . . I like things like that. I like things step by step."

The band's first U.S. appearance was scheduled for May. For Paul, it was the first time in a decade he had performed in the States.

"There's no point in getting too hepped up about it," Paul told the *Sunday Times,* referring to the critics. "I know in America the press will be sitting in the front three rows, their pencils ready. It doesn't really matter what they say. I'm not as precious about Wings as I used to be. If (the tour) folds, it folds. Hard luck. I'll be very upset. I'll say, 'Sod it,' but we'll survive. I feel very secure with Wings now.

"We'll have to just go out and do the best we can," Paul said. "If it's the end of Wings, then it's the end of Wings."

Linda, however, was worried. She knew the American press was none too supportive of her playing with Wings. Outside the confines of a recording studio, she felt that playing in concert would again subject her to further criticism. "What worries me most about America is that we'll have to start again . . . I'll obviously be criticized and I'll hate it. I'd love to put the critics up there on stage and see them do better. You lose a few years of your life on stage. You live on your adrenaline. When it's over I want to crash out and go and live in Scotland for a while. We've got to do America and prove we can do it." Linda also added, "I don't want to spend my life touring."

The first American concert was held in Ft. Worth, Texas, on 3 May. "When the lights dimmed . . . virtually everyone in the arena stood in anticipation of what was clearly the most notable return to rock concerts since Bob Dylan's 1974 appearance in Chicago," the *Los Angeles Times* relayed. Under the headline McCARTNEY, WINGS SOAR OVER TEXAS, the newspaper applauded the concert. "Not only did the two hour concert demonstrate McCartney's ability to satisfy audiences with his post-Beatles work, it also enabled many in the audience to relive—at least indirectly—some of the magic of the heralded Beatles era. It was, then, a double triumph."

The 1976 Wings Over America portion of the world tour was described by one employee as a "military operation," with an entourage of thirty-three people plus publicists, playing twenty cities for thirty-one performances in large arenas. Orrin Bartlett, formerly of the FBI, was hired to scout out each concert venue and make inquires about bomb threats and grudge calls. *Time* noted, "Paul worries about snipers."

The American press heralded the arrival of Paul and Wings to the United States. "Mr. McCartney established himself and his band, Wings, as concert artists in their own right. And he did so triumphantly," wrote the *New York Times*. "(The audience) had good reason to like the Wings material, for on the whole it sounded better than it does on records. The arrangements were often very similar, but the whole tone was harder-edged, and Mr. McCartney's music benefited from the difference."

Billboard praised all of the band's members, particularly Joe English's excellent drumming, and commented that Linda served a key role in Wings. The *Washington Post* called the concert "an almost ideal display of what live rock & roll should be . . . as exciting visually as it was musically."

One news report announced: "The sound of his (is) new and is sweeping the land. Some critics think McCartney is making the same

During the world tour: Joe English stands in back, with Jimmy McCulloch on left and Denny Laine sitting next to his future wife JoJo.

sort of musical impact the Beatles made a decade ago, with a new sound, a new generation. McCartney says he's more interested in rocking with Wings than recalling the past.

"Ten years after his last tour on these shores with the Beatles, McCartney has returned to the U.S. victorious. (It) is the popular music event of the year."

"Paul didn't feel confidence in the band before," Linda told *Melody Maker*, "whereas this (line-up), he really knows he can get up there and sing. Because he knows that everybody else knows what they're doing . . . With this, we've listened to it and criticized it . . . Denny has been with us always, and he'd always fit in . . . Henry (McCullough) didn't really fit in. Jimmy is great and I think he'll improve a lot, he'll get better and really get his own style. And Joe English is a very good drummer, who has never really done anything big before. He's great on rhythms, and he doesn't come on like 'I'm a great drummer.' He just gets behind it . . . You can't ever say what's going to be in the future, but I'd like to see this band carry on."

During the tour, a reporter told Paul he felt that at thirty-three, McCartney was too old for rock and roll. He asked Paul if he felt he was too old. "I'll tell you what," Paul answered, "I don't . . . no, I wouldn't be here if I thought I was. You come to the show." Paul added if the reporter thought he was still too old, to come and see him. "And if you tell me I am," he joked as cameras recorded his reaction, "it's coats off outside!"

Most of the tour was pleasant, however. At an awards presentation during the tour, the band walked into a room full of reporters, one of whom was sleeping in one of the chairs reserved for the band. Wings entered, and upon seeing the sleeping "reporter," sat on either side of him, pretending that they, too, were sleeping. It was perhaps the most fun the group ever had with the press.

The "reporter" awoke, shocked and embarrassed. He took his place among the other reporters and asked Paul a question: "After being married all day . . ."

"All day, eh?" Paul interrupted.

"Yeah, and then at night having to perform together on stage, do you find it difficult? Don't you sometime like to say 'not tonight. Thanks darling, but I have a headache'?"

" 'Not tonight' jokes?''

"It's called henpecking . . .''

Paul laughed and handed a framed gold record to the smiling man, then promptly pulled it back. The man then asked Linda if she had been involved in Beatlemania, to which she answered no, but admitted she had liked the Rolling Stones.

"Oh, really? Which one?''

"Mick Jagger,'' she answered.

"Mick Jagger was?'' he turned to the side and commented to another reporter about Paul, "She got him on the rebound." He then realized his faux pas, then complimented the couple by saying that their marriage was going well.

"Yeah, but you're not helping matters any," Paul replied to the laughter that filled the room.

Paul arranged for rental homes in New York, Chicago, Dallas, and Los Angeles so that he, Linda, and the girls could stay in a home base rather than be cooped up in hotel rooms. They simply flew to the nearest home after each show. As for the rest of the crew, they flew or drove to the next city where Wings were scheduled to perform.

With each venue, Paul and the band arrived early for a full sound check to make sure the lighting and especially the sound system were up to par. Such perfectionism paid off with fans and reviewers, who complimented Wings on the clarity and precision of their sound. The tour went smoothly, as did most of the concerts. An accident did occur, however, when someone accidentally kicked one of the dozens of power cables one night. Unfortunately, that cable was a main one that cut out half of the sound system. It was soon corrected and considered a minor sideline to the concert series.

"In ten years, I'll be looking back and remembering everything about it. At the moment, I'm just zooming through it all," Paul commented. "If I were able to get away from the tour for awhile and come back to it through some sort of time machine, I'd definitely be freaking out. I'd be going, 'Wow. This is great.' Occasionally, on the place, we'll get the group together and say, 'Oh great, isn't it?' But most of the time, it's hard to see what is really happening until you get away from it."

Although Paul oversaw everything associated with the tour, the other male band members at times grew bored. On more than one occasion, the guys snuck into the cockpit of the band's jet to take a turn at the controls. Once, the jet went into a tailspin that threw Paul into the aisle. Fortunately, the aircraft was brought under control. When Paul found out that members of the band and entourage had been taking turns at the controls, he severely reprimanded each of them for their carelessness.

As the tour continued, so did the boredom of singing the same songs, setting up the same stage, following the same procedure, for all but a handful of the crew. The routine after-concert parties became more depressive than euphoric, and booze, pot, and cocaine were readily available. JoJo Laine once said that she stole some prime tickets from one of the road managers and scalped them. She used the money to buy cocaine for herself and Jimmy McCulloch.

By the end of June, the band played thirty-four concerts in twenty-one cities before more than 600,000 people. Tickets for the New York Madison Square Garden shows sold out in four hours, and 40,000 tickets for the Los Angeles Forum concerts sold out in three hours and fifteen minutes. Tickets sold out at some places within two hours. This was in the day when people actually stood in line to buy tickets, long before the era when the Internet and Ticketmaster enabled almost immediate sellouts.

The 67,100 people who turned up at the Seattle Kingdome broke the record for the largest turnout for an indoor concert by a single act. The massiveness of the Kingdome required three days for the crew to build the concert's set. Wings grossed $336,000 in Philadelphia, making that appearance one of the biggest box office receipts of 1976. In addition, the two-hour and fifteen-minute concert featured only Wings. Unlike most concerts by other artists, there was no opening act.

The Wings Over America tour was covered more extensively than perhaps any other concert of the decade. The major television networks and major newspapers carried several accounts of the tour, and such was the magnitude of Wings Over America that the *New York Times* even ran a story on the concert ticket sales. The concerts attracted celebrities including Cher, who saw the show with Elton John, Jack Nicholson, Angelica Huston, Carole King, Jackie Kennedy Onassis, and Neil Sedaka.

Paul remembered Sedaka visiting the band backstage after a concert. "He's a very sort of sweetie guy," Paul said. "He said to Linda, 'Oh, I listened so hard. I listened to every single note you sang, honey, and there was not one note out of tune. You were great!' She loved that."

"This tour has been a beauty for Paul," Linda said. "It has been the most positive thing that has happened to him in years, and he works very much on positive vibes. When it's possible, he flowers.

"He's very much his old self again. He's got his thinking cap on again. He has got a team together in Wings and the audiences have accepted it. Seeing him on this tour, I can realize now what he had before the Beatles broke up."

At the last U.S. concert, held at the Forum in Los Angeles on 23 June, Ringo Starr appeared after the last encore. The audience cheered,

Joe English and Denny Laine arrive in Cleveland, Ohio on 10 May 1976, during the U.S. leg of Wings' world tour.

thinking the pair would sing a song or say something publicly. But such wasn't the case. Ringo simply escorted his former band mate off the stage.

Afterwards, Paul held an $80,000 party at the mansion of late film star Harold Lloyd in Hollywood. The Los Angeles Ballet performed, and a chamber orchestra played Beatles and Wings songs. The swimming pool was drained and converted into a dance floor, and Nelson Riddle's Orchestra provided music. The invitations asked guests to wear white clothes. Paul and Linda hired Hawaiian artists to spray-paint designs on the guests' clothes. Rod Stewart, Warren Beatty, members of the Beach Boys, Tony Curtis, and David Cassidy were a few who attended that gala. The American leg of the tour lasted seven weeks and grossed more than five million dollars, a phenomenal amount at the time.

Returning to Europe, Paul remarked that the U.S. concert series "convinced us that we're a group, and I think it has convinced the audience, too. This wasn't just a one-time trip. This is going to be a working band. We'll be back." But the first Wings over America tour would eventually prove to be the band's last.

Before commencing the last leg of the world tour in Europe, Paul organized and held the first annual "Buddy Holly Week" in London. Paul had always been a fan of the late singer, who, with his band the Crickets, had achieved great success in the 1950s. Holly's career and life were cut short in 1959, however, when he died, along with Ritchie Valens and the Big Bopper, in an airplane crash near Clear Lake, Iowa. Through Linda's father, Paul had acquired Holly's song catalog a couple of years earlier as an investment.

In September 1976, Paul held a round of Holly events. An MPL luncheon honored Holly's producer, Norman Petty, who was flown in especially for the event. Eric Clapton, Elton John, and members of Queen, 10cc, and Roxy Music attended the luncheon, where Petty presented Paul with a pair of Holly's cuff links. In addition, a memorial dance was held at the Lyceum Ballroom in the Strand.

Paul also produced an album of Buddy Holly songs recorded by Denny Laine during this break in the tour. Entitled *Holly Days*, the idea for it originated when Linda's father, Lee Eastman, suggested that Denny should record the songs. Denny had also had the same idea.

"It's a tribute to Buddy Holly, really," Denny said. "Originally, it was that I like Buddy Holly songs." The cuts were recorded at Rude Studios in Scotland, "a little 4-track studio. Well, it wasn't a studio," Denny recalled, "it was a shack which we hired for and gave it a name." The entire album took less than three weeks to make, with Paul and Linda helping with backing tracks and harmonies. When released the following year, *Holly Days* did not sell, and reviewers dismissed the tribute as, in the word of *Rolling Stone*'s John Swenson, "an insult to Holly's memory."

Wings resumed the world tour on 19 September, with a quick tour through Europe including Vienna, Munich, and Zagreb, Yugoslavia. The latter stop was hailed as the first concert by a major rock artist in a communist country.

Wings also played a much-publicized UNESCO concert in St. Mark's Square, Venice, Italy on 30 September 1976. Venice had been long in need of restoration, and city officials were attempting to save the city through financial appeal. In September 1976 a series of concerts were held to raise money for the city. Peter Ustinov, Ravi Shankar, and the La Chunga Flamenco Ballet were a few who gave benefit performances.

The city approached Wings about doing a benefit concert, and the group agreed to perform. The organizing committee paid for hotel accommodations for the entourage, erected a stage, and provided seating for the audience. Wings agreed to pay for the transport of their equipment and to donate their services to the cause. Because of the decay on the Piazza and the fact that the area sits on wooden piles sunk into the sea bed, strict limitations were imposed on the audience size and the weight of the band's equipment. It was rumored, however, that the trucks hauling Wings' sound equipment were so heavy they cracked some ancient paving flags.

Authorities controlled the number of seats in front of the stage for fear of the weight. These limited seats were given to the press and dignitaries. The public viewed this action as separating the rich from the poor. As a result, 30,000 people turned up for the concert as a partial protest, but also to view Wings in a historic concert.

Although Wings played virtually the same set they had during the world tour, the crowd didn't mind, as most had never seen the group in concert. They were entertained with perhaps the best concert Wings had ever done, given the natural setting and the lighting crew's utilization of the open area. After the "Soily" encore, the laser lights shone on the red brick tower at the opposite end of Piazza from the stage, and converged into Wings' "W" emblem. The event raised $50,000 for the city of Venice.

Wings concluded the world tour in October with three nights at the Wembley Empire Pool. The Rolling Stones had appeared there in May, and their performance was generally judged a failure, but Wings tri-

"Silly Love Songs" single, Belgium, 1976.

umphed with their concerts there. For the 1976 portion of the world tour, the band had played forty-two concerts in ten countries.

In November 1976, it was announced in trade publications that Wings would perform and act in a science fiction film musical. Paul had met with Gene Roddenberry, the producer of television's *Star Trek* series, which had resulted in the proposed film project. But the plans fell through, especially when Steven Spielberg's *Close Encounters of the Third Kind* went into production.

In December 1976, Linda produced a solo project. It was not a recording, but a book called *Linda's Pictures*, which showcased her talent as a photographer. The book contained a wide selection of her works, from the Rolling Stones in New York in her early days, through her time at Fillmore East. The work contained photos of many of the great recording artists from the 1960s and also a large section devoted to Paul and the kids.

Some people felt that Linda was simply setting herself up for continued public humiliation by the critics. But this was different. This was the art of photography, and although she knew she wasn't the most accomplished or talented musician to be playing in one of the top bands in the world, she felt confident about her talents with photography.

With typical gutsiness, she had the work published. To her credit, the majority of reviews were excellent. Terry O'Neill, a foremost and accomplished photographer of noted personalities, reviewed Linda's work in *Melody Maker*: "I fully expected this book to be an unmitigated disaster. However, I was very pleasantly surprised and can only take my hat off as one professional to another. Well done! Very few good photographers emerge from the rock world and against that criterion, she has done more than well . . . her work of her husband and family is simply excellent; she tells a story with every shot."

In the meantime, Paul decided to release the world tour concerts in LP form. Nearly all of the American concerts were recorded, and after the tour Paul listened to each concert. He selected the five best recordings of the twenty-eight songs. For six weeks during the autumn of 1976, working as much as sixteen hours per day, seven days per week, Paul made the final selections and supervised the mixing and mastering of the chosen songs. The result was a live, three-record set of the tour, issued just before Christmas 1976.

The triple-record set *Wings over America* caught the ambiance of the concert tour and was the next best thing to actually being there. Critics hailed the album a great work and one of the best live rock recordings ever assembled. Dave Marsh of *Rolling Stone* called the album "nearly perfect . . . the band's toughness is firmly established."

Rick Mintz of *Stereo Review* thought Wings' "same songs, oddly enough, removed from the studio candy box and set on the stage of the concert hall, work brilliantly, displaying some hard, rough edges that make us think more of sandpaper than of sand castles.

"The album has fortunately avoided the pitfalls that await live-in-concert albums. Worst of these is the Greatest Hits trap, usually baited with enough sweetened laughter and applause for a *Lucy* rerun. The album does contain McCartney's hits, but there are also enough never-before-recorded songs to make the whole thing a new dish rather than a platter of leftovers. . . . Everyone *knows* McCartney is a rock-and-roll star. But it's nice to learn from this album . . . that he is such an accomplished *performer.*"

One reviewer proclaimed *Wings over America* to be an invaluable recording of "the best rock band in the world, at their best."

As usual, there were the usual snide remarks against Linda. *Cream* informed its readers to "Rest easy, neither Linda's keyboard work nor her background vocals offend—in fact, they're hardly noticeable."

Wings over America sold four million copies in the United States. As the industry counts each disc as one unit, the album sold the equivalent of twelve million copies. *Wings over America* holds the distinction of becoming the first triple album by a group to go to number one in the United States, and only the third triple set (up to that time) to hit number one, joining the *Woodstock* compilation concert series and George Harrison's *All Things Must Pass.*

"Maybe I'm Amazed," the single-that-never-was from Paul's 1970 *McCartney* album, was finally released under the Wings name as a live version from the album. Strangely, it did not appear until two months after the release of *Wings over America.* Although it hit the top ten in the United States, the record was not the huge success it deserved to be. Perhaps the majority of record buyers had already owned *McCart-*

ney or *Wings over America*—or both albums—by the time the song was issued as a single.

Wings over America also included the five Beatles songs ("The Long and Winding Road," "I've Just Seen a Face," "Lady Madonna," "Blackbird," and "Yesterday") that the band performed on the tour. Paul had the songwriting credits printed as "McCartney-Lennon," which some people felt was smug and petty. Although the pair had agreed that their writings would read "Lennon-McCartney," many of their later songs were not true collaborations. It was John Lennon who broke the tradition years earlier when he dropped Paul in favor of Yoko Ono as his songwriting partner. Paul was subtly letting people know he was the true author of these classic songs.

In addition to the recordings, the concert tour also produced two other (if belated) projects: a television documentary called *Wings over the World*, which was shown on television in 1979, and a theatrical film (*RockShow*) that had been filmed primarily at the Seattle Kingdome concert. *RockShow* did not make its premiere until November 1980.

By the end of 1976, Wings and Elton John were running neck and neck as the world's most popular recording artists. In the 1976 *Daily Mirror*'s British Rock & Pop Awards, Wings was named both Best Rock Band and Best Pop Band. Paul captured the Best Male Group Singer award.

"Wings are settled for years," Jimmy McCulloch proclaimed in late 1976. "It would be a shame if anything happened. I can't see anything cracking Wings in the foreseeable future." But in the new year, Wings ruffled its feathers and was left with only its core members once again.

6

Spin It On

In early 1977, Linda learned that she was pregnant again. Paul decided to scrap plans for more tours and to concentrate on other projects, primarily recording. Although Linda was pleased at not being on the road, she was put off whenever she felt that Paul spent too much time recording. In fact, friends said the only arguments they saw Paul and Linda have were regarding the time he spent working in the recording studio. One acquaintance close to the couple recalled, "all Paul cares about is music and Linda and the kids and smoke. When he was a Beatle, all he cared about was music and dope and sex. It really hasn't changed that much, has it?"

Joe English returned to the United States and wed his girlfriend Dayle Betts on 13 January 1977 in Forsyth, Georgia. After spending their honeymoon there, Joe went back to England to begin work on the next Wings album. Preliminary work began in February 1977 at Abbey Road Studios and continued through the end of March. The album was originally called *Water Wings*, but evolved into the released title, *London Town*.

There was, however, a lack of inspiration during the recordings in London, as the foggy, rainy days did little to lift the group's moods and creativity. Denny Laine mentioned to Paul that when he had been in Los Angeles he had visited a recording studio on a boat, and he told Paul he thought it might be an interesting way to record an album. Denny was surprised when Paul agreed that the group should try doing just that.

Paul chose to record in the U.S. Virgin Islands. At the end of April, the *Fair Carol* set sail from St. Thomas to Francis Bay on the island of St. John, where it awaited Wings' arrival. The yacht was equipped with a recording studio complete with a twenty-four-track tape recording system. Three other yachts were brought in as well: *The Samala*, a converted British mine-sweeper used for eating and sleeping, and the *El Toro*, which was for the McCartney family. A fourth yacht, *Wanderlust*, was also rented for the band's use.

Recording a performance on a boat may have sounded impossible, from salt water possibly affecting the equipment to the boat rocking in the water. But fortunately for the band and the fifteen or so others who joined them for recording, they were able to tape a track on their first day of recording.

It was idyllic for a time. As Mark Vigars, an assistant engineer for EMI who was with Wings, recalled: "By Monday, May 2, 1977, serious recording began and a pattern emerged of three or four hour sessions in the morning, the same from late afternoon to evening, interspersed with yet more swimming, water skiing and fantastic meals on *Samala*, prepared by no less than the captain, Tony Garton, a sound seaman but also a superb chef. On the morning of the 5th, Paul recorded a track playing acoustic guitar on the stern deck looking out over a sun-splashed sea. A dolphin surfaced to enjoy the super sound and splashed around the boat for some time."

At night the yachts were lit up with colored lights while Wings music floated across the bay. It was one of the most tranquil times the group experienced.

But on the first night out to sea, the captain of Paul's yacht smelled marijuana smoke and threatened to turn Paul over to the authorities. Eventually during their stay on the boats, they were visited by suspicious U.S. customs officials. This provoked Paul to write the song "Wanderlust" about the incident; the song eventually appeared on his 1982 solo album *Tug of War*.

There were additional mishaps. Denny suffered sunstroke, and a roadie broke his heel after slipping. Geoff Emerick electrocuted his foot, and a member of the boat crew lost his false teeth.

Jimmy McCulloch brought along his girlfriend, who happened to be a *Playboy* model, but Joe English's wife and Denny Laine's then-girlfriend JoJo were not allowed to join the band for the sessions. Of the women who were there, some romped around at times in bikinis, which did little for the confidence of Linda, who was self-conscious about being heavily pregnant. Eventually, Linda drummed up enough confidence to don a bikini, which not only exposed her swelling belly, but made public the fact that she followed the European women's custom of not shaving her legs or her armpits.

While in Jamaica that June, Wings recorded the standards "Sugar-

Paul McCartney & Wings—Best of the Best, *a 1976 greatest hits package released in Singapore.*

time" and "Mister Sandman" with Linda on lead vocals. The group recorded nine songs, and then returned to England for further work.

As to exactly why Paul decided to record on international waters, it was partially for tax reasons: Entertainers are taxed wherever they perform. For example, Wings were taxed in Los Angeles for their concerts there, just as they were in Seattle, Chicago, and New York. Songwriters are taxed by the locale where the song is composed, so authorities need to be given this information to determine where the composition will be taxed. (John Lennon had a habit of giving details of where Beatles songs were written and where they were recorded.) Most countries have tax experts who do nothing but track down what entertainers are doing and where they are doing it. According to an MPL employee, that was the reason why Paul decided to use international waters to compose and record. Although he willingly paid his 98 percent tax in England, he was less enthusiastic about paying taxes elsewhere.

As for other projects, Paul and Linda decided to give more attention to the Wings Fan Club. The club had been in existence in some form since its announcement on the back cover of the *Red Rose Speedway* album in 1973, but subscribers received only an occasional newsletter that was copied on a duplicating machine. The newsletters had been restyled and improved in 1974 with a glossy cover, and they were now published quarterly, more or less.

In 1977, Paul and Linda decided to revamp the newsletter altogether into a regular, professional-looking product. The couple had their ideas: it would be loaded with pictures (taken mainly by Linda); the paper on which it was printed was not to be shiny; and Paul's doodle was to be the paper's new logo. They wanted the product to look like a newspaper, so copies were printed at the Westminster Press in London because the business had the technology to produce the saw-edge side that newspapers have.

The new Wings Fun Club produced the official *Club Sandwich*, a newsletter by Paul and Linda that not only told its readers of the latest happenings in the lives of Wings, but also offered its members memorabilia and albums. (Twenty years later, these original early issues were selling for up to two hundred dollars per copy.)

In addition to his work on the formal Fun Club newsletter, Paul released an instrumental version of the *Ram* album, entitled *Thrilling-ton*, in April 1977. It had been recorded six years earlier. The tapes had been sitting around all this time, and Paul simply decided now to release them, issued under the pseudonym Percy "Thrills" Thrill-ington.

The public wasn't buying. The record (like "Walking in the Park with Eloise" before it) did not chart or gain any airplay. The public wasn't going to purchase a McCartney record unless they knew it was a McCartney record. By the time the public discovered the artist's true identity, the record had become a collector's item.

The Linda McCartney and Wings song "Seaside Woman" was also released in 1977, under the pseudonym Suzy and the Red Stripes. This record, however, did hit the American charts as word spread that it was Wings in disguise, but "Seaside Woman" had a very short chart life. It was a complete bomb in the United Kingdom, not making any of the charts.

Although this period kept Paul and Linda occupied with their proj-ects, it provided very little creatively for Joe English and Jimmy McCulloch. All too infrequently, Paul called the group in to record on a whim, and the pair was frustrated that there wasn't more to do. In his boredom, McCulloch began drinking more and taking more drugs.

In late summer, the band returned to the McCartneys' farm. McCul-loch was tired of the way Paul treated him like a session man. McCul-loch felt that there was no winning—or compromising—with the leader. He also hated living on the farm. His "cottage" had no hot water and no television, and his bed was simply an old urine-stained mattress.

There were many arguments between Paul and McCulloch. Paul had tried in vain to help McCulloch curtail his drinking, drugs, and mood swings. But McCulloch did not feel that there was a problem. Although he spent an enormous amount of time trying to straighten McCulloch out, Paul grew weary of this temperamental Wing. When McCulloch complained one time too many, Paul told him he could leave. According to McCartney biographer Geoffrey Giuliano, McCul-loch, in his frustration, told JoJo that he was going to murder Paul and the pregnant Linda in their sleep.

One night he had pulled out his hidden, illegally purchased handgun and walked outside to the McCartneys' bedroom window. McCulloch peered through the window and saw the couple asleep. He stretched out his nervous, shaking arms and pointed the gun. But he changed his mind and raced to a stream that ran through the property. There he put the gun in his mouth, intending to kill himself instead. At the last moment, he heard Denny and JoJo's van driving up to the farm. He decided not to end his life, but to end his tenure as a Wing instead.

A few days later, on 12 September, Linda gave birth by Cesarean section to a boy, James Louis. "I'm over the moon!" Paul told the British papers. "When I knew the baby was a boy I really flipped. He has fair hair and looks like Linda. She's still a bit tired, but otherwise smashing. I don't know how she does it."

Shortly after, McCulloch left Wings to join the reformed Small Faces. He publicly said that he was disappointed Wings hadn't evolved into a total band. "I'm sure (Paul) knows, and everyone knows that it can never be. As a touring band, it'll never be like other bands where you see the other members when you're not working. With Wings, it's get the work done and get home."

"I left amicably," McCulloch later said. "I don't think anyone was too upset about the parting. We had some very good times together. Though Linda doesn't know much about music, she's really a nice chick. And I certainly learned a lot over the past two years."

When Paul was asked about Jimmy McCulloch's exit, he replied, "It was just one of those things. When you think about it, it's really difficult to set up something like a stable group, because in my position you get all sort of weird little problems that you can't do much about. Say I decided to do it one way and a guitar player wants to do it another way. It becomes very difficult then, unless he comes up to me and tells me, 'Look, I wanna do it this way.'

"What was happening was that tension was just building up a bit and we didn't really feel like we (were) quite fitting. It was just getting to the point where we were either gonna do another album that was going to be hard to do and keep on arguing, or else we were just gonna decide that we don't need all that stuff and get on with the music. That's exactly what happened. Jimmy decided to leave . . .

Luckily he'd done all the required stuff on the album that we wanted him to do, so it worked out quite well for us."

Joe English followed suit, longing as well to be part of a real musical team. He complained that Linda was pulling the band down and that he was not a fan of Denny Laine, either. Like others before him, English had not seen any of the royalties he said were promised when he joined the group.

In regard to Joe English, Paul said he left because "he wanted to spend more time with his family in Georgia . . . He just wanted to go back home, really. He'd had enough of England after four years." Denny felt that English left because "he'd made some money, bought a house and got his Porsche."

Having gone through five members in seven years, Paul failed to realize that perhaps it was his unbending ways that had caused the upheavals in Wings. Or was he simply a poor judge of character? "I tend to forget people have to more or less live together and if there's a bit of bitchiness on a tour or during something boring like rehearsals," Paul admitted. "We need people who make that side of it very easy for each other . . ."

The pair's leaving did not bring an end to Wings, as Denny Laine continued to remain faithful to the McCartneys. Clipped to the core once again, Paul and Denny got together to collaborate. One of the songs they worked out was "Mull of Kintyre."

Paul had written the chorus in the summer of 1976, and then put the song away until the following year, when he showed it to Denny. Together the pair completed the music and lyrics. The song became the unofficial anthem of Scotland, complete with bagpipes and guitars.

Paul said he didn't know why he wrote a somewhat traditional sounding Scottish song. "I started off with the basic idea," Paul said, "because I thought that most Scottish songs you hear these days are either old tunes that people redo, or comedy songs about football or something like *Up Your Kilt*. So we decided that we'd get something together that was a new song with a modern feel to it, and see if we could make it sound as traditional and Scottish as possible."

Writing with Paul worked well, Denny indicated, even if he wasn't always given credit for his efforts. "Arrangement-wise we come with

"Seaside Woman" by Suzy and the Red Stripes was really by Linda McCartney and Wings in disguise. Sheet music, 1977.

better things," he said of collaborating, "word-wise better things. Things that suit our voices for harmonies."

As for the actual Mull of Kintyre, Denny recalled that the place had an old lighthouse, a decrepit hotel, and a cemetery. "It was the worst shithole in the world," Denny told author Geoffrey Giuliano. "I wouldn't wish the place on my worst enemy." But the lyrics and arrangement to the song compensated for any beauty that may have been lacking in the actual place.

While preparing to record "Mull of Kintyre," Denny suggested the Campbeltown band to play the bagpipes on the record. Paul invited the band's leader to his farm, where he showed Paul the notes a bagpipe can play, as they can't change key or modulate. Paul and Denny rewrote the song to incorporate the instrument, then had the bagpipers join them in recording the song on the farm. "It was quite a night—and quite a noise," Paul recalled. "We had a few beers and a hit."

Of "Mull of Kintyre," Paul wasn't terribly concerned about public or critical opinion as he personally felt the piece was one of Wings' best. "I hope they will be a bit surprised," he said, "because that's the whole idea, really. I mean, I heard a fellow on the radio the other day saying while he played it, 'There you go Paul. You keep them guessing.' And I think that's great."

The "Mull of Kintyre" single (backed with the hard-rocking "Girls' School") was released in November 1977. Although several Wings singles had hit the top of the charts in the United States, none had managed to hit number one on England's leading music chart, BMRB. In less than three weeks, "Mull of Kintyre" was number one on all three major English charts, including BMRB.

"It's been a long time coming," Paul said when he learned that the single had become his first post-Beatles number one BMRB song. "This should just about make our Christmas, and Hogmanay to boot."

The purchaser of the one millionth British copy of "Kintyre" was David Ackroyd, a soldier from St. Albans, who found a notice inside the record sleeve notifying him to contact EMI. He did so and received a special Christmas basket presented to him by Denny Laine. "Kintyre" soon after became the first single in Britain to go double platinum, and it eventually sold more than 2.5 million copies in Britain alone. The previous best-seller in the United Kingdom was the Beatles' "She Loves You." "Kintyre" stayed atop the U.K. charts for nine weeks. Wings had their first number one single in Germany and France with the song, and it also hit the top of the charts in several other countries as well, including Australia, Belgium, Holland, and New Zealand. Its worldwide sales exceeded 10 million.

"When we heard 'Mull of Kintyre' we knew it was going to be a biggie," remarked Leslie Hill, then-managing director of EMI, "but it has exceeded our greatest expectations. It's a great song, beautifully arranged and performed. There could be no better tribute than for it to become our biggest selling single ever." (NOTE: In 1984, Band Aid's "Do They Know It's Christmas?" became the United Kingdom's all-time best-seller, besting "Mull of Kintyre" by a few thousand copies, and in 1997, Elton John's "Candle in the Wind '97" became not only the biggest seller in the United Kingdom, but the world. Interestingly, McCartney was featured as a member of Band Aid, and thus he holds the distinction of being involved in three of the top four all-time best-selling singles in the United Kingdom.)

"Mull of Kintyre," however, failed to hit the top one hundred on any of the U.S. charts. The song's complete chart failure in the United States was then, and remains today, a mystery. The United States had grown to expect two styles of songs from Wings: either a ballad or a rocker. As "Mull of Kintyre" was considered a ballad, it was, perhaps, no accident that Paul had made the B-side a rock and roll song.

"The idea there is that people go buy the record and wanna dance and leap around," Paul reasoned, "they can just flip it over and they've got something completely different, rather than two of the same kind of thing. There might be a few people who still prefer the more rocking side, 'Girls' School.'" That's exactly what the American disc jockeys did, making "Girls' School" the A-side. It hit the Top 40 on the U.S. charts, but was considered a disappointment.

When "Mull of Kintyre" became such an astounding success, some members of the Campbeltown bagpipers who played on the recording started complaining to the press. They had been paid only scale wages (the going rate for musicians) for their work, and their sound contributed greatly to the song's success. Paul eventually doled out approximately three hundred dollars to each of the bagpipers.

Wings continued working on the *London Town* album into early 1978. At that time, Paul, Linda, and Denny recorded the song "Waterspout," which would have worked well with the water theme of *London Town*, but it was never commercially released.

After working on the album on and off for nearly a year, Paul released *London Town* in the spring of 1978. It was a generous offering, with thirteen cuts and fifty minutes' worth of music, and it contained five McCartney/Laine collaborations—more than any other Wings album. The album shipped platinum (the advance orders were such that it "sold" a million copies before being stocked in stores) and had a major hit song pulled from it ("With a Little Luck," which hit number one in the United States). *London Town* stalled at number two for a month and a half in the United States. It was kept from the top slot by the *Saturday Night Fever* soundtrack, which was the biggest-selling album in the country up to that time.

Some fans were disappointed with *London Town*. "Why wasn't 'Mull of Kintyre,' my biggest seller, on the album?" Paul recalled in 1990, voicing the fans' upset. "I didn't feel like it. When the (record company) man rang and said, 'We're going to put it on,' I said, 'No, we're not.' Don't ask. Just don't ask. It's my fault."

Robert Hilburn of the Los Angeles *Times* echoed most critics' feelings, in that he found the album Paul's "most confident and comfortable work. That doesn't mean, however, that it's also his boldest, a point that is going to make many critics look on it with disfavor. (It) lacks the hard, adventurous edges of *Band on the Run* and *Venus and Mars*, but the melodic fibers and arrangements are as solidly crafted as anything he has done in the '70s."

"I think I've some idea of the way Paul feels about things," Denny said in an interview to promote *London Town*. "I know the kind of pressure he's under because I've been through a lot of the same stuff myself. The longer you go on, the tougher it is in a lot of ways. People expect more and more from you. For Paul, having been part of the best rock 'n roll band in history . . . it must be very heavy. I admire him so much for the way he handles it and doesn't let it interfere with his music."

The interviewer responded: "It has been a remarkable relationship, to say the least."

"No problems," Denny replied. "None whatsoever."

After *London Town* was released, Paul hired two more musicians to replace Jimmy McCulloch and Joe English.

Laurence Juber was born on 12 November 1952 in the east of London, in a neighborhood called Stepney. His family later moved to north London, where he grew up and attended school. Juber joined the National Youth Jazz Orchestra in which he learned many musical styles, and he earned a Bachelor of Music degree in 1975. Among the many sessions he played were ones with John Williams, Shirley Bassey, and Jimmy Rafferty, and his ambition was to become a top studio musician. In the back of his mind there had been a dream to play with Paul McCartney or the Beatles.

Juber was working on *The David Essex Show* when Denny Laine appeared as a musical guest. Apparently, Juber made an impression on Denny, because six months later, he received a phone call from MPL: was he interested in joining Denny for a jam session? Of course he was. "By the way, Paul and Linda will be there," he was told.

Wings 1975–1978: From left, Joe English, Denny Laine, Linda, Jimmy McCulloch, Paul.

Juber arrived at Abbey Road Studios at the appointed hour. "We jammed to Chuck Berry tunes and reggae-sort of things, and then they asked me what I was doing for the next year. I thought it over for about a millisecond!" Juber recalled. He accepted the offer to join Wings "because you don't turn down that kind of job. I was 25 and ripe for a change of direction, and I looked at it as a furthering of my musical education. Sort of my Masters at McCartney University."

Steve Holly was also British, having been born in Isleworth, Middlesex on 24 August 1953. He had always wanted to play drums, and he eventually played with G. T. Moore and the Reggae Guitars, Kiki Dee, and Elton John. In March 1978, Holly was invited by friend Denny Laine to play, and he began casually jamming with Wings on occasion. In fact, he appeared with Wings on the "With a Little Luck" promotional video and is seen briefly playing drums.

When the time came for a formal audition, Holly traveled to London with Denny, where he was left waiting for a couple of hours before the McCartneys arrived. After they played together for "a good long time," Paul arrived at an immediate decision. "Fine," Paul said. "That's a good group. Sounds good—let's go."

Years later, Paul commented on the large turnover rate with Wings: "You'd like to think that if you get a band you can just get happy with each other and the chemistry will work. I think one of the main things was they were very conscious of being the follow-ups to the Beatles. I know people thought when the Beatles broke up, 'follow that.' It's not easy to just go and get another band. A lot of people wouldn't even attempt it. That's why I went very basic, and didn't try and sort of come in with the new Beatles. That's why I wanted to go the back route and try to work the band up. And if we were going to be as good as that then we would have done it on our own merit, and not on the fact that I'd been in the Beatles. Yeah there were a few personnel changes.

"We were trying to get it right, really. Various people would leave, and we'd have arguments and stuff. That's bands."

Juber and Holly were offered $450 per week each, at a time when bands of Wings' caliber earned group members as much as $2,500 per week. But Juber and Holly both felt that Paul's offer was enough to live comfortably.

The newly formed Wings recorded their first song together in May 1978: "Same Time, Next Year," a proposed song for the film of the same name. In late June 1978, the group converged at Paul's Spirit of Ranachan Studios, which he had built on his Scottish farm. The group began recording various songs for a new album, but on 5 July, they broke to work on songs that Paul wrote for another project. A dozen songs were recorded on that day for a planned full-length film on Rupert the Bear, the beloved cartoon character, to which Paul owned the rights. The songs were never released.

Work resumed on the album, entitled *Back to the Egg*, which Paul envisioned to be harder-sounding, mixed with the punk/new wave style that was then emerging. Paul enlisted Chris Thomas, who was intimately involved with punk/new wave in his associations with the Pretenders and the Sex Pistols, to co-produce the album. Thomas also had been an assistant to George Martin on *the Beatles* (the White Album) a decade earlier and worked on the sound problems with the upcoming film of Wings' 1975–76 world tour.

"It was a back-to-basics, garage band kind of feel," Juber recalled of the recordings for *Goldmine*. "That was probably why Steven (Holly) and I had a great deal of freedom—they really wanted to bring some kind of edge to things. There weren't too many times when Paul gave me specific things to play."

The band joked about the punk style and how they could change their names to fit in with the style. Paul chose "Noxious Fumes," and Linda was going to be "Vile Lin." Paul later remarked that Linda was the most likely punk contender from Wings. "(T)rying to sing straight, like soul or melodic, was not really her forte. But the minute she started yelling the songs, she was great. She never got to do that on stage . . . because I'm not really into that."

Late one evening on the farm, Linda confessed to Steve Holly that she really didn't care to be in the group. "All I truly want," she said, "is to be here with my family." Holly also knew that Paul had Linda in the group for the "comfortability of the situation." He appreciated the needs of both McCartneys but refused to take sides.

Working with Wings, Holly found that Paul was open enough to accept anything that was offered to him creatively, and to listen to suggestions. But as with the other Wings lineups, this incarnation also had its problems. Prior to recording the song "Old Siam, Sir" for the new album, Holly claimed to have written one of the main riffs for the song and accused Denny Laine of "borrowing" it prior to Paul's arriving for the recording. Holly said he dreamed it up, then Denny claimed the same, and the argument almost resulted in a fistfight. Paul broke it up when he sided with Denny.

Perhaps the most ambitious tracks recorded for the album were "Rockestra Theme" and "So Glad to See You Here," which included the all-star lineup "Rockestra." Along with Wings, the participants of Rockestra included Tony Ashton, Gary Booker, and John Paul Jones on piano and keyboards; John Bonham and Kenney Jones on drums; Pete Townshend, David Gilmore, and Hank Marvin on guitars; Bruce Thomas and Ronnie Lane on bass; and Ray Cooper, Tony Carr, Speedy Acquaye, and Maurice Pert on percussion. The *At the Speed of Sound* and *Wings Over America* tours' brass section, Howie Casey, Tony Dorsey, Thaddeus Richard, and Steve Howard, were also recruited.

The Rockestra lineup gathered at Abbey Road on 3 October 1978 for recording of the two tracks. Beginning at half past eleven o'clock in the morning, Paul took the group through rehearsals and five takes of "Rockestra Theme" alone. After a break, they began work on "So Glad to See You Here." Sixty microphones were used, along with two mixing consoles and a sixteen-track recorder to accommodate the huge group. As Paul wanted the event filmed for posterity, director Barry Chattington was hired and brought a full sound and camera crew, plus five Panavision cameras, to capture the group from various angles.

Wings continued recording songs for the album throughout the autumn at Lympne Castle in Kent, EMI Studios in London, and at Replica Studios in the basement of the MPL office. Paul also employed former Apple artists the Black Dyke Mills Band for recording. Many of the songs recorded at this time, including "Night Out," "Robber's Ball," and "A Love for You," remain unreleased but have found their way onto illegal bootlegs and into fans' collections.

After spending more than five years together and having two children, Denny and his longtime girlfriend JoJo were married in November 1978 on a boat outside of Marblehead, near Boston. Not only did

Paul and Linda not attend the ceremony, they did not give their best wishes. Several weeks passed before the McCartneys actually sent a wedding gift—a pair of silk sheets and pillowcases—not gift wrapped, but in a shopping bag with no card.

For the band's 1978 holiday gift to Wings fans, EMI packaged a collection of McCartney and Wings' greatest hits. Paul and Linda designed the cover themselves. Linda had purchased an art deco statuette of a woman with arms stretched out, and the couple decided to put it on the cover. They also felt that the statuette would look good surrounded by snow against the background of a clear blue sky.

As an example of their habitual overindulgence, Paul and Linda dispatched a full production crew to Switzerland to have the cover photographed there. An entire week was spent preparing the shoot, with personnel making a proper snowdrift and a chartered helicopter to take aerial photographs. But in the end, no one could imagine why such time was taken with the shoot or why such lengths were gone to (especially as the *London Town* cover looked thrown together). The *Wings Greatest* cover looked as if Linda could have done it by herself

Postcard of Wings 1978 promotion for the London Town *album.*

in the backyard of her home. The final cost of the cover alone: eight thousand dollars.

Paul chose the song content, which was not an easy task considering that the group had amassed almost two dozen top forty hits and that only twelve would fit on a single vinyl disc. *Wings Greatest* was welcomed by collectors, as five of the album's cuts had never before appeared on a Wings album. One faux pas, however, was the inclusion of Paul's solo hit "Another Day," recorded before Wings had been formed. In addition, "Mull of Kintyre" was included, even though it was Wings' least successful single in the United States, and "Uncle Albert/Admiral Halsey" was included although it had not been issued as a single in Britain. Many fans felt that a true Wings' greatest hits package would have included "Helen Wheels" and "Maybe I'm Amazed" (both U.S. top tens), or the remixed single version of "Venus and Mars Rock Show," which was not on any Wings album. In addition, "Listen to What the Man Said" was not included, although it was surely one of Wings' greatest, and "C Moon" and "Mary Had a Little Lamb" were both top tens in the United Kingdom. Both were also left off the album.

Robert Christgau of the *Village Voice* dismissed *Wings Greatest*, calling it "pop for potheads." *Rolling Stone*, however, welcomed the collection, which "demonstrated Paul's attention to the art of the single. (The album) is better than any individual album the group did except *Band on the Run*."

Although the collection sold more than a million copies in the United States, EMI hoped for bigger sales. It was the only Wings album not to crack the U.S. top ten, although it did so in Britain. *Wings Greatest* fulfilled Paul's EMI contract, which enabled him and the group to sign with another label. After fifteen years with EMI/Capitol, Paul decided to sign with the highest bidder.

Columbia Records (CBS) was the winner, in what was described as the worst deal CBS ever offered—and conversely the best deal Paul ever made. Rumored to be in the fifteen-million-dollar range, the deal included deferments, payouts, buybacks, release windows, tour support, et cetera, all in favor of Paul McCartney and Wings. In addition, Paul was given Frank Music, the publishing catalog of Frank Loesser, known for creating *Guys and Dolls,* among other shows. This acquisition fit nicely into Paul's already growing publishing catalog.

It was obvious to the industry that CBS president Walter Yetnikoff was bagging a trophy and had bought himself a Beatle. "It was all prestige for the company," a former CBS employee told McCartney biographer Chet Flippo. "It was too much money for an artist who was obviously past his prime. We knew we would have to really work our asses off to try to earn some of that money back. None of us who had to actually work (with) him felt that Paul had much left to say, but how can you argue with buying a Beatle? You should have been here in Black Rock (the CBS headquarters) the day Paul came in to press the flesh. It was like royalty. I've never seen anything like it. Everybody in the building came out of their offices and were just shaking."

The deal with CBS also gave Paul the then-remarkable royalty rate of twenty percent for every album sold. At the time, that amounted to $1.80 per album, regardless of any discounts involved. The label also acquired Paul's back catalog, and CBS could reissue those releases five years after their original release dates. The rights to the records then reverted back to Paul as long as he remained with the label. Another plus for Paul and another negative for Columbia.

Wings' first release under the Columbia label was the disco-inspired "Goodnight Tonight" single, which was promoted with a simple yet stylish video of the band dressed in 1920s gear, intercut with the band in present-day 1979. The song was completely different from anything Wings had done, and it showcased Laurence Juber's excellent classical guitar work throughout the cut.

The B-side of "Goodnight Tonight" was "Daytime Nighttime Suffering," a song penned by Paul a few months earlier. When Wings were recording *Back to the Egg,* Paul had announced to the other band members that if they could come up with a good enough song, it would be recorded and put on the B-side of the single. Such a generous gesture opened financial doors for the other band members, as the song could earn a small fortune as the flip side of a hit single. Each member—including Linda—spent the weekend trying to compose *the* song, but when Monday morning rolled around, Paul announced that he had written "the one." It was included as the B-side of "Goodnight

Tonight," which hit the top ten on both sides of the Atlantic in the spring of 1979 and went gold in the United States.

On 16 March 1979, the documentary of the 1975–76 world tour was belatedly and finally televised as *Wings over the World* in the United States (8 April in the United Kingdom). The delay was primarily due to the quality of the sound that was recorded with the film footage. "The sound wasn't that excellent," Paul said. "If you try and re-record the sound again, you'll lose the whole atmosphere." He and Chris Thomas worked with various electronic equipment to remedy the problem. Although interesting to view, the Wings of 1976 was not the Wings of 1979, and the project was simply two years overdue to capture any new fans.

In late spring, *Back to the Egg* was released, but it was not the success the band—or CBS, in particular—had hoped. "McCartney has become increasingly involved with the business side of music," one critic of the album snapped, "and the hours spent in boardrooms can hardly be the ideal environment in which to conceive musical flair."

Rolling Stone was particularly cruel: "It is just about the sorriest grab bag of dreck in recent memory . . . *Back to the Egg* doesn't contain one cut that's the least bit fleshed out or brought to any logical conclusion." Perhaps if Paul had formed the album as more of a concept, as simple as boy meets girl and boy gets girl, or if he had slow songs on one side and the hard rock songs on the other side, the album may have had more success. Or, had he remained focused on the original idea of a rock/punk album, there may have been more buyers. But in retrospect, Laurence Juber feels that there was "no way that it could ever be punky enough for what was going on in the music scene at the time."

When *Rolling Stone* asked Paul if *Back to the Egg* branched out into "new areas," Paul replied that was his intention, "slightly. You start off really wanting to do something very new, but eventually you come back to what is you. So it always gets an imprint of what is you and you always do what you do. The sort of magnetic forces, or whatever it is around you, make a certain mold, I think."

Columbia promoted the album heavily. There was a party at EMI's Abbey Road studios in England to celebrate the album's release. Blackened to resemble the inside of a frying pan, the tables were decorated with fried egg-printed tablecloths. A video of the Rockestra supersession was shown, and the event was rumored to have cost twelve thousand dollars. The album was issued in a special boxed set in Britain, and a thirty-minute promotional film was made for syndicated television.

It did not help. *Back to the Egg* peaked in the bottom half of the U.S. top ten, and although the album sold more than a million copies, CBS had hoped for more sales. Two singles were pulled, but neither sold in large numbers. The company quickly soured on Paul: he was the only major artist the company never had a welcoming party for.

"The records he delivered to us didn't help much," said a former CBS executive. "He came in with a fair hit single, 'Goodnight Tonight,' but he refused to put it on (*Back to the Egg*). So we had nothing to work with."

"It was a contest of wills," said the executive. "Paul wouldn't bend. He's a Beatle. He didn't have to have us. But we really wanted him."

The fact that the album "failed" in comparison to the previous Wings albums was not a complete surprise to the band. Steve Holly recalled that the group thought *Back to the Egg* was going to be a great album but that it was during the final mixing at Abbey Road that it "dawned on us that there might be problems."

"That wasn't one of our better albums," Paul confessed years later. "We'd come into it thinking (it) was going to be quite good, that one. You just can't get it right all the time. Name someone who has. Can't think of anyone—Stones, Elvis had 'deft' albums."

When asked if *Back to the Egg* was a concept album, Paul joked that it was a "bomb-cept."

During the summer of 1979, Paul spent much time recording— without Wings. These sessions eventually evolved into 1980's *McCartney II* album.

On 27 September 1979, Jimmy McCulloch was found dead in his London apartment. His brother Jack had stopped by to visit when he smelled a strange odor and thought there was a smoldering fire inside. Jack broke open the door and discovered the body of his brother, sitting in a chair as if watching television.

A pathologist discovered evidence that Jimmy had been smoking

Laurence Juber and Steve Holly with Linda, Paul, and Denny Laine in the final Wings lineup. 1979.

pot and drinking alcohol before dying of a huge overdose of morphine. But there were no traces of alcohol or drugs inside the apartment. In addition, the security chain on the door had been ripped out by someone other than Jack McCulloch, and there was no cash inside the apartment. The police felt that the apartment had been straightened up after McCulloch's death, yet there were no leads as to who may have been involved in his death. An open verdict was recorded at the inquest.

Two days earlier, Steve Holly had received a phone call from the former Wings guitarist. McCulloch had asked Holly if he was interested in doing some recording with him. Holly had said yes and was waiting for the date when he read of McCulloch's death in a newspaper.

McCulloch's funeral was attended by the McCartneys' housekeeper Rose Martin, as well as by the bands Stone the Crows and Maggie Bell; however, no one from Wings made an appearance. Denny Laine was working in a studio that day, and although he planned to attend, he debated whether or not to go to the service. He was "pissed off" with McCulloch over different things that had happened during their Wings years, and ultimately, Denny decided to stay in the studio working as he was told. He also did not wish to upset Paul. JoJo Laine, however, was present at the funeral.

By the fall of 1979, Wings had sold more than 100 million records around the world, and at the time they had achieved the unthinkable by outselling the Beatles. In fact, in October 1979 the *Guinness Book of World Records* presented Paul with a specially made rhodium disc to commemorate his achievement in becoming the most successful composer of all time, the holder of the largest number of gold records, and the world's most successful recording artist.

Despite the "failure" of *Back to the Egg*, Paul planned to tour again. The men of Wings were happy with the announcement because it meant more money, as the band members would share in the profits from each concert. Linda, however, could not have cared less. She dreaded going out on the road and wanted to simply retreat to their country home, be with family, and work on projects. Paul's insistence on Linda's staying with Wings strained their marriage at times. "(I)t caused a lot of trouble between us," Paul admitted years later.

Originally, Paul wanted to tour in a fashion similar to the 1972 University Tour. "At the moment we don't want a great big tour of the world with everything it entails," Paul said in *Club Sandwich*, "so it looks as though we'll just be turning up with our guitars and plugging them in wherever they want to listen to us. Another reason is that we've commissioned a screenplay by Willy Russell to be built around a group on the road, and for him to write it we have to be a group on the road again." Neither of these ideas came to fruition.

Paul instead went ahead with a major tour of twenty dates in Great Britain in late November into December. The tour began with a benefit concert at the financially troubled Royal Court Theater in Liverpool. At Steve Holly's suggestion, Paul hired Earl Okin as the opening act. Okin recalled not seeing a lot of drugs on the tour, and he never witnessed Paul and Linda smoking pot. He noted, however, that Paul constantly smoked Senior Service, a brand of strong cigarettes.

Okin remembered Linda fondly, said that she made him feel at home and welcome on the tour. "Nobody treated her like a star; she mucked in with everyone and was often ignored in favour of somebody else in pecking order. She never pulled rank! Indeed, she was often funny, with a very self-deprecatory sense of humour."

In Paul's mind, the tour never seemed to gel, a fact that bothered him greatly. At the Edinburgh Odeon concert, there was a power failure close to three-fourths into the song "Spin It On." After their initial shock, the band treated it as a joke. Denny Laine took center stage by providing acrobatics and a mock striptease to entertain the crowd. Musicians in the horn section walked onto the stage and started playing "When the Saints Go Marching In." Linda then led the audience in a sing-along to accompany the horn players. Shortly after, the power was restored, and Wings returned to their script and completed the concert. No mention was made of what Paul did during the outage.

Critics noted that the concerts weren't as polished as those on the previous world tour, and the song selection wasn't terribly strong. Such oddball songs as Linda's "Cook of the House," Paul's "Hot as Sun" from his first solo album, and Denny's "Again and Again and Again" were selected over Wings songs more suited for live performances like "Jet," "Hi, Hi, Hi," and "Girls' School."

"Everything about this performance," Mick Brown wrote in a *Rolling Stone* review of the sold-out 5 December concert at the Rainbow Theater in London, "seemed designed to take the spotlight off Paul McCartney and spread it among the rest of Wings . . . the impression given was not that of a deity with a boxful of thunderbolts, but a band on-stage for the hell of it."

Paul wasn't happy with the way the tour was going. He felt that the band had not rehearsed sufficiently to perform in public. When Holly stopped by Paul and Linda's dressing room to compliment them on how well the concert went one evening, Paul replied, "It sucked."

The drummer recalled that one-fourth of the way into the tour, he felt that the band was just going through the motions with the concerts. At one concert, Paul missed his queue in singing "Old Siam, Sir," something he would have found unacceptable in previous years. "But it wasn't all terrible, looking back," Holly told author Geoffrey Giuliano. "There were actually quite a few fine magic moments as well."

Perhaps the most magical moment occurred during Wings' final concert at the Apollo Theater in Glasgow. When the band returned for an encore, Paul played the opening chords to "Mull of Kintyre," which was a crowd pleaser. The audience rose to its feet when the Campbeltown bagpipers appeared onstage and joined in the song. "It was one of those incredible emotional high points you can never really adequately describe," Holly said.

During the tour, Paul followed in the footsteps of his former colleagues and released a holiday song. Although John Lennon's "Happy Xmas (War is Over)" had become a holiday standard and George Harrison's "Ding Dong, Ding Dong" had been a top forty entry in 1975, Paul's "Wonderful Christmastime" was not a welcomed holiday song at the time of its release. Although the video of the song featured Wings, the single was credited to Paul McCartney—sans Wings—and was recorded earlier in the summer. This was Paul's first solo credited single since 1971's "Another Day." Although "Wonderful Christmastime" was a top ten hit in Great Britain, the single did not chart on two of the United State's leading trade magazines—the first time a McCartney single did not chart since his leaving the Beatles.

In the fall of 1979, secretary-general of the United Nations Kurt Waldheim asked Paul if he'd consider reuniting with the three ex-Beatles for charity. Waldheim hoped the group would play a concert to raise money for the starving refugees of Kampuchea (formerly Cambodia). Paul telephoned George and Ringo, who agreed to appear together, but as part of a larger group. John, however, said he was not interested. Unfortunately for Beatle fans, news of the possible reunion was leaked to the press, and both George and Ringo scrapped their plans to take part. Paul contacted Waldheim and said that he didn't feel that the other members would reunite, but that he could deliver Wings.

Wings appeared at the last concert of the Concerts for the People of Kampuchea series, held December 26–29, 1979 at Hammersmith Odeon. For their set, Paul regrouped Rockestra and supplied gold lamé top hats and suit coats for the members to wear. Pete Townshend, however, took one look at the gaudy outfit and refused to wear it. As the others had consented to wearing the outfit, Townshend looked oddly out of place when he appeared onstage. Regardless, the polished concert was a shining triumph for Wings, and they were given high marks by both critics and the fans who attended the event.

An abbreviated two-record set of songs from the concert series was released several months later to raise additional money for the cause. A strange occurrence happened when Paul heard a cut from the concert played on the radio. He angrily telephoned the director of London's Capital Radio and demanded to know why the station was playing a Wings bootleg record. Paul was informed that the music that was aired was part of the legitimate album *Concerts for the People of Kampuchea*, then available at most every record store. Paul was stupefied, to say the least.

The decade ended on a high note, as Wings had become one of the top record sellers of the decade, and their 1975–76 world tour was regarded one of the three best tours of the 1970s. In Norway alone, Paul was voted the top composer and musician of 1979. Wings placed number three in that country as the top group of the year, and *Back to the Egg* was the number three album. The group also had three singles in the yearly top twenty-five, and three Wings albums placed in the top twenty of the decade: *Back to the Egg* at number twenty; *Band on the Run* at number five; and *London Town* at number four.

But like the Beatles before, Wings would not last through a second decade. In an interview with U.S. reporter Tom Snyder at the end of 1979, Paul and Linda appeared bored. "It doesn't appear that Wings is in any kind of trouble right now," Snyder said. After a pause, Paul replied, "Well, we keep trying, y'know." Snyder asked Paul how he kept the band and touring "fresh." "I think the trick is we enjoy doing it," he answered. "I suppose when we don't enjoy it we'll knock it on the head. But at the moment, we're still enjoying it." At that point, Linda turned to Paul and pretended to hit him on the head. Paul grinned.

7

Letting Go

After the holidays, Paul was set to continue touring. The band flew from Heathrow Airport to New York on the Concorde on 12 January 1980 to spend a few days in the Big Apple before embarking on a series of concerts.

While spending a belated holiday with Linda's family in New York, Paul telephoned John Lennon to see if he could stop by John's house for a visit. Yoko Ono took the call and told Paul that it wasn't a good time, as they were much too busy for company. It is unknown if John was ever told that Paul had called.

Regardless, Wings were in flight when Paul finally received permission to play Japan, which had been denied for the 1975–76 tour. Eleven sold-out dates were set in Japan, from 21 January through 2 February, including seven days at Tokyo's Budo Kan Hall. The concerts at Budo Kan sold out within four hours, with more than one hundred thousand tickets purchased.

Wings arrived at Tokyo's Narita Airport on 16 January 1980 and were met with an onslaught of fans, reporters, and photographers numbering in the hundreds. The group went through customs, and it was there that an official discovered a plastic bag in Paul's luggage. It contained 7.7 ounces of marijuana.

"It's all a mistake," Paul said quietly to the police officers as he was being handcuffed. "A serious mistake." He was immediately taken into custody. The remaining Wings had already gone through customs and were waiting on a bus for Paul and Linda. They were informed of a "minor" complication and were sent to a hotel without any explanation. Exhausted from the flight, Steve Holly simply retreated to his room and fell fast asleep. That evening, Linda telephoned and told him that Paul was in jail. Holly thought she was joking, but when he arrived in the hotel bar to meet the band for dinner, Holly saw the MPL staff members with forlorn expressions; police officers were questioning them. He realized Linda was not kidding.

Meanwhile, Linda had made frantic telephone calls to her family and MPL. During the interrogations, Paul had told the officials that the pot was his. But many close to the couple felt that it was Linda who had packed the pot in the bag without Paul's knowledge.

Paul knew that possession of pot in Japan was a serious offense. But he did not know that the maximum sentence for drug offenses in Japan was five years' imprisonment for possession and seven years, plus a fine, for smuggling. It was reported that Paul may have gotten eight years in prison if the Japanese government had wanted to make an example out of him. The government had begun to do just that, in fact, by banning all Wings songs from the national radio and television stations.

Although the world in general did not feel that the Japanese would keep the world's most successful composer incarcerated for eight years for marijuana possession, there were times when Paul and Linda both thought differently. So did many fans. Kenneth Lambert, a twenty-nine-year-old McCartney fan, went to a Miami International Airport reservation counter and demanded a ticket to fly to Japan. His intention was to "free Paul." When Lambert did not have the money to pay for the ticket, he was refused. Lambert continued to ask for a ticket and, after he was politely asked to leave several times, an argument broke out. Lambert pulled out a realistic-looking toy gun and began waving it wildly overhead. Airport officers saw the gun and shot the man dead.

The Japanese tour was canceled, and MPL decided to altogether scrap any plans of touring other countries as well. Tickets were refunded, and Paul was required to reimburse every expenditure, from hall rentals to promotional expenses, at a cost of more than five hundred thousand pounds. When the concert series scheduled for

Budo Kan Hall was canceled, only 37 percent of the ticket holders asked for a refund. The others preferred to keep their tickets as a souvenir of the tour that never was.

The aborted tour not only cost Paul money, but also took potential earnings from fellow Wings members. Although they were paid their weekly salaries, the canceled tour cost the members tens of thousands of dollars that they were to earn from the concerts. While Linda remained in Japan with Paul, the three other Wings left the country on 21 January after strong suggestions by MPL executives. As for Denny, his anger moved him to record a single called "Japanese Tears" with former Wings members Denny Seiwell and Henry McCul-

"Adios a la Noche" ("Goodnight Tonight") single, Spain, 1979.

lough. It was a song about a Japanese Wings fan who was hoping to see the group, only to have her heart broken by Paul's arrest. Denny's anger toward Paul and Linda did not subside for several months, and his disappointment lingered for years.

"(The band members) were all very annoyed with me, rather than sympathetic," Paul said years later, "because me being busted had blown one of their big pay days. (T)hey weren't too happy with me. But I think Wings (was) really finished in my mind then. It had sort of lost its charm. It wasn't fun anymore and the bust had definitely sort of cemented that. It was like, 'Oh God, who needs all this?'" But Paul waited several months before making a final decision in disbanding Wings.

After ten days in jail, Paul was released and deported. On the flight back to Britain, Paul told members of the media who were on the plane: "I have been a fool. What I did was incredibly dumb. I had just come from the States and still had the American attitude that marijuana isn't really too bad. I didn't appreciate how strict the Japanese are about it. I was really scared, thinking I might be in prison for so long. I've made up my mind. I've been smoking marijuana for more than eleven years now, but I'm never going to touch that stuff again."

But Paul and Linda would be busted again in the coming years.

Whether Linda packed the dope (as rumored) or if Paul was the actual possessor (as he claimed) remains unknown. One source says the Japanese customs men believed that Linda was the possessor and had begun questioning her when Paul stepped forward to claim responsibility. Other sources said Paul was acting "suspiciously" as he went through customs, which led to a search of the luggage.

John Lennon felt that the bust was "somebody's cheap trick" and that Paul "was set up and that's the long and unfortunate short of it." Lennon thought a customs official may have planted the marijuana on Paul for the purpose of publicity or notoriety. "(T)he minute the Beatle steps up, it's presto—headlines," Lennon believed.

Rumors circulated that Yoko Ono made phone calls to a relative of hers in Japan who had connections with customs and that she alerted this relative that the McCartneys may have marijuana in their possession. Yoko denied this, and in fact, she wrote a letter along with John to the Japanese authorities requesting Paul's release from prison.

In the spring of 1980, Paul released *McCartney II*, ten years after the first *McCartney* appeared. Like the first, it was a homemade LP, with Paul playing all of the instruments and doing all of the vocals. Linda provided a few backing vocals, but it was mainly a Paul McCartney album, made entirely by Paul McCartney. "There's nothing against Wings in this," Paul stated. "Everyone's got a lot of solo stuff. Denny has got one (album), Laurence had got one, I've got one. Sometime we'll just pick it all up again."

The album was a large disappointment to critics. *Billboard* commented that it was "another exercise in pop insignificance. . . . Again, the decline of McCartney's lyrics are evident, with most songs coming across as cute throwaways. Even the melodies don't seem as penetrating."

One of the more surprising aspects of the *McCartney II* project was the release of the single "Coming Up," which was pulled as a preview to the upcoming album. As Paul played all of the instruments on the cut, the promotional video showed Paul in various characters, from Frank Zappa to Beatle Paul, playing in a band called the Plastic Macs.

Although the studio release of "Coming Up" marked McCartney's second solo single in a year, it was the B-side that became a smash hit in the United States. The B-side was none other than Wings' "Coming Up (Live at Glasgow)," which had been recorded at the Glasgow Apollo in Scotland during their 1979 U.K. tour.

Although "Coming Up" (the studio version) was climbing the U.S. charts in the spring of 1980, radio station programmers and listeners preferred the live version rather than the speeded-up vocals and techno-pop-sounding A-side. So, Paul's version was overtaken by Wings' version, and that side became a number one gold single. (Paul's version officially had reached number one on the *Billboard* charts, but it was rarely heard on American radio stations as the other version's popularity grew. Wings' live version replaced the McCartney solo at the top spot during the single's second week at number one, and the single stayed at number one for an additional week. In the United Kingdom and most of the world, though, Paul's solo version was the hit.)

The Wings version was such a huge hit that the American public wanted "Coming Up (Live at Glasgow)" included on the *McCartney II*

LP. Paul wouldn't allow CBS to include the song on the album because it was, after all, a *solo* album. As a compromise, CBS pressed a special one-sided seven-inch disc of Wings' "Coming Up (Live at Glasgow)" and included it with initial copies of the U.S. *McCartney II* release to satisfy consumer demand—and Paul.

Although Wings as a group remained dormant through most of 1980, each of the individual members branched out creatively. Denny Laine and Steve Holly went on the road with JoJo Laine, Andy Richards of the Alex Harvey Band, and Mike Piggot. The group performed gigs on weekends throughout the summer in Britain, not unlike Wings' University Tour in 1972.

Laurence Juber went off on his own. He visited the United States to find "inspiration for some songs I've been writing," and also completed an album of guitar versions of some standard songs from the MPL publishing catalog.

Linda continued her photography. She invited animator Oscar Grillo to make an animated film of her song "Seaside Woman." The completed piece was selected as the official British entry for the short film category at the 1980 Cannes Film Festival, where it won the Palm d'Or prize in May. "Paul and I would have loved to have flown to Cannes to accept the award," Linda said, "but I have to collect the children from school this afternoon." *Seaside Woman* was later shown with the Peter Sellers hit film *Being There*.

Paul continued with his music. In July, he flew to France to help Ringo Starr with his new album. Paul supplied the songs "Private Property" and "Attention," both of which appeared on Ringo's *Stop and Smell the Roses* work. Laurence Juber also played guitar on the cuts, and Linda provided background vocals. In the fall, Paul and Wings entered the studios to begin work on another album. The work was intended as part of a collection of post-1970 McCartney outtakes and unreleased songs, similar to the postponed 1974 work *Cold Cuts*. These were Wings' last recording sessions as a group and were never legally released.

In August 1980, John Lennon (with Yoko Ono) also returned to the studio to record *Double Fantasy*, his first album in five years. In 1975, Lennon had decided to help care for his newborn son, Sean, and had thus retired from the music scene. Now that his son was no longer an infant, Lennon felt comfortable enough to return to making records.

The *Double Fantasy* album and its first single, "(Just Like) Starting Over," were climbing the charts during late autumn. Both Lennon and Yoko Ono were enjoying favorable press for their joint effort, especially Ono, whose work was considered progressive like the punk/new wave style that was popular at the time.

After working on additional recordings the evening of 8 December 1980, Lennon was shot by a deranged fan while entering his New York apartment complex, the Dakota. Although she miraculously escaped

"Rockestra Theme" single, France, 1979.

injury, Yoko Ono endured having to witness the incident. Lennon died en route to the hospital.

The morning after Lennon's death, Paddy Moloney, leader of Ireland's band the Chieftains, flew into London to help with Paul's album session. "Paul looked stunned," Moloney recalled. "He said it was tragic and useless, and it didn't make any sense. I don't think at the end of the session that it had really penetrated either . . . that John was dead, gone forever. I'm sure it took a few days before that finally sank in."

Paul spent part of the day in the studio working on the song "Rainclouds" with Denny Laine. When Paul left the studio to return home, the press descended upon him like vultures and expected a statement. Still shocked by Lennon's death, all Paul could say was, "It's a drag." Although he meant Lennon's death was "the unholiest drag of all drags," as Paul later explained, the original statement hit the news and portrayed Paul as uncaring, even flippant. Photographs taken at the time of the statement, however, reveal Paul with a pale, drawn face; he appears to be in shock.

Of course, Paul mourned Lennon's passing, but he did so in private, as his friends and family have attested. Lennon's death impacted Paul beyond the loss of one of his old friends. As death threats against Paul and his family trickled in, he hired security guards and decided he did not want to tour anymore. Apart from Linda, though, the other members of Wings wanted to tour. Unbeknownst at the time, the death of John Lennon ultimately helped bring about the breakup of Wings.

In early 1981, Paul, Linda, and Denny Laine sang backing vocals on George Harrison's tribute to John Lennon, "All Those Years Ago." The recording was a Beatles reunion of sorts, as the song featured Ringo Starr on drums. Denny believed that Paul always felt superior to George Harrison, and he recalled that when they were working on the song at Harrison's estate, it was uncomfortable. After Paul and Linda left, the atmosphere became light and relaxed. Perhaps it was because Paul was a perfectionist and wanted everything just so. But Denny believed it was due to the fact that Paul "doesn't trust people and it shows."

"All Those Years Ago" was released in the spring and shot up to near the top of the worldwide charts. Denny Laine said he was never paid for the session.

Paul and Linda traveled to Montserrat on 1 February to resume work on the new Wings album. Paul then made a public announcement that there would be no Wings tours in the near future, mainly due to the fact that there were death threats against him in the aftermath of Lennon's murder. Also, the revised *Cold Cuts* album from the previous autumn was shelved, as its release didn't seem appropriate so soon after John Lennon's death. Since the work-driven McCartney had no tour to plan and no album to promote, he concentrated on the new recordings. At first, the Montserrat setting was not ideal, as the seemingly eternal rift within Wings crested once again. This time, it was between Paul and Denny Laine. Denny felt that his income throughout the past ten years was too little, and he was also upset at how his wife JoJo had been treated in the past. At times, Paul would make remarks about JoJo, like "I can't work with people around." Also, Denny felt that Linda envied JoJo, who was very much the extrovert that Linda never was. There was no compromise to address Denny's concerns, so Denny packed his bags and left the island and the group.

Denny says the primary reason he left Wings was because of the drug bust in Japan. "We'd been waiting for five years to get there," he said. "One reason is the fact that we couldn't do the tour. That was the biggest upset of all." Denny viewed Paul and Linda's casual handling of marijuana as careless. Countless times throughout the years, he had witnessed them smuggling the drug, including secreting it away in places such as the hood of their daughter Stella's coat and baby James' diaper, where it would not be found.

Paul and Linda returned to England in March, where Paul was honored with an inclusion in *Who's Who*, receiving a forty-one-line listing—more than several judges, politicians, and other noted public figures had been given. There was no mention of George Harrison or Ringo Starr in the famous red book. Soon after, Paul decided to finally shed his ties with Wings.

In the beginning, Wings had served to help Paul. No one could have predicted the group's success. No one thought Wings would ever hold the world's record (at the time) for the largest stadium concert, that being the one at the Seattle Kingdome with sixty-seven thousand people in attendance—besting the previous record held by the Beatles' Shea Stadium appearance by two thousand. The Beatles had garnered eleven Grammy Award nominations during the course of their years as a group. By 1980, Wings had achieved the same.

By 1974, Paul had earned more money with Wings than he had in the so-called "boom years" with the Beatles, and by 1980, the group had sold more records than the Beatles. Both facts were circulated widely around the world, and there were several Beatles purist who scoffed at the facts. They felt that no group—let alone Wings—could ever outdo the Beatles in any form or manner. Still, John Lennon most likely went to his grave knowing that the unthinkable had been done—by Paul McCartney's other group, no less.

The music industry had been buzzing about the breakup of Wings for several months; however, no public comment was forthcoming. Paul McCartney, it was felt, simply had no use for Wings any longer. He accomplished what he had set out to do, and there was no need to continue. But before Paul could make a formal announcement, the news media discovered the truth.

On 26 April 1981, the story hit the newspapers. The Associated Press ran the following:

> Ex-Beatle Paul McCartney, who formed the group Wings after the Beatles split up in 1970, is now facing problems with his band.
>
> Denny Laine, the band's drummer since it was formed in 1971, quit suddenly Tuesday in a disagreement over McCartney's decision to halt the group's public appearances temporarily.
>
> The departure left only two permanent members of the group, McCartney and his wife, Linda.
>
> "There is no row," said Laine's manager Brian Adams. "But Denny likes to tour and Paul has decided that Wings will not make any tour plans for the future."
>
> A London newspaper reported Laine, 36, decided to quit the group during a recent recording session in the West Indies, where the next Wings album was made. It claimed McCartney halted public appearances because he had received several death threats since the murder in New York of fellow ex-Beatle John Lennon on Dec. 8.

A McCartney spokesman denied that report, adding that Wings would still exist.

Steve Holly learned about the breakup by reading the story in a newspaper. It was the first he had heard of the group disbanding. He telephoned Paul to ask him about it.

"What is this? I read that Wings is no more."

"Yeah, well, I've been meaning to call you . . ." Paul stammered. He relayed to Holly that George Martin felt that it may be better if *Tug of War* (the upcoming album) was completed as a solo project. Holly felt that Paul was simply using the producer as a scapegoat.

Although initially angry and disappointed, Holly later realized that in the time he was with Paul and Wings, he had gained an enormous amount of experience and credibility. He has often wondered what may have transpired had the final Wings lineup made another album.

Laurence Juber had a similar telephone conversation with Paul. "If I'd been aggressive about it, I probably could've ingratiated myself in on some of the *Tug of War* sessions. But I just didn't see the point." Although the band officially broke up in April 1981, Juber had already moved to New York the previous January. "I think as the band progressed, the dichotomy between his own creativity and the momentum the band generated was starting to show."

"I had a lot freedom (with Wings)," Juber later said, "and creatively I thoroughly enjoyed it because it was very challenging and it was quite an education watching Paul McCartney work."

Although understandably disappointed with the disbanding, Juber went on to great success on his own. He continued with a successful solo career, releasing several acoustic guitar instrumental albums and winning a Grammy award. He also composed music for such television shows as *Home Improvement, Boy Meets World,* and *Roseanne* and for films such as *The Brady Bunch Movie* and *Dirty Dancing*. Juber also continued with studio work, including Belinda Carlisle's number one song "Mad About You."

Wings' *Club Sandwich* reported of the breakup simply: "As I'm sure most of you know, Denny, Steve and Laurence have left Wings to concentrate on their solo careers, and I know you'll join me in wishing them well." Other than a three-picture tribute to Denny Laine, there was no discussion in the magazine as to why the group dissolved. (After the breakup of Wings, the *Wings Fun Club* was changed to *The Paul McCartney Fun Club* and survived until October 1998. After the death of Linda McCartney, Paul decided to end the *Club Sandwich* newsletter after twenty-one years and eighty-six issues. He felt that "it is not appropriate to continue without [Linda].")

Paul later said that one of the jokes he had been waiting to use for when the group disbanded was to say "Wings Fold." "But as it turned out, when it did happen, Wings didn't actually fold," Paul recalled, "it sort of dissolved. Like sugar in tea."

Denny Laine was gone and would not return to the group. After the disappointment of the Japanese drug bust, he knew the group would have problems organizing another tour. Denny also felt that Paul's word in regard to promised royalties did not mean a thing. There were no signed agreements or contracts—nothing on paper in Denny's defense. Denny no longer trusted his boss, partner, and friend.

Back in 1974, Denny had said: "(W)e went to Nashville with the idea that we'd get this group together and we'd all sign contracts and be Wings, as a business thing . . . but then it seemed as if it was being a bit rushed. I thought, 'hang on—let's make sure that this is the right group.' Then I started thinking about contracts, and I decided that I could be in any group without signing a contact . . . It just didn't seem necessary to me, and the minute I said this to Paul he said, 'great, that's the way I want it too,' and then I realized that we were only going through this thing with contracts because we'd all been advised to do it. It wasn't what we wanted."

In 1973, Denny had received a "retainer fee" of £5,730, which fell to £3,408 in 1974. For services up to August 1974 "to include albums to *Band on the Run* and singles to 'Junior's Farm,'" Denny received £40,000. By 1975, Denny had earned approximately $100,000, far less than what should have been his share of the millions of dollars Wings earned in that year alone.

Paul's attitude toward Denny was a "stick by me and you'll do all right" attitude. But many times Denny did not feel he was being paid adequately. At one time he had gotten so angry with Paul regarding his salary that Paul wrote him a check for £30,000. "I was kept in the dark all the time about money," Denny said, "just given a check now and again."

In February 1975 during the *Venus and Mars* sessions, Denny purchased a large estate in Laleham, Suffolk for the cut-rate price of £37,500. Rather than purchase the estate outright as he wanted to, Denny was convinced by MPL and the Eastmans to let them buy the property on his behalf for tax reasons. Denny then paid MPL a monthly installment based on a monthly mortgage. In a few short years, when Denny was out of Wings, he could not afford to pay the mortgage and eventually lost the house.

As for co-writing "Mull of Kintyre" and the million of dollars he should have been paid for that song alone, Denny said he got "very little" from it. Denny was on salary, not on a percentage of records sold. Although Denny said he was promised more money, he says "it never came." Allegedly, Denny was paid twenty thousand dollars for his contributions to "Mull of Kintyre"—a minuscule amount to a co-writer and performer of a song that eventually sold more than ten million records worldwide. In a Paul McCartney exposé for the London *Sun*, it was reported Paul had paid Denny ninety thousand pounds for Denny's publishing rights for the songs he had written with Wings, including "Mull of Kintyre."

Regarding Denny's earnings while with Wings, Paul told *Rolling Stone* in 1989: "I've got receipts in the office for a million pounds paid to him. Now, you tell me a guy in any group who got that for the period we were together. Now, okay, if you think I sound mean after that, I've got to disagree with you. I mean, these people like Denny say, 'He didn't pay us enough.' Well, what I think is, 'Yeah, well, I did.' I know exactly what I paid him. It's a million. And that was worth more than a million is worth now."

On 16 December 1986, Denny Laine appeared before the London Courts to declare bankruptcy. He claimed debts amounting to £76,035, with zero assets.

Paul McCartney has become rock music's first billionaire, earning more than fifty million dollars per year from various investments, primarily music publishing. He owns the rights to such works as "Sentimental Journey," "Stormy Weather," and "One for My Baby," and to such musicals as *Grease*, *A Chorus Line*, *Annie*, *The Music Man*, and *La*

Cage Aux Folles. In addition to the Buddy Holly catalog (including such standards as "Peggy Sue" and "It's So Easy"), Paul owns the copyrights to more than ten thousand songs. Unfortunately for him, though, acquiring the Beatles' catalog (or at least the songs Paul himself wrote as a Beatle) will more than likely never happen. After Michael Jackson outbid Paul in the mid-1980s when the Beatles catalog came up for sale, Jackson later sold part of the catalog to the huge Sony entertainment group.

With all the others gone, only Linda McCartney remained, just like when she and Paul first started out together. Perhaps she was relieved that Wings was no more. She confessed that she had thought of quitting Wings "a hundred thousand times." Now she was free to explore other avenues she had more interest in.

But the slagging of Linda, although not as frequent as before, nonetheless continued on occasion, despite the raves she received as an accomplished photographer and despite her entrepreneurial endeavors in vegetarian cookbooks and frozen foods. In fact, during the 1981 Beatlefest held in New Jersey, any appearance of Linda in a promotional film resulted in the crowd's booing and jeering at the screen.

Yoko Ono visited Paul, Linda, and their children on the Scottish farm after John Lennon's death. Yoko appreciated the luster and beauty of the farm and the fact that it was an actual working farm, not a manicured estate. She also paid attention to the McCartney children, especially how they interacted with Linda.

"What I noticed with sadness was that (the) children were living with the pain of what their mother went through," Yoko recalled. "Their mother was attacked by the world and for a long time not recognized for her achievements. Everything that was good was considered the work of her husband, and everything the public did not approve of was considered her doing. I didn't hear any of this from Linda. But when I met her children and saw how protective they were of their mother, I felt the pain of their knowledge that the world was not always kind to her."

One female fan recalled running into Paul and Linda while they were working on *Back to the Egg*. She asked Linda if she and Paul would allow her friend to take a picture of the three of them. Linda agreed and put her arm around the fan.

A few months later, the fan was walking past MPL and noticed Paul and Linda in a first floor office. Linda looked out the window, remembered the fan, and waved to her.

"I think it's time somebody wrote a few kind words about (Linda)," the fan wrote in the *Beatles Monthly Book*. "She is not as horrible as some people try to make her sound. Unfortunately, not many people have had the chance to meet her and see how friendly she is."

In fact, all the members of Wings' last incarnation liked Linda as a person and gave her credit. Many people felt that the main reason she was in the group was because she was Paul's wife. But the last Wings members knew that Linda was in the group because Paul wanted her there beside him. There is a difference.

As for the end of Wings, Paul told *Music Express* in 1982: "I hate the pressure of a group. . . . Anyway, I got bored with the whole idea, and I thought, 'Christ! I'm coming up to forty now. I don't really have to stay in a group. There's no rule anywhere that says I have to do it that way.' At the time Denny and I were writing together. He was going to stay on, but we had a bit of a falling out. It was nothing madly serious, but he decided to go his own way, saying that he wanted to tour.

". . . it was his own decision (to leave). I can never remember these things because once they're gone, they're gone."

Music Express then asked Paul, "Could it be that with Wings you were not personally satisfied with the music that was being produced?" He answered: "And that's why I (ended Wings), you mean? Yeah, probably that kind of thing."

Paul's solo *Tug of War* album was released in 1982 to glowing reviews, the best he had seen since *Band on the Run*. Denny Laine was credited as playing on five of the album's cuts. *Tug of War* became Paul's first LP to hit number one in the United States since 1977. It was also his last solo album to hit number one on the U.S. charts.

For many years, Paul spoke very little about his Wings days, not unlike the way that, when he led Wings, he did not talk much about the Beatles. The song lineups during his two post-Wings world tours included very few Wings hits, to the disappointment of fans. It was almost as if he dismissed that part of his life. In fact, when the video film version of his solo 1989–90 world tour was released, the song

The long-awaited and much-delayed Cold Cuts *still has not been legitimately released.
Containing unreleased Wings songs, bootlegged copies of this album have found their way
into fans' collections. This copy is dated 1980.*

"Band on the Run" was intercut with footage not of Wings, but
strangely enough, of the Beatles.

When the 1989–90 world tour hit the United States, it was the first
time in thirteen years Paul had played there; he had not played the
United States since the *Wings over America* tour. He had a new lineup,
but the group was not called Wings. This was Paul McCartney and
His Band. This and his subsequent New World Tour a couple of years
later were mostly sellouts, and Linda, of course, was with him on both
tours. It was during this era that radio stations around the world

acquired a bootlegged copy of the band playing "Hey Jude," which was performed late in the show. At the particular performance this recording came from, Linda had been tired when the time came to sing the tune.

The song was a from show in Knebworth Park, England and had been recorded by sound engineers at the concert, who removed all of the instruments and vocals from the track except for Linda's. As a cruel and cheap joke, the tape was sent to radio stations. Many dee-jays aired the recording of Linda's voice—which was off-key—to embarrass her. They succeeded. It was as if she were the only perfor-mer who ever sang off-key. "Denny Laine (sang) off-key," Linda once remarked during the 1975–76 world tour. "So what?"

And as Jack Douglas, who produced John Lennon and Yoko Ono's *Double Fantasy* album, has attested, Lennon did not always sing in key either. "(I) didn't really have to push him," Douglas said. "I just had to direct him."

Longtime McCartney publicist Geoff Baker broke the news about the "Hey Jude" recording to Linda. "Lin just took it on the chin," Baker said. "But it did hurt her . . . a lot. She used to say 'sticks and stones may break my bones, but words will break my heart.' There's a lot of musicians who wouldn't thank anyone for isolating their voice."

During the tour, Paul telephoned Denny Laine. By then Denny and JoJo Laine had divorced, and it had been years since the former band mates had spoken. The tour must have brought back a flood of memo-ries of Wings' triumphant world tour, as well as the group's other tours, all of which Denny had taken part in.

When Paul's call came through, Denny was unfortunately out. Paul arranged for him to attend a show and meet him backstage after-wards. When the show was over, Denny and a friend went backstage and waited as Paul was being interviewed. After half an hour of wait-ing, Denny gave up and left, not knowing why Paul had wanted to see him, or what—if anything—he had to tell him.

One day in the mid-1990s, Denny Seiwell decided to telephone Paul. More than two decades had passed since Wings' original drummer had abruptly left the group. Seiwell told Paul how sorry he was that he left the group. "It was the shittiest decision that I ever made,"

Seiwell later remarked. "That is my only regret in life." Paul and Seiwell eventually became closer, and today they speak regularly.

In 1995, Linda McCartney was diagnosed with breast cancer. The cancer eventually spread to her liver and, knowing she had little time to live, she convinced Paul and their children to go on vacation in April 1998. The family flew to their private farm near Tucson, Arizona, which was Linda's favorite place. The last days were spent laughing, talking, eating, and even riding horseback for two days. Then Linda took a turn for the worse.

On 17 April, as she was lying in her bed and surrounded by her family, Paul's was the last voice she heard. He said to her, "You're up on your beautiful Appaloosa stallion. It's a fine spring day . . . and the sky is clear blue." He had barely finished the sentence when Linda closed her eyes and passed away. (While in Texas during the 1976 *Wings over America* tour, Paul and Linda had taken a wrong exit on the freeway and chanced upon an Appaloosa grazing in a pasture. They purchased the horse and took it back to Britain for breeding.)

Paul and Linda had spent only eleven nights apart in their twenty-nine years of marriage. Theirs was one of the most successful marriages ever in the entertainment world, not only in longevity, but in that they were each other's best friends and confidants and that they were completely devoted to each other. And although Paul had grieved quietly and quickly when others close to him had passed away, Paul's grief over the loss of Linda was so deep and lengthy that friends were concerned for his own well-being.

Paul later finished assembling a compilation of Linda's songs, which she had in fact been working on for the past several years. "Cow" and "I Got Up" were aimed at those who sneered at her activism roles, and "The Light Comes from Within" was a middle-fingered gesture to those who had savaged her. The collection was released as *Wide Prairie* in autumn 1998. *Entertainment Weekly* reviewed the CD:

> . . . The simpleminded domestic anthem "Cook of the House" is genuinely terrible, but the poignant "Love's Full Glory" manifests a sweetly unaffected amateur charm and the animal-rights broadside "Cow" makes its point with subtle passion . . .
>
> Though the late Wings singer and songwriter received little respect during her lifetime, this compilation of 16 of her solo tunes . . . isn't quite so easy to dismiss.

Epilogue

With the advent of Linda McCartney's illness, few realized that any possibility of a Wings reunion no longer existed. Despite her lack of formal musical training beforehand, she had learned to play musical instruments under the scrutiny of the public and critics. She won many of them over as the years progressed. She had a place in Wings, and she earned it.

One must realize that Paul McCartney had wanted to perform again, to entertain, to sing and write songs. Linda gave him the courage and strength he needed after the Beatles broke up, a fact Paul himself pointed out on countless occasions. So, then, credit must go to Linda for Wings, for Paul could not, would not have continued in the early days without her by his side. It is obvious today that she did not want to be in the band, but her love for her husband was much stronger than many knew. Not many people could have survived the criticism and harsh words Linda endured in her tenure with Wings, which is in itself a testament to the woman very few people in the rock world truly knew.

"In Wings I was innocent," Linda said in the late 1980s. "So they said I sang out of tune. Big deal. Most punks do, and I love punk. I like the rough edge. I don't like perfect and beautiful. So I fit in nicely. I'm the rough edge."

The "rough edge" musically perhaps, but one distinction Wings had that set them apart from other groups was its flawless harmonizing, to which Linda contributed greatly, along with Denny Laine. Music has not heard that before or since Wings.

"It's a shame that Linda died," Denny Laine commented recently. "It really finished everything. . . ."

In March 1999, a twenty-fifth anniversary limited edition of Paul and Wings' most popular album was rereleased. *Band on the Run* was remastered and, although it was released four months late from the actual anniversary, it was greeted with revived interest in the album and in the group that Paul spoke of less and less with each passing year.

The *Band on the Run* anniversary package was a surprise hit and debuted in the United States at number one on *Billboard's* Pop Catalog Album charts. It included the original U.S. song listing (with "Helen Wheels") and also a second disc, which comprised interviews and

Wings' last incarnation, 1978–1981: From left, Laurence Juber, Denny Laine, Linda and Paul McCartney, and drummer Steve Holly in front.

snatches of different versions of songs that had appeared on the album. Also featured were new and archival interviews with Linda, album engineer Geoff Emerick, and arranger Tony Visconti. A majority of the interviews were with Paul, of course.

Although he was a major force with Wings and contributed to *Band on the Run*, there was only one short interview clip from Denny Laine included on the disc. More time was spent on the recollections of James Coburn and Kenny Lynch, whose sole contributions were that they had appeared on the album's cover. The lack of Linda's, and especially Denny's, remembrances made the package almost a tombstone—more so than a celebration—of the album. Apparently, whatever grudge Paul McCartney had against Denny Laine in 1981 continues to this day.

Paul McCartney as a solo artist has been unable to capture a glimmer of the success he found with Wings, let alone the Beatles. Aside from chart-topping duets with Stevie Wonder and Michael Jackson, only three solo McCartney songs have hit the U.S. top ten, and those were before 1987. After 1982's *Tug of War*, Paul had to wait another fifteen years before another of his albums hit the U.S. top ten, that being 1997's *Flaming Pie*.

In the spring of 2001, a Wings anthology appeared worldwide in the form of a documentary and compact disc compilation. Entitled *Wingspan*, it was produced by Paul's daughter Mary and her husband. Although it provided an intimate look at the group, with Mary's interviews of Paul and some previously recorded anecdotes by Linda, it was far from a satisfying history of the group. As the documentary did not include any interviews with other members of the group, the work was not a fair, well-rounded representation of Wings.

Laurence Juber remarks that the film made it appear that the band fell apart right after Paul's bust in Japan. He felt that this was not true, pointing out that the group won a Grammy Award for "Rockestra Theme" in the spring of 1980 and that "Coming Up (Live at Glasgow)" was a huge summer hit. "There was still life in (Wings)," he says. "And we worked pretty consistent throughout 1980."

The two-CD *Wingspan* set was a greater disappointment. Divided into two parts, "Hits" and "History," the forty-track set featured a dozen McCartney solo songs, including half of the *McCartney* album alone. Even Wings' hit rendition of "Maybe I'm Amazed" was passed over in favor of Paul's solo version. "Helen Wheels" and "Venus and Mars Rock Show" appeared on the "History" portion of the set, and "Getting Closer," "Mary Had a Little Lamb," "I've Had Enough," "Sally G.," "London Town," "Letting Go," "Girls' School," "Arrow Through Me," and "Give Ireland Back to the Irish"—all U.S. top forty hits—were left off the compilation to make room for non-Wings cuts.

Wings' albums were also treated with disregard, as *London Town* and *At the Speed of Sound* were represented with two cuts each and *Back to the Egg, Wild Life,* and *Red Rose Speedway* had one each (not counting an improvisational medley of "Bip Bop/Hey Diddle" featuring only Paul and Linda). *Wings over America* fared the worst, in that not one song was included from that set. Conversely, five songs from *McCartney* and such non-Wings/Paul solo cuts as "Pipes of Peace" (1983), "Waterfalls" (1980), "Tug of War"(1982), "Take It Away" (1982), and two versions of "No More Lonely Nights" (1985) did make it into the set. As to where the logic was in Paul's song selection, the question remains unanswered. Although a booklet included with the set provided several photographs, the liner notes were minimal, not making any detailed references to the successes the band achieved.

But all of these things were somewhat forgiven when the CD set was released. Critics now regarded Wings as a true band, and *Wingspan* debuted at number two in the United States. The 224,000 copies sold during its first week of release in the United States stunned music retailers and insiders, simply because they had felt that there wouldn't be a large audience for Wings after all these years. The compilation later went double platinum. By comparison, greatest hits compilations by current acts such as the Backstreet Boys and Mariah Carey each sold fewer than two hundred thousand copies in their first weeks of release. Apparently, the public's hunger for Wings had gone unnoticed not only to Paul but also to the music industry.

Wingspan hit number five in the United Kingdom and hit near the top of the charts worldwide. Considering that all but one of the songs had been previously released—and some reissued up to ten times— the success of *Wingspan* was one of the year's music surprises. Six months after the release of *Wingspan,* Paul issued *Driving Rain,* a CD of new solo material. This was his first CD of original material in four

To celebrate the thirtieth anniversary of Wings' birth was the documentary and double CD compilation set Wingspan. *Ad, 2001.*

years, and reviews were positive for the work. But in its first week, *Driving Rain* sold a disappointing sixty-six thousand copies in the United States.

Thirty years after Wings' debut, Paul remarked to *Billboard* magazine about the problems he had encountered in attempting to form a new band. "For me, it was like, 'What do you do—how do you follow the Beatles?' We'd always thought it's impossible. And we were always in the shadow of the Beatles. That was the big difficulty with Wings.

"We really were trying to get good as a band, and we never really thought we did, because everything (we did) was stacked up against the Beatles. So it was, 'Well, that's not quite as good as the Beatles' tour' or 'That's not quite as good as a Beatles record.'"

Long after Wings had disbanded, David Bowie paid Paul and Linda a visit. The trio peered through *Billboard's* compilation book of rock music listings, which included the music chart histories of various artists. They looked up the Beatles and others including James Brown. Then they looked up Wings. There, Paul saw that each of the group's singles had hit the American top forty and that most of Wings' albums had peaked at number one. He read that the 1975–76 world tour was considered one of the best concert tours of the decade and that Wings' "Mull of Kintyre" was one of the world's ten biggest-selling singles of all time.

Paul had not realized that Wings had been so successful.

"Bloody hell. We did amazingly well," he recalled of the discovery. "Anyone else would have given their right arm for a career like that."

Appendix:
Interview with Henry McCullough

Garry McGee: *Denny Laine suggested you to Paul to join the group in 1971.*
Henry McCullough: That's right. That's perfectly true.

GM: *What were your impressions of "Give Ireland Back to the Irish"?*
HM: That was my first record with Wings. I joined the band and then
    we came out with "Give Ireland Back to the Irish" and I thought,
    "God, I have to be careful where I stand here." In saying that, I had
    a brother who was in an Irish pub in London and he was asked if
    he was my brother and he said he was. And he was asked again,
    "Did he play on that record 'Give Ireland Back to the Irish'?" And
    he said, "He did." And he ended up with a bottle in his face over
    it. Nothing that would warrant anything apart from a few stitches.
    At that particular time, Ireland was at the height of the war here.
    It's a difficult thing, with my being Irish as well, it was a little diffi-
    cult for me, but nothing that one wasn't able to handle at the end of
    the day and thankfully I wasn't living in Ireland at the time or I
    think it could have been a lot worse.

GM: *I heard EMI requested the song not be included in the* Wingspan *set.*
HM: It doesn't surprise me. People would be . . . the final deal has yet
    to be done with Northern Ireland and the Republic, the north and
    south. But that's been going on for thirty years. But you live with it.

But I don't think it would have been a good idea myself to put it on something like that.

GM: *But it's part of the band's history.*
HM: I suppose it is but there are other songs that were part of the band's history that weren't included in *Wingspan* . . .

GM: *One was "Mary Had A Little Lamb." What were your impressions of that song?*
HM: I was able to cope with it because I had my apprenticeship in music in Ireland. They were like four piece horn sections and "Top of the Pops" and old time waltzes, stuff like that. So I was well educated. Comedy as well as corniness, all part of the trip, along with half a dozen tracks from the English top twenty. So, "Mary Had a Little Lamb" was a little strange, and it was one of the reasons why I . . . I went along with it. I didn't know what the hell was going on.

GM: *Did you ever confront Paul with suggestions like, "Perhaps if we played or recorded some song more appropriate?"*
HM: No, that wouldn't have come about. He was the leader so to speak and the way it worked, at that particular time, he was strictly the boss and that's the way it was. And it stayed until myself and Denny Seiwell parted . . . we left in the same week. A little strange, but at the same time, I wouldn't get embarrassed about it or anything like that but I would think, "Oooh." I wouldn't do it twice, let me put it that way.

GM: *"Mary Had a Little Lamb" was a top ten hit in the U.K.*
HM: I can't honestly remember to tell you the truth. What I remember is playing the mandolin, leaning up against a tree in white trousers, white shirt and white shoes or something. I don't know what his plan was there. I think he's a very hard working man and I wouldn't begrudge him anything because he works extremely hard at what he does, all the time. Not only does he play music and all the rest, but he has a fairly good business head on him too. He's a thoroughly professional man in all aspects of his life. That in itself warrants a certain respect.

GM: *In Wings' first tour—the University Tour—the money from each performance was collected and divided among the group.*

HM: That's exactly true. We didn't have any plan, we'd just pull up to a university. The first one may have been Oxford. No it would've been [Nottingham] and we sort of pulled up to the student's union and asked if we could play. On several occasions, they didn't believe that Paul McCartney was sitting in this van with dogs and a couple of kids and no windows. And they had to come out to double check, so to speak. But once they realized it was Paul McCartney with his new band Wings, then it was no problem. And after the gig it was, there'd be a bag of money and it'd be "two for you, two for me." It was great. It was like pocket money. It was a great way to work.

GM: *All of you—not just Paul—had experienced better working conditions before Wings—but touring in a van?*

HM: We had a van with no windows and Paul's kids, and we had a small truck come from behind with equipment. It was like going back to the very, very basics and the freedom to be able to call anywhere en route at the same time. So that made it easy because Paul was with the band, but there isn't a band in the world that does that sort of thing because it's a bit like a seaside holiday—with no sunshine.

GM: *Were you only on a salary while with Wings, correct?*

HM: That's right. We were on a retainer. We were promised different things initially in the beginning about when things got up and rolling as Wings then we would be sort of treated a little bit better financially, but it never came about. I think that was one of the problems that occurred. It was also part of Denny Seiwell's reasons for getting out of it as well. We'd been up to Scotland rehearsing *Band on the Run* for like two weeks prior to going to Lagos to do it, and the day before—no, four days before we were due to go—I couldn't take it anymore. And I don't think Paul could. I think that at the end he would have wanted me to have [stayed], but he didn't want to tell me.

At this particular time, so long after, I know he would have thought of the band as "Paul McCartney and Wings." But in hindsight, I saw him on television, he didn't realize until the time came that he didn't just have a bunch, he had an actual band there. Wings were a band in their own right. We were always clawing to try to get involved in it, not only for our own sake, but to make it a better thing, to try and change McCartney's image. He's a great rock and roller, but there is a lot of stuff he does like "Mary Had a Little Lamb" that I don't know what it is or what it's for, and I never bothered to ask. I think in hindsight, he now realizes that he had another group on his hands and he didn't realize it.

GM: *Wings was the biggest selling act of the 1970s in the United States in terms of records sold.*

HM: It doesn't surprise me. There's a lot of money there, that's for sure, with the Wings thing. But Paul's been very, very good and I've had corresponded to him by letter. I haven't spoken to him by phone. . . . He's had it hard. Linda, George Harrison, John Lennon. He's making a whole new start I think. It's like another lifetime for him has appeared on the horizon.

GM: *I've always enjoyed your guitar solo in the song "My Love." Had you rehearsed your piece or was it improvised?*

HM: We were in the studio. I think it was AIR Studios in London, I'm not quite sure. I can't remember what was to be played, but it was most certainly to have been something [that could be improved]. We had done it before and the backing track had been done. I had to put on the solo and I said literally before running the tape that I wanted to change the solo. I can't remember what it originally was, but I knew it wasn't up to my standard. And so I put myself in that position where I had George Martin hanging at my fingertips, Paul McCartney wondering what the hell was going on and when the solo came I did it in one take and I swear I did it off the cuff, and because of that, it was the first time McCartney had been challenged musically. We were always saying, "Let me try to work on the guitar part. Let me try and do it rather than going through rehearsals and parts that are low." We all wanted, not for our own sakes, but for McCartney's as well to make this, "please let me be part of the band." It was still Paul McCartney. It's something very difficult to get away from, with an ex-Beatle as your boss.

But I did the solo in one take, and I think because the way I approached and the way that it came out of the blue, I think that in itself showed Paul McCartney that, "Hell, if he can do that without even thinking about it, what can he do when he (does) sit down and think about it." I think it was the only time he was challenged musically and because of that I've heard him mention on several occasions about that particular solo. So I live with that and I'm very happy for it to have occurred in front of the eyes of one of the greatest stars. I was able to walk out of there with a smile on my face.

I was in front of a fifty piece orchestra, just me and the guitar and the orchestra and when the drop in came, they were playing along with me and that in itself terrified me so I was in a very strange situation. So I did it and I got away with it. It wasn't worked on, it was played much as you would a blues. I said a prayer afterward, if only to myself, thanking whoever concerned for landing it right on my plate and it didn't take more than the length of the solo to record it.

GM: *Many feel the members of Wings had to live in the shadow of the Beatles and their music. Was that difficult for you personally?*

HM: We were very much like in a bubble, like the Beatles would have been, not such a small bubble but we were still in a bubble. In fact, were together twenty-four hours a day—there was a long bonding period.

We all grew up with the Beatles, in my generation, and we were in love with music and we were in love with very much the outcome of the Beatles—the long hair and everything. We all looked up to the Beatles until they finished. They had a huge influence on the world. There wasn't any comparison at all. It wasn't even brought up.

GM: *Paul was going through many lawsuits to resolve the Beatles' business affairs when you were with Wings. Do you recall any talk of the lawsuits or Allen Klein?*

HM: Three of them were with Klein and Paul stuck to his guns and went off with Linda's brother and father. And at the end of the day, it showed you who was right—McCartney. They got screwed with Allen Klein and everything else, their assets froze as was McCartney's. I think McCartney's clear headedness and general being, he would want to lay the cards on the table a little bit better than what maybe Allen Klein [wanted]. It doesn't make for good vibes when you have people like that for whatever reason. At the end of the day it was proved that was the case.

GM: *You also played on "Live and Let Die," another classic.*

HM: We attended the film's premiere as well. That was great. It was just another song. It worked great, but it wouldn't have made any difference. Anything was acceptable. And the fact that if you're working with Paul McCartney and he's [written] a song for a movie, there's not much you can do but play it and that's about as far as you can get with it.

GM: *You also were in the television special "James Paul McCartney." Were you concerned with the special or was it just another gig to you?*

HM: It's just another gig. Just like when Woodstock came about and I was there with Joe Cocker. It made its mark, that's for sure. I don't think any of the promoters or the bands involved realized not until two days before exactly what was going on because of the size of it, with TV stuff and everything else. [In the end] it sounded like everyone in the world was attending Woodstock.

GM: *During the European tour while Wings played in Sweden, a man apparently threatened Paul's life while the group was in a bar. You, in turn, took control of the situation and possibly saved Paul's life.*

HM: I remember the incident. I think because of the whole situation, I felt, I would've probably felt very protective of Paul McCartney because of his vulnerability . . . and I think everyone felt protective of him because he was going out to show the world what he wanted to do with [Wings]. But it was one of those incidents that happens a thousand times on a Saturday night in any given city or time. People just get a little bit funny and if you don't get out of that quick it can get a little bit nasty . . . he needed a strong helping hand from whoever was around him. He wanted to do as well with Wings as he did with the Beatles, if not better—but that would've been impossible.

GM: *Looking back, what are your impressions of the other members of Wings—Denny Laine and Denny Seiwell?*

HM: I did keep in touch with Denny Seiwell, but I don't see anything of Denny Laine . . . but I think I got along very well with Denny Laine during my time with Wings [but] we never kept in touch and I don't know what Denny Laine is doing. You see, Denny sold his story, so to speak to the *Sun* which is a daily paper—something like, not quite as bad as the *National Enquirer*—but he sold a story to this particular paper, a bit of a disgrace, I think. And I have never, ever— and I've had the opportunity as well—to speak of Joe Cocker or Paul McCartney, but we were too good of friends. But Denny Laine, I don't think it would've bothered him too much.

GM: *Denny Laine once remarked he felt you were eager to leave Wings because you made enough money to purchase a house and a car.*

HM: That's not true. We didn't get paid for tours, we didn't get paid accordingly. We didn't make money with Wings. You were with one of the most famous bands in the world at that point—but we were still on a smallish retainer. We didn't get weekly wages, we got a weekly retainer, you know, so it wasn't a case of getting paid largish amounts of money and onto to larger things. It wasn't that at all, that's for sure.

In the last couple of weeks, because of this *Wingspan* thing, Paul has been in touch with myself and Denny Seiwell. So at the end of the day we made a little money, but when you break it down over a period of years it's [little]. So that end, which is McCartney's back catalog, there's no open door . . . being the man he is, he wanted a clean sheet from the day he was born, really, so there's no comeback from anything or anybody, but he's been in touch recently and has helped a little bit. So, life goes on.

GM: *What about Linda?*

HM: Whether she was playing the keyboard with two fingers or whether she was playing it with three, it didn't make any difference because she was playing a part. Once she learned what had to be done, and Paul would've showed her, she learned exactly what was required of her. But there was a sort of meeting of the minds. It was brought up, "Why don't we bring in a rock & roll piano player?" But it never came about and it wasn't meant to be. Paul and Linda started the whole thing up in Scotland and they would've been sing- ing Everly Brothers songs, a little bit of harmony, a fire going and a couple acoustic guitars. I think they wanted to take it farther, which they did do. But then they had to bring in an electric guitar like myself, so everything changed. And as it was going to change. It sort of went a little different, I think, than what Paul had imagined.

I have nothing but good to say about Linda McCartney, and I must be very honest about that. She was a lovely woman . . . (critics) didn't know the strength of the woman. She was very, very brilliant about the whole thing. Paul & Linda were beautiful people, and very vulnerable at that particular point, and so protective of each other. They were always together. It became OK, there was nothing wrong with it at the end of the day.

I think up until the end she really wanted to be as good as everyone wanted her to be.

GM: *What are your favorite Wings songs?*

HM: "Maybe I'm Amazed" is a bit of a cracker. But there's so many. I enjoyed *Wild Life*, that album. It was so sparse, the production and the size. It was very, very raw. I like "My Love" for the song and the way it worked. I enjoyed them all to be honest with you. I got a little weary of "Mary Had a Little Lamb" and I think that's the best way to put it. The one I wouldn't attach myself to. But all the others I enjoyed. I mean, he's one of the best songwriters in the world, and to have the opportunity to be there through it with him . . .

GM: *In the 1990s, Paul had two huge world tours. It appeared that would have been an ideal time to reunite Wings for the world tours. Do you think that could have been possible?*

HM: I don't know. The second Wings could have been, but it wouldn't have been the same. I don't think any Wings effort that would have been after the initial Wings, like with ourselves, I don't think there was a band that could match it although they all played great parts and everything else. But it's a little different if you could imagine somebody coming out from a hole that has been there for a couple of years and they don't know whose part this is or what's going on here. Once it's up and rolling, I don't think it's the same. It just had to stop, the Wings thing, and he had to go back to being Paul McCartney. But the original Wings was the definitive Wings. He knows it now. And after so long, if we had sorted out our differences right at the table as they arose, then I think Wings may have been going today.

GM: *Do you have any regrets about leaving Wings?*

HM: You played a role with Wings. The only thing I regret is the fact that we didn't stay together, that we didn't talk before the whole thing blew itself out. Different situations arose and nobody said anything. That would always add a little layer to something that would bring it to a boiling point. That I regret. Apart from that, I really don't have any regrets and I am thankful for the experience and I enjoyed it tremendously and I learned a lot. But I certainly . . . I would like to try and do it again . . . in my dreams.

Official Wings Lineups

WINGS STAGE I (AUGUST 1971 TO AUGUST 1973)

Paul McCartney	Linda McCartney	Denny Laine	Denny Seiwell*	Henry McCullough

WINGS STAGE II (AUGUST 1973 TO APRIL 1974) AND STAGE V (AUTUMN 1977 TO JUNE 1978)

Paul McCartney	Linda McCartney	Denny Laine

WINGS STAGE III (JUNE 1974 TO JANUARY 1975)

Paul McCartney	Linda McCartney	Denny Laine	Jimmy McCulloch**	Geoff Britton

WINGS STAGE IV (JANUARY 1975 TO SEPTEMBER 1977)

Paul McCartney	Linda McCartney	Denny Laine	Jimmy McCulloch	Joe English

WINGS STAGE VI (JUNE 1978 TO APRIL 1981)

Paul McCartney	Linda McCartney	Denny Laine	Laurence Juber	Steve Holly

*Seiwell joined Paul and Linda McCartney on their duet album *Ram* in early 1971.
**McCulloch joined Wings in April 1974.

Concert Tours

1972 GREAT BRITAIN TOUR
("THE UNIVERSITY TOUR")

Songs performed included:
"Lucille"
"Wild Life"
"Give Ireland Back to the Irish"
"Blue Moon of Kentucky"
"Help Me Darling"
"Some People Never Know"
"Bip Bop"
"Help Me"
"Seaside Woman"
"The Mess"
"Say Darling"
"Smile Away"
"Henry's Blues" (Henry McCullough)
"Long Tall Sally"
"Turkey in the Straw" (partial performance of this song)
"The Grand Old Englande of York" (partial)

Dates:
Feb 9 Nottingham University
Feb 10 York University

Feb 11 Hull University
Feb 14 Lancaster University
Feb 16 Leeds University
Feb 17 Sheffield University
Feb 18 Manchester University
Feb 21 Birmingham University
Feb 22 Swansea University
Feb 23 Oxford University
(Wings consisted of Paul & Linda McCartney, Denny Laine, Henry McCullough, and Denny Seiwell with this and the following tours until the 1975–76 World Tour)

1972 WINGS OVER EUROPE TOUR

Songs performed included:
"Smile Away"
"The Mess"
"Hi, Hi, Hi"
"Mumbo"
"Bip Bop"
"Say You Don't Mind" (Denny Laine)
"Wild Life"
"Seaside Woman" (Linda McCartney)
"I Would Only Smile"
"Blue Moon of Kentucky"
"Give Ireland Back to the Irish"
"Henry's Blues" (Henry McCullough)
"1882"
"I Am Your Singer"
"Junk"
"Eat at Home"
"Cottonfields"
"Maybe I'm Amazed"
"My Love"
"Long Tall Sally"
"Mary Had a Little Lamb"

"Soily"
"Best Friend"
"Mama's Little Girl"

Dates:
Jul 9 Theatre Antique, Chateau Vallon, France
Jul 12 Theatre Antique, Les Pins, France
Jul 13 Theatre Antique, Arles, France
Jul 16 Olympia, Paris, France (two shows)
Jul 18 Circus Krone, Munich, Germany
Jul 19 Offenbach Halle, Frankfurt, Germany
Jul 21 Kongresshaus, Zurich, Switzerland
Jul 22 Pavilion, Montreux, Switzerland
Aug 1 K.B. Hallen, Copenhagen, Denmark
Aug 4 Messuhalli, Helsinki, Finland
Aug 5 Kupittaan Urheiluhalli, Turku, Finland
Aug 7 Kungliga Hallen, Stockholm, Sweden
Aug 8 Idretshalle, Orebro, Sweden
Aug 9 Njardhallen, Oslo, Norway
Aug 10 Scandinavium Hall, Göteborg, Sweden
Aug 11 Olympean, Lund, Sweden
Aug 12 Fyns Forum, Odense, Denmark
Aug 14 Vejlby Risskov Hallen, Aarhus, Denmark
Aug 16 Stadthalle, Hanover, Germany
Aug 17 Doelen, Rotterdam, the Netherlands
Aug 19 Evenementenhall, Groningen, the Netherlands
Aug 20 Concertgebouw, Amsterdam, the Netherlands
Aug 21 Concertgebouw, Amsterdam, the Netherlands
Aug 22 Ciné Roma, Antwerp, Belgium
Aug 24 Deutschlandhalle, Berlin, Germany

1973 UNITED KINGDOM TOUR

Songs performed included:
"Big Barn Bed"
"Soily"
"When the Night"

"Wild Life"
"Seaside Woman" (Linda McCartney)
"Go Now" (Denny Laine)
"Little Woman Love"/"C Moon"
"Live and Let Die"
"Maybe I'm Amazed"
"Say You Don't Mind" (Denny Laine)
"My Love"
"The Mess"
"Hi, Hi, Hi"
"Long Tall Sally"

Dates (note that more dates were later added to this tour than had been originally planned):
May 11 Hippodrome, Bristol
May 12 New Theatre, Oxford
May 13 Capitol, Cardiff
May 15 Winter Gardens, Bournemouth
May 16 Hard Rock, Manchester
May 17 Hard Rock, Manchester
May 18 The Empire, Liverpool
May 19 Leeds University
May 21 Guildhall, Preston
May 22 Odeon, Newcastle
May 23 Odeon, Edinburgh
May 24 Green's Playhouse, Glasgow
May 25 Odeon, Hammersmith
May 26 Odeon, Hammersmith
May 27 Odeon, Hammersmith
Jul 4 City Hall, Sheffield
Jul 6 Odeon, Birmingham
Jul 9 Odeon, Leicester
Jul 10 Newcastle City Hall

1975–76 WINGS OVER THE WORLD TOUR

Songs performed included:
"Venus and Mars"
"Rock Show"

"Jet"
"Let Me Roll It"
"Spirits of Ancient Egypt" (Denny Laine)
"Little Woman Love"/"C Moon"*
"Maybe I'm Amazed"
"Long and Winding Road"
"Live and Let Die"
"Picasso's Last Words"
"Richard Corey" (Denny Laine)
"Bluebird"
"I've Just Seen a Face"
"Blackbird"
"Yesterday"
"You Gave Me the Answer"
"Magneto and Titanium Man"
"Go Now"** (Denny Laine)
"Call Me Back Again"
"My Love"
"Listen to What the Man Said"
"Letting Go"
"Junior's Farm"*
"Waltzing Matilda"* (partial)
"Medicine Jar" (Jimmy McCulloch)
"Band on the Run"
"Hi, Hi, Hi"
"Soily"
"Let 'Em In"**
"Silly Love Songs"**
"Time to Hide"** (Denny Laine)
"Beware My Love"**

*1975 tour only
**added to later 1976 tour dates

Dates:
1975:
Sep 9 Gaumont, Southampton, England
Sep 10 Hippodrome, Bristol, England

Sep 11 Capitol, Cardiff, Wales
Sep 12 Free Trade Hall, Manchester, England
Sep 13 Hippodrome, Birmingham, England
Sep 15 Empire, Liverpool, England
Sep 16 City Hall, Newcastle, England
Sep 17 Odeon, Hammersmith, England
Sep 18 Odeon, Hammersmith, England
Sep 20 Usher Hall, Edinburgh, Scotland
Sep 21 Apollo, Glasgow, Scotland
Sep 22 Capitol, Aberdeen, Scotland
Sep 23 Caird Hall, Dundee, Scotland
Nov 1 Entertainment Centre, Perth, Australia
Nov 4 Apollo Stadium, Adelaide, Australia
Nov 5 Apollo Stadium, Adelaide, Australia
Nov 7 Horden Pavilion, Sydney, Australia
Nov 8 Horden Pavilion, Sydney, Australia
Nov 10 Festival Hall, Brisbane, Australia
Nov 11 Festival Hall, Brisbane, Australia
Nov 13 Myer Music Bowl, Melbourne, Australia
Nov 14 Myer Music Bowl, Melbourne, Australia

1976:
Mar 20 Falkoner Theater, Copenhagen, Denmark
Mar 21 Falkoner Theater, Copenhagen, Denmark
Mar 23 Deutschlandhalle, Berlin, Germany
Mar 25 Ahoy Sport Paleis, Rotterdam, Switzerland
Mar 26 Pavillion, Paris, France
May 3 Tarrant County Convention Hall, Fort Worth, Texas
May 4 The Summit, Houston, Texas
May 7 Olympia, Detroit, Michigan
May 8 Olympia, Detroit, Michigan
May 9 Maple Leaf Gardens, Toronto, Canada
May 10 Richfield Coliseum, Cleveland, Ohio
May 12 Spectrum, Philadelphia, Pennsylvania
May 14 Spectrum, Philadelphia, Pennsylvania
May 15 Capitol Center, Largo, Maryland
May 16 Capitol Center, Largo, Maryland

May 18 Omni, Atlanta, Georgia
May 19 Omni, Atlanta, Georgia
May 21 Nassau Coliseum, Long Island, New York
May 22 Boston Garden, Boston, Massachusetts
May 24 Madison Square Garden, New York
May 25 Madison Square Garden, New York
May 27 Riverfront Stadium, Cincinnati, Ohio
May 29 Kemper Arena, Kansas City, Missouri
Jun 1 Chicago Stadium, Chicago, Illinois
Jun 2 Chicago Stadium, Chicago, Illinois
Jun 4 Civic Center, St. Paul, Minnesota
Jun 7 McNichols Arena, Denver, Colorado
Jun 10 Kingdome, Seattle, Washington
Jun 13 Cow Palace, San Francisco, California
Jun 14 Cow Palace, San Francisco, California
Jun 16 Sports Arena, San Diego, California
Jun 18 Community Forum, Tucson, Arizona
Jun 21 Forum, Los Angeles, California
Jun 22 Forum, Los Angeles, California
Jun 23 Forum, Los Angeles, California
Sep 19 Stadhalle, Vienna, Austria
Sep 21 Dome Sportova, Zagreb, Yugoslavia
Sep 25 St. Mark's Square, Venice, Italy
Sep 27 Olympiahalle, Munich, Germany
Oct 19 Empire Pool, Wembley, England
Oct 20 Empire Pool, Wembley, England
Oct 21 Empire Pool, Wembley, England
(Wings consisted of Paul & Linda McCartney, Denny Laine, Jimmy McCulloch, and Joe English)

1979 UNITED KINGDOM TOUR

Songs performed included:
"Got to Get You into My Life"
"Getting Closer"
"Again and Again and Again" (Denny Laine)

"Goodnight My Love"
"Cook of the House" (Linda McCartney)
"Old Siam, Sir"
"Maybe I'm Amazed"
"Coming Up"
"No Words (For My Love)"
"Arrow through Me"
"Let It Be"
"Hot as Sun"
"Every Night"
"Spin It On"
"Lucille"
"Goodnight Tonight"
"Twenty Flight Rock"
"Wonderful Christmastime"
"Band on the Run"
"I've Had Enough"
"Go Now"
"Fool on the Hill"
"Yesterday"
"Mull of Kintyre"
"Rockestra Theme"

Dates:
Nov 23 Royal Court Theater, Liverpool
Nov 24 Royal Court Theater, Liverpool
Nov 25 Royal Court Theater, Liverpool
Nov 26 Royal Court Theater, Liverpool
Nov 28 Apollo in Ardwick, Manchester
Nov 29 Apollo in Ardwick, Manchester
Dec 1 Gaumont, Southampton
Dec 2 New Conference Centre, Brighton
Dec 3 Odeon, Lewisham
Dec 5 Rainbow Theater, Finsbury Park
Dec 7 Empire Pool, Wembley
Dec 8 Empire Pool, Wembley
Dec 9 Empire Pool, Wembley

Dec 10 Empire Pool, Wembley
Dec 12 Odeon, Birmingham
Dec 14 City Hall, Newcastle
Dec 15 Odeon, Edinburgh
Dec 16 Apollo, Glasgow
Dec 17 Apollo, Glasgow
Dec 29 Hammersmith Odeon, London
(Wings consisted of Paul & Linda McCartney, Denny Laine, Laurence Juber, and Steve Holly with this tour, the Concerts for the People of Kampuchea appearance on 29 December, and the aborted Japan tour in 1980.)

Album Releases

(NOTE: Quoted comments in this section are from Paul McCartney, unless otherwise indicated.)

RAM
(PAUL AND LINDA McCARTNEY)

U.S. label, catalog number, and release date: Apple SMAS 3373; 17 May 1971

British label, catalog number, and release date: Apple PAS 10003; 21 May 1971

Song listing on original release: Too Many People/3 Legs/Ram On/ Dear Boy/Uncle Albert—Admiral Halsey/Smile Away/Heart of the Country/Monkberry Moon Delight/Eat at Home/Long Haired Lady/Ram On (Reprise)/Back Seat of My Car

Cover photograph by Linda McCartney

"(*Ram*) was quite hard work because it was mainly just me and Linda doing it. One of my nephews, it's his favourite album of mine. It's funny, you know, people have these different favourites and sometimes they want to pick the offbeat one that didn't do well, just to be cool. There's something in all of those albums even if they're my worst ones. I know I did them intending for them to be the greatest things I ever did."

181

Although credited to Paul and Linda McCartney, *Ram* featured Denny Seiwell on several tracks. Shortly after the release of *Ram*, Seiwell was asked to join Wings.

Billboard review, 29 May 1971: "Paul and Linda debut like the sweethearts of rock 'n roll reborn, as the ex-Beatle continues to play the rock Romeo with little else on his musical mind. A good part of the fun is McCartney's light, clever arrangements and superb rhythm changes."

WILD LIFE
(WINGS)

U.S. label, catalog number, and release date: Apple SW 3386; 7 December 1971

British label, catalog number, and release date: Apple PCS 7142; 3 December 1971

Song listing on original release: Mumbo/Bip Bop/Love Is Strange/ Wild Life/Some People Never Know/I Am Your Singer/Tomorrow/Dear Friend

Cover photograph by Barry Lategan

"I must say you have to like me (to like this album).
"When *Wild Life* came out, all the critics said it was rubbish, so I started thinking like them that it was rubbish. But when I heard it later, I really liked it and I still think it's quite good. Okay, I didn't make the biggest blockbuster of all time. But I don't think you need that all the time."

Billboard review, 18 December 1971: "The McCartneys (Paul and Linda) have solicited the talents of the Dennys (drummer Seiwell and guitarist Laine) to become the first supergroup of 1972. The LP is more acoustic and less gimmicky than McCartney's last two and among the eight songs, four are triumphs: 'Bip Bop,' 'Tomorrow,' 'Wild Life,' and Mickey and Sylvia's 'Love Is Strange.'"

RED ROSE SPEEDWAY
(PAUL McCARTNEY AND WINGS)

U.S. label, catalog number, and release date: Apple SMAL 3409; 30 April 1973

British label, catalog number, and release date: Apple PCTC 251; 3 May 1973

Song listing on original release: Big Barn Bed/My Love/Get on the Right Thing/One More Kiss/Little Lamb Dragonfly/Single Pigeon/When the Night/Loup (1st Indian on the Moon)/Medley: Hold Me Tight—Lazy Dynamite—Hands of Love—Power Cut

Cover photograph by Linda McCartney

"(The album) wasn't named after Rose, my housekeeper, to debunk another myth. I remember the evening we did the album cover, Linda took that photo of me as I sat next to a motor bike with a rose in me mouth all evening, listening to *Innervisions*, Stevie's (Wonder's) album. At one point while I had some of the tunes going, we were up in Scotland at my sheep farm . . . There was one lamb we were trying to save. We stayed up all night and had him in front of the stove, but it was too late and he just died. I wrote a song about it, 'Little Lamb Dragonfly' . . . my little tribute to him."

Billboard review, 5 May 1973: "Best effort from McCartney since his break with the Beatles, featuring powerful rock material as well as the great ballads he was so well known for when the (Beatles were) together. Arrangements are tighter than the previous LP's, with guitar work of Henry McCullough and Denny Laine as well as vocal backup of Laine and Linda McCartney giving added strength to disk."

BAND ON THE RUN
(PAUL McCARTNEY AND WINGS)

U.S. label, catalog number, and release date: Apple SO 3415; 5 December 1973

British label, catalog number, and release date: Apple PAS 10007; 30 November 1973

Song listing on original release: Band on the Run/Jet/Bluebird/Mrs. Vandebilt/Let Me Roll It/Mamunia/No Words (For My Love)/ Helen Wheels/Picasso's Last Words (Drink to Me)/Nineteen Hundred and Eighty-Five (NOTE: "Helen Wheels" on American pressings of album only)

Cover photograph by Clive Arrowsmith

"There is a thread, but it's not a concept album," McCartney said. "It sort of relates to me escaping.

"(It) was great. Everyone just freaked. When we got back people said, 'Out of adversity has been born a good album.' I hate that theory. It may be true as well. That's why I hate it. I hate the idea that you've got to sweat and suffer to produce something good. It turned out successful anyway.

"I love the album, I must say. When you make an album you're waiting for everyone to criticize, waiting for everyone to put it down. You're living on your nerves, really, for the first couple of weeks, wondering if it's going to be the biggest blow-out of all time, or whether it's going to be as good as you think it is."

(NOTE: The working title for *Band on the Run* was *Son of Always*.)

Billboard review, 13 March 1999: "A watershed album for Paul McCartney and Wings, a massive hit, and one of the most enduring pieces of work in the rock era. A well-deserved return to the spotlight."

VENUS AND MARS
(WINGS)

U.S. label, catalog number, and release date: Capitol SMAS 11419; 27 May 1975

British label, catalog number, and release date: Capitol PCTC 254; 30 May 1975

Song listing on original release: Venus and Mars/Rock Show/Love in

Ad for the long-awaited album Venus and Mars, *1975.*

Song/You Gave Me the Answer/Magneto and Titanium Man/Letting Go/Venus and Mars (Reprise)/Spirits of Ancient Egypt/Medicine Jar/Call Me Back Again/Listen to What the Man Said/Treat Her Gently—Lonely Old People/Crossroads Theme

Cover photograph by Linda McCartney

"When we had a party in the States to celebrate having finished the album, someone came up and said 'Hello Venus. Hello Mars.' I thought, 'Oh no.' It never occurred to me. I wrote a totally imaginary song and just bunged the line in, like I do a lot of lines. I didn't even know they were our neighboring planets. I just thought of naming any two planets.

"I don't think of particular themes for an album," Paul said. "There wasn't one on *Venus and Mars*. I thought of a bunch of tunes. They have a sort of family, love-ish, warmish feel. I can never analyze me own stuff."

Billboard review, 7 June 1975: "A much more musically intricate project than Wings' other (efforts) without losing the feelings of fun and spontaneity that good rock has always offered. And, to serve up the old cliché, all possible singles."

AT THE SPEED OF SOUND
(WINGS)

U.S. label, catalog number, and release date: Capitol SW 11525; 25 March 1976

British label, catalog number, and release date: Capitol PAS 10010; 26 March 1976

Song listing on original release: Let 'Em In/The Note You Never Wrote/She's My Baby/Beware My Love/Wino Junko/Silly Love Songs/Cook of the House/Time to Hide/Must Do Something about It/San Ferry Anne/Warm and Beautiful

Cover photograph by Linda McCartney (NOTE: The group sketched on the inside sleeve of the album is Ian and the Kilburns [alias for Kilburn and the High Roads with Ian Dury].)

"We fit (*At the Speed of Sound*) in (during the tour) . . . it didn't take long. But we didn't rush it—just let the ideas blossom. We (tried) to make it as hard as possible, but sometimes you just don't bring off in a studio what you can bring off in a live thing.

"There were a few things I especially wanted to do. I put a backing track down (on 'Must Do Something About It') and then got the idea of getting Joe English to do it, because he's got a very good voice. Linda's got this track called 'Cook of the House.' The band came together for rehearsals at Elstree and a nice thing was the way the brass players worked out a bit for a song called 'Silly Love Songs.' They can really get behind it, because it's theirs. The object with anything I do (is) to try and get out of a rut and do something different."

Billboard review, 3 April 1976: "Good, solid album of individual songs which works much better than McCartney's concept *Venus and Mars* set. The album is a sneaky one in a way, because first listen does not find any real standouts. The key, however, is a steadiness that sees the LP running on an even keel."

WINGS OVER AMERICA
(WINGS)

U.S. label, catalog number, and release date: Capitol SWCO 11593; 11 December 1976

British label, catalog number, and release date: Capitol PCSP 720; 10 December 1976

Song listing on original release: Venus and Mars/Rock Show/Jet/Let Me Roll It/Spirits of Ancient Egypt/Medicine Jar/Maybe I'm Amazed/Call Me Back Again/Lady Madonna/The Long and Winding Road/Live and Let Die/Picasso's Last Words (Drink to Me)/Richard Corey/Bluebird/I've Just Seen a Face/Blackbird/Yesterday/You Gave Me the Answer/Magneto and Titanium Man/Go Now/My Love/Listen to What the Man Said/Let 'Em In/Time to Hide/Silly Love Songs/Beware My Love/Letting Go/Band on the Run/Hi, Hi, Hi/Soily

Cover painting by Richard Manning

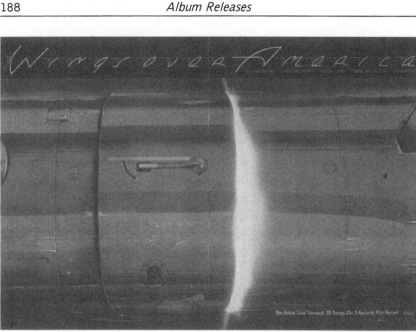

Ad for Wings over America *album, 1976.*

"Everything I have done since the Beatles split has been leading up to this (tour). I would have said [no] if you asked me in 1969 if a group could have done it after the Beatles; if any of the Beatles could have had the strength to actually do something else, because it's a hell of a thing when you've been in one group all your life."

Billboard review, 18 December 1976: "McCartney live with this well-honed group is an endless fascination. No LP in the future is likely to deliver us this much of McCartney in so many effective settings. The set is listed at $13.98 which is actually a generous price for an out-pouring of three LPs of music at such a high level."

LONDON TOWN
(WINGS)

U.S. label, catalog number, and release date: Capitol SW 11777; 31 March 1978

British label, catalog number, and release date: Capitol PAS 10012; 31 March 1978

Wings' first studio album in two years, London Town, Germany, 1978.

Song listing on original release: London Town/Café on the Left Bank/
I'm Carrying/Backwards Traveller/Cuff Link/Children Children/
Girlfriend/I've Had Enough/With a Little Luck/Famous Group-
ies/Deliver Your Children/Name and Address/Don't Let it Bring
You Down/Morse Moose and the Grey Goose

Cover design and photograph by Paul McCartney, Linda McCartney,
and Denny Laine

"The big problem with recording on a boat was that maybe once
we got out there we might find that salt water had gone through the

machines and the equipment, or that they just wouldn't work. You know, with any new studio you need to spend at least a couple of weeks sorting out the wrinkles and breaking it in. But we were dead lucky actually because we got out there and were able to record a track the very first day . . . and they sound as good as a normal studio recording."

(NOTE: The album was originally called *Water Wings*.)

Billboard review, 8 April 1978: "*London Town* demonstrates that McCartney still has a flair for writing clean, intelligent rock 'n roll. The music flows unrestrained, the material is varied and polished and McCartney's singing comes across with all its vitality and precision intact. *London Town* is not a skimpy album either. The love songs are tender, the rockers move along at a riveting pace and the instrumental interludes are solid."

WINGS GREATEST
(WINGS)

U.S. label, catalog number, and release date: Capitol SO 11905; 22 November 1978

British label, catalog number, and release date: Capitol PCTC 256; 1 December 1978

Song listing on original release: Another Day/Silly Love Songs/Live and Let Die/Junior's Farm/With a Little Luck/Band on the Run/ Uncle Albert—Admiral Halsey/Hi, Hi, Hi/Let 'Em In/My Love/ Jet/Mull of Kintyre

Cover design by Paul and Linda McCartney; photograph by Argus Forbes

"To me, (*Wings Greatest* was) just a repackage. I'm not into Beatles repackages or anything myself because it seems like a second-class item to me. It's understandable that kids who don't want to buy sin-

A dozen worldwide million-selling songs in an $8,000 cover,
Wings Greatest, *Philippines, 1978.*

gles will be waiting for the album, and when it's not on the album, they feel a little bit cheated.

"The companies would like a single on the album. It makes more sense merchandising wise. But sometimes I just have to remember that this isn't a record retail store I'm running; this is supposed to be some kind of art. And if it doesn't fit in, it doesn't fit in."

Billboard review, 2 December 1978: "Many acts use padding (to fill out a Greatest Hits package). Wings has done the opposite . . . omitting eleven Top 40 hits. Best cuts—all twelve."

BACK TO THE EGG
(WINGS)

U.S. label, catalog number, and release date: Columbia FC-36057; 24
   May 1979
British label, catalog number, and release date: Parlophone PCTC 257;
   8 June 1979
Song listing on original release: Reception/Getting Closer/We're
   Open Tonight/Spin It On/Again and Again and Again/Old Siam,
   Sir/Arrow Through Me/Rockestra Theme/To You/After the Ball—
   Million Miles/Winter Rose—Love Awake/The Broadcast/So Glad
   to See You Here/Baby's Request

Cover photograph by John Shaw

"The New Wave thing was happening and . . . I sort of realized,
'Well, so what's wrong with us doing an uptempo?' I always am getting influenced. *Back to the Egg* was influenced just as what I had
wanted to do at the time, the direction I felt I hadn't been in for a
while—do a bit of that. And the sales, by most other people's standards would be like very healthy. By our standards, they weren't that
good.

"I'm used to all that by now. You know nearly everything I've ever
done or been involved in has had some of that negative critical reaction . . . We went in there thinking it was going to be a good album.
Who is there whose every single album is incredible? I can't think of
anyone."

(NOTE: *We're Open Tonight* was the working title for the album, and
Wings in the Wild was the original title of *Back to the Egg*.

Billboard review, 23 June 1979: "The music features typical McCartney fare of late with nothing here that will distinguish it as one of his
classics. The arrangements, though, are interesting, encompassing a
variety of styles."

CONCERTS FOR THE PEOPLE OF KAMPUCHEA
(VARIOUS ARTISTS)

U.S. label, catalog number, and release date: Atlantic SD 2 7005; 30 March 1981

British label, catalog number, and release date: Atlantic K 60153; 3 April 1981

Paul McCartney and Wings songs on original release: Got to Get You into My Life/Every Night/Coming Up; w/Rockestra: Lucille/Let It Be/Rockestra Theme

In December 1979 during their tour of the United Kingdom, Wings performed a benefit in London to raise money for the people of Kampuchea (formerly Cambodia). Wings' concert took place on 29 December, the last night of the series. They were joined by most of the members of Rockestra, the all-star ensemble that appeared on *Back to the Egg*.

This two-record set was released way too late after the event to be fresh in the minds of record buyers, and despite the fact that entire sides of this two-record set featured the Who and Wings, the set never reached the top thirty on the charts. It also became the last album featuring Wings, as the band announced its breakup shortly after this release hit the stores.

Single Releases

Quoted comments in this section are from Paul McCartney, unless otherwise indicated.

"UNCLE ALBERT/ADMIRAL HALSEY"
(B/W "TOO MANY PEOPLE")

U.S. label, catalog number, and release date: Apple 1837; 2 August 1971 (single was only released in the United States)
Artist: Paul and Linda McCartney
Producer: Paul and Linda McCartney
Writer: A-side: Paul and Linda McCartney; B-side: Paul McCartney
A- and B-sides: From the LP *Ram*

McCartney's first post-Beatles number one single in the United States was this duet with Linda, released two and one-half months after the debut of their LP *Ram*, from which the single was pulled. McCartney felt that, rather than issue the songs off the album as singles, why not wait until the album is released, then pull whichever song the public demanded for a 45 release? Although this concept is not widely used, it worked to McCartney's advantage.

In an interview with Paul Gambaccini, Paul said that "Uncle Albert" was based on his own uncle. "I did have an Uncle Albert who used to quote the Bible to everyone when he got drunk. He used to read from the Bible. It was the only time he ever read the Bible, but it was when he was drunk. He died a few years ago and he was a good man.

"(H)e's someone I recalled fondly, and when the song was coming it was like a nostalgic thing. 'I think I'm gonna rain' was the wistful line, really, and I thought of him. As for Admiral Halsey, he's one of yours, an American admiral. I use these things like a painter uses colors. I don't know where I got Halsey's name, but you read it in magazines and sometimes they just fall into your songs because they scan so well."

"THE BACK SEAT OF MY CAR"
(B/W "HEART OF THE COUNTRY")

British label, catalog number, and release date: Apple R 5914; 13 August 1971 (single was only released in the United Kingdom)
Artist: Paul and Linda McCartney
Producer: Paul and Linda McCartney
Writer: A-side: Paul McCartney; B-side: Paul and Linda McCartney
A- and B-sides: From the LP *Ram*

"'The Back Seat of My Car' is the ultimate teenage song, even though it was a long time since I was a teenager and had to go to a girl's dad and explain myself. It's the kind of meet-the-parents song . . . obviously 'back seat' is snogging, making love."

This single was released in the United Kingdom instead of "Uncle Albert/Admiral Halsey," which was issued in the United States. The rest of Europe and other parts of the world saw the single "Eat at Home"/"Smile Away" from the *Ram* album. "The Back Seat of My Car" was not a hit, entering only one of the British charts and stalling at number thirty-nine.

"GIVE IRELAND BACK TO THE IRISH"
(B/W "GIVE IRELAND BACK TO THE IRISH"
[INSTRUMENTAL VERSION])

U.S. label, catalog number, and release date: Apple 1847; 28 February 1972
British label, catalog number, and release date: Apple R 5936; 25 February 1972

Artist: Wings
Producer: Paul McCartney
Writer: the McCartneys
Originally released as a non-album single

McCartney's newly formed band, Wings, got off to a rocky start with its panned debut album *Wild Life* and the group's first single. Although a top twenty hit in Britain, the single peaked at number twenty-one in the United States. The song was banned by the BBC for its obvious political overtones, but McCartney felt it important to directly respond to the Bloody Sunday massacre in Northern Ireland that had occurred in January of that year.

"Our soldiers, my country's army had gone in and killed some people," Paul said. "And I'd grown up with this thing that the Irish are great, they're our mates, our brothers. We used to joke that Liverpool was the capital of Ireland. Suddenly we were killing our buddies and I thought, 'wait a minute, this is not clever and I wish to protest on behalf of the people.' I did that song and was rung up by a lot of people who said, 'Please don't release this. We don't need this right now.' And I said, 'Yes we do. Gotta have it.'"

"MARY HAD A LITTLE LAMB" (B/W "LITTLE WOMAN LOVE")

U.S. label, catalog number, and release date: Apple 1851; 29 May 1972
British label, catalog number, and release date: Apple R 5949; 12 May 1972
Artist: Wings
Producer: the McCartneys
Writer: McCartney and McCartney
Originally released as a non-album single

"I just found out what the words to the nursery rhyme were, wrote a little tune up around it, went and recorded it. I had an idea in my head that it would be interesting for everyone to find out what the words to the original nursery rhyme were. I see now it wasn't much of a record. That's all. It just didn't really make it as a record, and that's what tells, the black plastic.

"I didn't give that much thought to it. I've got a daughter named Mary and she always pricks up her ears at this tune. I thought I'd record a song for her. I do things that aren't necessarily thought out."

"HI, HI, HI"
(B/W "C MOON")

U.S. label, catalog number, and release date: Apple 1857; 4 December 1972

British label, catalog number, and release date: Apple R 5973; 1 December 1972

Artist: Wings

Producer: Paul McCartney

Writer: Paul and Linda McCartney

Originally released as a non-album single

McCartney and Wings quickly rebounded from the lackluster success of their previous releases with this hard-rocking song. And once again, the song was banned by the BBC, this time for "inappropriate lyrical content" and drug references.

"I think 'Hi, Hi, Hi' is now kinda dated. It's got words and phrases in it like 'bootleg' and 'we're gonna get high in the midday sun,' and it's very much a song of the times when there were festivals and everyone had long hair, flared trousers and macramé jackets: very sixties. To me, that was my parting shot at those days."

As for the flip side, "C Moon," Paul explained: "Remember Sam the Sham and 'Woolly Bully'? Well, there's a line in that that says, 'Let's not be L7.' Well, L7, it was explained at the time, means a square—put L and 7 together and you get a square . . . So I thought of the idea of putting a C and a moon together (a half-moon) to get the opposite of a square. So 'C Moon' means cool, in other words."

"MY LOVE"
(B/W "THE MESS")

U.S. label, catalog number, and release date: Apple 1861; 9 April 1973
British label, catalog number, and release date: Apple R 5985; 23 March 1973
Artist: Paul McCartney and Wings
Producer: Paul McCartney
Writer: McCartney
A-side: From the LP *Red Rose Speedway*
B-side: Originally released as a non-album single

A sentimental ballad written by McCartney for his wife, "My Love" became the biggest U.S. hit by Wings thus far, spending a total of four weeks at number one in June 1973. In addition, the single earned a gold record award. In Britain, it made the top ten.

"When 'My Love' came out, John Lennon actually said, 'If only everything was as simple and unaffected as McCartney's new single, then maybe Dean Martin and Jerry Lewis would reunite with the Marx Brothers.' We were going through a slagging off period with each other, although most of the slagging was coming from him. He called me Engelbert, and Engelbert Humperdinck started getting annoyed with me."

"LIVE AND LET DIE"
(B/W "I LIE AROUND")

U.S. label, catalog number, and release date: Apple 1863; 18 June 1973
British label, catalog number, and release date: Apple R 5987; 1 June 1973
Artist: Wings
Producer: A-side: George Martin; B-side: Paul McCartney
Writer: McCartney (Paul and Linda McCartney)*
Originally released as a non-album single

*The soundtrack album correctly credits Linda as co-writer of "Live and Let Die."

"Live and Let Die" single, France, 1973.

"When I was asked to do a Bond film, I thought, 'Why not?' I said, 'Look, give me a week. If I can't do it, I'll back out of it.' I don't normally write to titles. But I read the book on a Saturday, and I wrote the song on a Sunday. I was ready to go to George Martin the next week. I found it came easily.

"But it was hard to do, the trick being how to combine my writing with the 'Bondiness' of the soundtrack orchestration riffs. I'll tell you who liked that song, and I was always surprised: Neil Young! I wouldn't have thought it'd be to his taste."

On the B-side is "I Lie Around" with Denny Laine on lead vocals, the first of three times Paul allowed another member of Wings to take the lead on a single. The second time was with Linda on "Cook of the House," the B-side to 1976's "Silly Love Songs" single. The third time was the flip side of 1978's "I've Had Enough," which featured Denny again on "Deliver Your Children," which Denny co-wrote with Paul.

"HELEN WHEELS"
(B/W "COUNTRY DREAMER")

U.S. label, catalog number, and release date: Apple 1869; 12 November 1973

British label, catalog number, and release date: Apple R 5993; 26 October 1973

Artist: Paul McCartney and Wings

Producer: Paul McCartney

Writer: McCartney

Originally released as a non-album single; A-side later added to the LP *Band on the Run*, U.S. version

"'Helen Wheels' was my Land Rover. It's a name we gave to our Land Rover, which is a trusty vehicle that gets us around Scotland. It takes us to the Shetland Islands and down to London.

"That song described a trip down the M6, which is the big motorway to get to Scotland down south to England. So that song was my attempt to try and put England on the map. All the Chuck Berry songs you've ever heard had things like 'Birmingham, Alabama!' shouted out, these American places like 'Tallahassee!' But you couldn't put the English ones in. It always sounded deft to us. 'Scunthorpe!' 'Warrington!' It doesn't sound as funky."

"JET"
(U.S.: B/W "MAMUNIA"; LATER ISSUE: "LET ME ROLL IT")
(BRITAIN: B/W "LET ME ROLL IT")

U.S. label, catalog number, and release date: Apple 1871; first issue 28 January 1974; second issue 18 February 1974

British label, catalog number, and release date: Apple R 5996; 18 February 1974

"Helen Wheels" single, Japan, 1973.

Artist: Paul McCartney and Wings
Producer: Paul McCartney
Writer: McCartney*
A- and both B-sides: From the LP *Band on the Run*

   "Some songs of mine are . . . about very definite things. Some of them aren't. I'd like to think, (I have) a kind of surrealistic streak and I don't necessarily have to know what it's about. The words just sound good together. 'Jet' is kind of one of those."

*The 1976 Capitol U.S. reissue of the single lists Linda as co-writer.

"We've got a Labrador (who) proceeded to have a litter (of seven puppies). Jet was one of the puppies. 'Suffragette' (in the song) was crazy enough to work. I make up so much stuff. It means something to me when I do it, and it means something to the record buyer, but if I'm asked to analyze it I can't really explain what it is."

An interesting aspect of this single is its U.S. history. On 28 January, "Jet" was released with "Mamunia" on the B-side. Three weeks later, "Jet" was re-released with a new B-side, "Let Me Roll It," thus deleting the original pressing.

"BAND ON THE RUN"
(U.S.: B/W "NINETEEN HUNDRED AND EIGHTY-FIVE")
(BRITAIN: B/W "ZOO GANG")

U.S. label, catalog number, and release date: Apple 1873; 8 April 1974
British label, catalog number, and release date: Apple R 5997; 28 June 1974
Artist: Paul McCartney and Wings
Producer: Paul McCartney
Writer: McCartney
U.S. A- and B-sides: From the LP *Band on the Run*
British A-side: From the LP *Band on the Run*
British B-side: Originally released as a non-album single

The title track from the immensely popular LP *Band on the Run* provided McCartney and Wings with another U.S. number one song, as well as the group's sixth consecutive trip to the top ten.

"There were a lot of musicians at the time who'd come out of ordinary suburbs in the '60s and '70s and were getting busted. Bands like the Byrds, the Eagles—the mood amongst them was one of desperados. We were being outlawed for pot . . . And our argument on ('Band on the Run') was, 'Don't put us on the wrong side . . . We're not criminals, we don't want to be.'

"So I just made up a story about people breaking out of prison.

Structurally, that very tight little intro on (the song)—'Stuck inside these four walls'—led to a hole being blasted in the wall and we get the big orchestra and then we're off. We escape into the sun."

"JUNIOR'S FARM"
(B/W "SALLY G.")

U.S. label, catalog number, and release date: Apple 1875; 4 November 1974

British label, catalog number, and release date: Apple R 5999; 25 October 1974

Artist: Paul McCartney and Wings

Producer: Paul McCartney

Writer: McCartney

Originally released as a non-album single; sides reversed in the United States on 7 February 1975

"To me, in a way, ('Junior's Farm') was reminiscent of Bob Dylan's 'Ain't Gonna Work on Maggie's Farm No More.' So the idea I thought was we'll have another farm, Macca's farm, and so the idea was to try and get a kind of fantasy about this person, Junior.

"The communicative value of a single is the big thing. That's why we turned 'Junior's Farm' over to 'Sally G.' Some people think, 'blimey, they're trying to get two records out of one.' But I think that if it's a song that people would like . . . then I like to see if we can give it an extra plug . . . we just wanted to expose the song.

"I didn't see anyone named 'Sally G.' when I was in Printer's Alley, nor did I see anyone who 'ran her eyes over me' as I sang 'A Tangled Mind.' That was my imagination, adding something to it, the reality of it."

"LISTEN TO WHAT THE MAN SAID"
(B/W "LOVE IN SONG")

U.S. label, catalog number, and release date: Capitol 4091; 23 May 1975

British label, catalog number, and release date: Capitol R 6006; 16 May 1975

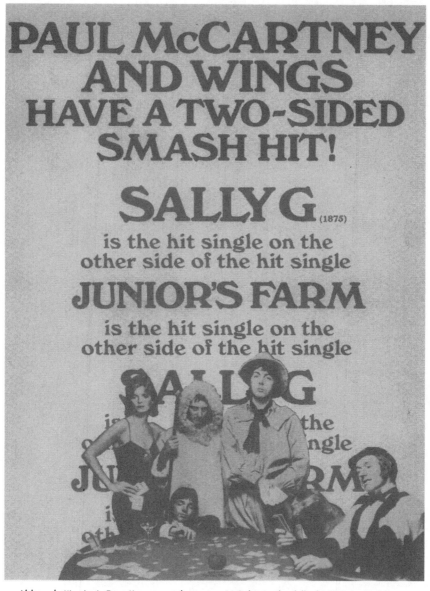

Although "Junior's Farm" was smash top ten U.S. hit in the fall of 1974, its B-side was pushed—and charted—in early 1975, both a rare practice and occurrence. Ad, United States, 1975

Ad for "Listen to What the Man Said" single, 1975.

Artist: Wings
Producer: Paul McCartney
Writer: McCartney
A- and B-sides: From the LP *Venus and Mars*

Wings' first release on the Capitol label not only extended the group's top ten streak to eight, but also resulted in another number one song.

"A pop hit has to have certain hooks you can hang your hat on," singer Neil Sedaka told *Time* in its 1976 cover story on McCartney. "The hook can either be musical or lyrical, but the best is a marriage of both words and music. McCartney does this. 'Listen to What the Man Said' is terrific."

"To me, I'm saying, 'listen to the base rules, don't goof around too much,'" McCartney remarked. "If you say 'the man,' it could mean God, it could mean women listen to your men, it could mean many things. It's a good summer single. It was one of the songs we'd gone in with high hopes for."

"LETTING GO"
(B/W "YOU GAVE ME THE ANSWER")

U.S. label, catalog number, and release date: Capitol 4145; 29 September 1975
British label, catalog number, and release date: Capitol R 6008; 5 September 1975
Artist: Wings
Producer: Paul McCartney
Writer: McCartney
A- and B-sides: Original versions appear on the LP *Venus and Mars*
A-side: Remixed single version originally available as a non-album single

"Letting Go" had the distinction of being the lowest-charting single by Wings to date. A complete disappointment for the band, especially as they had established one of the longest streaks of U.S. top ten hits in the 1970s. (Wings would ultimately tie with Elton John and the Bee Gees for the honor, with each having eight top tens in a row.)

The song was remixed, and this made for a very different tune than the version released on *Venus and Mars*. Although the song became a favorite with audiences during the 1975–76 Wings world tour, its lack of success on the charts still remains a mystery.

"VENUS AND MARS ROCK SHOW" (B/W "MAGNETO AND TITANIUM MAN")

U.S. label, catalog number, and release date: Capitol 4175; 27 October 1975

British label, catalog number, and release date: Capitol R 601; 28 November 1975

Artist: Wings

Producer: Paul McCartney

Writer: McCartney

A- and B-sides: Original versions appear on the LP *Venus and Mars*

A-side: Remixed single version originally available as a non-album single

"The song 'Venus and Mars' is about an imaginary friend who's got a girlfriend who's into astrology, the kind of person who asks you what's your sign is before they say hello. I just thought of naming any two planets. I didn't know they were the gods of love and war either, and I wasn't thinking about the Botticelli picture.

"Venus and Mars" segues into "Rock Show." "That just happened to coincide. I start off with an idea. 'Rock Show,' boom. Concertgebouw came into my mind, because that's one of the places you play in Amsterdam (Wings played there during their 1973 European tour), so I rhymed it with 'Rock Show' in an English pronunciation of Gebouw. 'Long hair' . . . Madison Square. 'Rock and roll' . . . Hollywood Bowl. Often these things that turn out to be great afterwards are just searches for a rhyme. I could see how you might think, 'well, he's doing this . . .' but for me it's just writing a song."

"Venus and Mars Rock Show" sheet music, 1975.

"SILLY LOVE SONGS"
(B/W "COOK OF THE HOUSE")

U.S. label, catalog number, and release date: Capitol 4256; 1 April 1976
British label, catalog number, and release date: Capitol R 6014; 30
   April 1976
Artist: Wings
Producer: Paul McCartney
Writer: McCartney
A- and B-sides: From the LP *At the Speed of Sound*

"I was getting slagged off for writing 'lurv' songs. You see, I'm looking at love not from the perspective of 'boring old love.' I'm looking
at it like when you get married and have a baby. That's pretty strong:
it's something deeper. I don't mind being sentimental, I love the old
movies. I've never been too ashamed of all that stuff.

"The hard nuts of the music business, the critics, are gonna hate (it)
because I'm not writing about acne. You weigh all those problems up
and you still write it. Unfortunately, it still gets to me. And it's great
when something wins a poll and you can say, 'Nyahh, nuts to you. I
thought I was right.' It's a vindication."

"LET 'EM IN"
(B/W "BEWARE MY LOVE")

U.S. label, catalog number, and release date: Capitol 4293; 28 June 1976
British label, catalog number, and release date: Capitol R 6015; 23 July
   1976
Artist: Wings
Producer: Paul McCartney
Writer: McCartney
A- and B-sides: From the LP *At the Speed of Sound*

"For me, 'Let 'Em In' is a sort of family song. I come from a big
rollicking Liverpool Irish family. If you go to one of my family parties,
there's just a lot of people . . . it's great and it's a fun time.

"Let 'Em In" single, Germany, 1976.

"It sort of said: let's have a party, why keep 'em outside?' So in listing the kind of people who might be outside the door, I just naturally went to . . . Auntie Gin, brother Michael—they all exist. I just wanted a parade of people that we could imagine outside the door, so I drew on all the people I knew."

The song was almost given to Ringo Starr to record for his 1976 album *Ringo's Rotogravure*, but Paul decided to record it with Wings. Ringo received and recorded the lesser-known McCartney-penned song "Pure Gold."

"MAYBE I'M AMAZED"
(B/W "SOILY")

U.S. label, catalog number, and release date: Capitol 4385; 7 February 1977

British label, catalog number, and release date: Capitol R 6017; 4 February 1977

Artist: Wings

Producer: Paul McCartney

Writer: McCartney

A- and B-sides: From the LP *Wings Over America*

"When you're in love with someone—I mean, God it sounds soppy—but when you are in love and it's new like that, as it was for me and Linda with the Beatles breaking up, that was my feeling. Maybe I'm amazed at what's going on—maybe I'm not—but maybe I am. 'Maybe I'm amazed at the way you pulled me out of time, hung me on the line.' There were things that were happening at the time, and these phrases were my symbols for them. And other people seemed to understand.

"It was for Linda and was about her."

"MULL OF KINTYRE"
(B/W "GIRLS' SCHOOL")

U.S. label, catalog number, and release date: Capitol 4504; 14 November 1977

British label, catalog number, and release date: Capitol R 6018; 11 November 1977

Artist: Wings

Producer: Paul McCartney

Writer: A-side: McCartney/Laine; B-side: McCartney

Originally released as a non-album single

Although "Mull Of Kintyre" was originally released as the A-side of the single, radio programmers in the United States decided to flip the record over and play the hard-rocking B-side, "Girls' School."

"Mull of Kintyre" / "Girls' School" single, Israel, 1977.

McCartney had written the song, originally titled "Love School," during a break in the Wings world tour. He was reading an American newspaper and was glancing at the movie advertisements. There he read the titles of the pornographic films that were being shown: *School Mistress, The Woman Trainer, Kid Sister.* "I rather liked the titles, so basically I took all of the titles and made a song out of them."

Paul added: "The whole thing with punk rock was boring to old farts. That was the expression that came in. Obviously there was the age difference. They were doing what we'd done ten years before.

"There was a bit of a divide around that time. And we just released 'Mull of Kintyre.' But I must say at the time I thought, we are kidding, of course, aren't we? Releasing a Scottish Waltz in the face of all this furious spitting and gobbing. So that turned out to be a bigger record than any of the punk records."

Paul noted that "There's a metal group called Girlschool . . . I always wondered if they took it off that song!"

Outside of the States, "Mull of Kintyre" became an outstanding hit. It hit number one in most European countries and spent ten weeks at number one in Australia alone.

"We felt it should sound very Christmasy and New Yeary. It's a kind of 'glass of ale in your hand, leaning up against the bar' tune," Paul recalled. "We had the Campeltown band and they were great—just pipes and drums. It was interesting, writing for them. They can't play every note in a normal scale. They've got the drone going all the time, so you have to be careful what chord you change over the drone."

"WITH A LITTLE LUCK"
(B/W "BACKWARDS TRAVELLER"/"CUFF LINK")

U.S. label, catalog number, and release date: Capitol 4559; 20 March 1978

British label, catalog number, and release date: Capitol R 6019; 23 March 1978

Artist: Wings

Producer: Paul McCartney

Writer: McCartney

A- and B-sides: From the LP *London Town*

When "With a Little Luck" hit number one, it partially made up for the lackluster success in the United States of "Mull of Kintyre." The single became another top ten record in England. Recorded in a twenty-four-track studio installed on a yacht off the Virgin Islands, the song recalled the simplicity of "Silly Love Songs" while still catching the interest of record buyers as well. The single broke a six-month streak of number one hits in the United States held by the record company RSO, which was then mainly succeeding with its *Saturday Night Fever* soundtrack hits.

"With a Little Luck" single, Italy, 1978.

"I'VE HAD ENOUGH"
(B/W "DELIVER YOUR CHILDREN")

U.S. label, catalog number, and release date: Capitol 4594; 12 June 1978

British label, catalog number, and release date: Capitol R 6020; 16 June 1978

Artist: Wings

Producer: Paul McCartney

Writer: A-side: McCartney; B-side: McCartney/Laine

A- and B-sides: From the LP *London Town*

Another rocker reminiscent of the 1950s, "I've Had Enough" received so much airplay in the United States upon its release, it was predicted that Wings would receive another top ten hit. But for some reason, the song stalled at number twenty-five. It missed the Top forty altogether in the United Kingdom.

"You can't win 'em all," McCartney commented on the single's failure. "Just didn't mean anything to people, I suppose. I can't pick 'em, but I'm very lucky. Out of all the ones I've released, quite a number of them have been hits, so I'm thankful for small murphies."

The B-side featured the lead vocals of Denny Laine, one of the few times Paul allowed another member of Wings to take the lead on a single.

"LONDON TOWN"
(B/W "I'M CARRYING")

U.S. label, catalog number, and release date: Capitol 4559; 21 August 1978

British label, catalog number, and release date: Capitol R 6021; 15 September 1978

Artist: Wings

Producer: Paul McCartney

Writer: A-side: McCartney/Laine; B-side: McCartney

A- and B-sides: From the LP *London Town*

Criticized at the time of release for being "prone to sleep" in an era of disco and punk music, "London Town" nevertheless was reminiscent of McCartney's "Penny Lane" and "Eleanor Rigby." The lyrics provided a picture of the variety of people one can find on the streets of London. Unfortunately, such images were not cared for by the record-buying public, and the song shared honors with "Letting Go" as the lowest-charting U.S. Wings single, peaking at number thirty-nine. It fared worse in England.

"GOODNIGHT TONIGHT"
(B/W "DAYTIME NIGHTTIME SUFFERING")

U.S. label, catalog number, and release date: Columbia 3-10939; 15
 March 1979
British label, catalog number, and release date: Parlophone R 6023; 23
 March 1979
Artist: Wings
Producer: A-side: Paul McCartney; B-side: Paul McCartney and Chris
 Thomas
Writer: McCartney
Originally released as a non-album single

"('Goodnight Tonight' is) the one that put me back on the map with
a top ten hit. I like dance tracks, and if I go to a club there's no point
in hearing ballads all night. You need something to get you up on the
floor, and I'm into a lot of that stuff. We recorded it in a long version,
as opposed to stretching it like they do now."

At one point, "Goodnight Tonight" was going to be the B-side of
"Daytime Nighttime Suffering." "We sat around for (what) seemed
like years discussing it," McCartney told *Rolling Stone* in 1979. "And
we decided, 'No, it isn't all right; we won't put it out.' So we scrapped
the whole thing. (Soon after) I thought, 'That's crazy, we've made it;
it's stupid, why not put it out? Just because people are gonna pan it?'
So we decided to (release) it."

An extended version of "Goodnight Tonight" was also released as
a twelve-inch disco single on 26 March 1979 (U.S.: Columbia 23-10940;
Britain: Parlophone 12Y R6023).

"GETTING CLOSER"
(U.S.: B/W "SPIN IT ON")
(BRITAIN: B/W "BABY'S REQUEST")

U.S. label, catalog number, and release date: Columbia 3-11020; 5 June
 1979
British label, catalog number, and release date: Parlophone R 6027; 10
 August 1979

Artist: Wings
Producer: Paul McCartney and Chris Thomas
Writer: McCartney
A- and B-sides: From the LP *Back to the Egg*

As the disco style of "Goodnight Tonight" had clicked with record buyers, now seemed to be a good time to try to capture the rock and punk music fans and to prove that Wings could rock with the best of them. Unfortunately, "Getting Closer" did not work despite its driving sound.

In Britain, "Getting Closer" was promoted as a "double A-side." It didn't help. Although the single became a top twenty hit in the United States, "Getting Closer" didn't reach any higher than number sixty in the United Kingdom.

"OLD SIAM, SIR"
(B/W "SPIN IT ON")

British label, catalog number, and release date: Parlophone R 6026; 1 June 1979 (single was only released in the United Kingdom)
Artist: Wings
Producer: Paul McCartney and Chris Thomas
Writer: McCartney
A- and B-sides: From the LP *Back to the Egg*

The marketing for *Back to the Egg* was very different from that of previous Wings albums, especially in the singles pulled from the album. Although "Getting Closer" was issued in the United States, this single was released in Britain. A few weeks later, "Getting Closer" became a single in Britain, and "Arrow Through Me" was issued in the United States. Regardless of this strange approach, none of the singles became very big hits on either side of the Atlantic.

"ARROW THROUGH ME"
(B/W "OLD SIAM, SIR")

U.S. label, catalog number, and release date: Columbia 1-11070; 14 August 1979 (single was only released in the United States)
Artist: Wings

"*Arrow Through Me*" *sheet music, 1979.*

Producer: Paul McCartney and Chris Thomas
Writer: McCartney
A- and B-sides: From the LP *Back to the Egg*

Another ballad, but in a techno-pop style, "Arrow Through Me" failed to make much of a chart impression, barely making the top thirty in the United States. "Old Siam, Sir," on the other hand, was another hard-driving sound that did not receive much, if any, airplay and went unnoticed.

Time has been good to "Arrow Through Me," however. It has been recorded by several artists, and many fans regard it as one of the band's most overlooked singles.

"COMING UP"
(B/W "COMING UP [LIVE AT GLASGOW]"/
"LUNCH BOX—ODD SOX")

U.S. label, catalog number, and release date: Columbia 1-11263; 15 April 1980
British label, catalog number, and release date: Parlophone R 6035; 11 April 1980
Artist: A-side: Paul McCartney; B-side: Paul McCartney and Wings
Producer: Paul McCartney
Writer: McCartney
A-side: From the LP *McCartney II*
B-side: Originally available as a non-album single

"I did 'Coming Up' in a reverse way of normal working. I did a drum track and then just built on it bit by bit. I put some guitars on, put the bass on, and built up on the backing track . . . I sped my voice up slightly, and did the vocals through a sort of echo machine.

"I always thought the (hit) was going to be the solo version.

"What happened was that I brought the solo track to the band when we were rehearsing for the last tour and they thought it would be a good number to do. It was recorded the last night in Glasgow and we put it on the B-side."

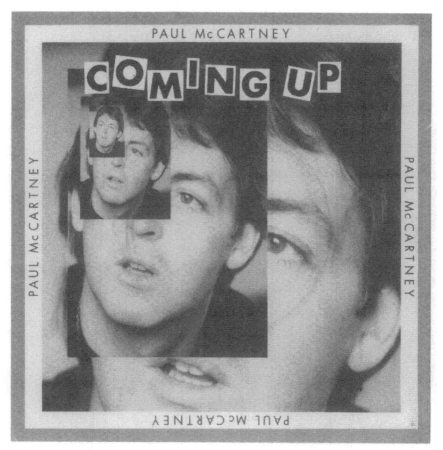

"Coming Up" single, United Kingdom, 1980.

Columbia suggested to certain dee-jays that the live version "was the one to go with," Paul recalled. "I didn't really know they were doing that or else I might have said, 'No, the other one is stronger.' But apparently something like forty top stations picked up the live one."

"Lunch Box—Odd Sox" was an instrumental from the *Venus and Mars* sessions.

Additional Wings Releases

"WALKING IN THE PARK WITH ELOISE"
(B/W "BRIDGE ON THE RIVER SUITE")

U.S. label, catalog number, and release date: EMI 3977; 2 December 1974

British label, catalog number, and release date: EMI 2220; 18 October 1974

Artist: The Country Hams

Producer: Paul McCartney

Writer: A-side: James McCartney; B-side: Paul & Linda McCartney

A- and B-sides: Originally released as a non-album single

This single was really Wings in disguise, along with the likes of Chet Atkins and Floyd Cramer.

"Well, (my father) used to have this one song, which he'd play over and over on the piano. It was just a tune; there were no words to it. Well, years later, I recorded it in Nashville. I told my dad, 'You're going to get all the royalties. You wrote it and we're going to publish it for you and record it, so you'll get the checks.' And he said, 'I didn't write it, son.' I thought, 'Oh, God, what?' He said, 'I made it up, but I didn't write it.' He meant he couldn't notate; he couldn't actually write the tune down. And, of course, that's like me. I can't write music."

"Walking in the Park with Eloise" single, Holland, 1974.
Wings in disguise as the Country Hams.

"SEASIDE WOMAN"
(B/W "B-SIDE TO SEASIDE")

U.S. label, catalog number, and release date: Epic 8-50403; 31 May 1977

British label, catalog number, and release date: A&M AASP 7461; 10 August 1979

Artist: Suzy and the Red Stripes

Producer: Paul McCartney

Writer: McCartney

A- and B-sides: Originally released as a non-album single

This single was Linda McCartney and Wings under a pseudonym.

Linda McCartney: " 'Seaside Woman' (is) very reggae inspired. That's when ATV was suing us saying I was incapable of (song)writing, so Paul said, 'Get out and write a song.' And then we (later) went in to a B-side for it of something I'd written in Africa, and we just talk over it. It's very sort of Fifties R&B, the Doves, the Penguins. I love that, that was my era.

"When we were in Jamaica, there had been a fantastic version of 'Suzie Q,' so they used to call me Suzy. And the beer in Jamaica is called Red Stripe, so that makes it Suzy and the Red Stripes."

The single was later re-released with remixed versions of both songs on a seven-inch single (Capitol B-5608) and on a twelve-inch single with extended mixes (Capitol V-15244). Both were issued on 13 August 1986. The single was also reissued in Britain on 18 July 1980 (A&M AMS 7458).

"WONDERFUL CHRISTMASTIME"
(B/W "RUDOLPH THE RED-NOSED REGGAE")

U.S. label, catalog number, and release date: Columbia 1-11162; 20 November 1979
British label, catalog number, and release date: Parlophone R 6029; 16 November 1979
Artist: Paul McCartney
Producer: Paul McCartney
Writer: A-side: McCartney; B-side: J. Marks
A- and B-sides: Originally released as a non-album single

"Wonderful Christmastime" marked Paul's first solo single since the 1971 single "Another Day." Although the song made the English top ten, it became the first solo McCartney single not to chart at all in the United States. Several critics felt that the song was some kind of a joke, but Paul was indeed serious. Although critics have not changed their assessment of the song, it has since become a standard on radio stations on both sides of the Atlantic during the holiday season.

Although this single was credited solely to McCartney, Wings played it in their 1979 U.K. concert tour, and appeared in the promotional video film. When the single was reissued in 1994 in the United States on the Capitol label, the credit was corrected as "Paul McCartney and Wings."

OTHER RELEASES

Wings' "My Carnival" song appeared on the B-side of McCartney's 1985 "Spies Like Us" single (Capitol B-5537). It was from the *Venus and Mars* sessions and had been left off the album, although it would have been a welcome addition in that it was a celebration of Mardi Gras in true New Orleans style.

Also, the Wings song "Mama's Little Girl" was released on the B-side of McCartney's 1990 single "Put It There." The British twelve-inch single of "Put It There" also included the previously unreleased Wings' tune "Same Time Next Year."

Wings' "I Would Only Smile" (from the *Red Rose Speedway* sessions), "Send Me the Heart" (1974 Nashville sessions), "Robber's Ball," and "Weep for Love" (*Back to the Egg* sessions) were released on Denny Laine's 1980 *Japanese Tears* album.

Grammy Awards

The Grammy awards are given out annually by the National Academy of Recording Arts and Sciences and are based in the United States. The organization honors all aspects of recording, focusing primarily in music.

It is interesting to note that in the 1970s—as well as in years prior—the Grammys did not have very many categories, thus, the competition for a nomination was much fiercer than it is for the awards today. For example, for quite some time, there was not a "Rock" category separate from "Pop" or "Easy Listening." Instead, everyone competed together in the same category. Thus, Wings' eleven nominations were impressive considering the limited number of categories.

Following is the listing of Paul McCartney and Wings' Grammy nominations, as well as the group's co-nominees in those categories. The winner of each award is printed in boldface.

1971

Best Arrangement Accompanying Vocalists

- Burt Bacharach and Pat Williams: "Long Ago Tomorrow," B. J. Thomas
- Richard Carpenter: "Superstar," the Carpenters
- Michael Colombier: "Freedom and Fear," Bill Medley

- Paul McCartney: "Uncle Albert/Admiral Halsey," Paul and Linda McCartney
- David Van Depitte: "What's Going On," Marvin Gaye

1973

Best Pop Vocal Performance by a Duo, Group, or Chorus

- The Carpenters: "Sing"
- Dawn, featuring Tony Orlando: "Tie a Yellow Ribbon Round the Ole Oak Tree"
- **Gladys Knight and the Pips: "Neither One of Us (Wants to Be the First to Say Goodbye)"**
- Paul McCartney and Wings: "Live and Let Die"
- Seals & Crofts: "Diamond Girl"

Best Arrangement Accompanying Vocalists

- Tom Baird and Gene Page: "Touch Me in the Morning," Diana Ross
- Richard Carpenter: "Sing," the Carpenters
- Dave Grusin: "Lady Love," Jon Lucien
- Dave Grusin: "Rashida," Jon Lucien
- **George Martin: "Live and Let Die," Paul McCartney and Wings**
- Gene Puerling: "Michelle," Singers Unlimited

Best Original Score Written for a Motion Picture or Television Special

- *Jonathan Livingston Seagull*, **Neil Diamond**
- *Last Tango in Paris*, Gato Barbieri
- *Live and Let Die*, Paul and Linda McCartney, George Martin
- *Pat Garrett and Billy the Kid*, Bob Dylan
- *Sounder*, Taj Mahal

1974

Album of the Year

* *Back Home Again*, John Denver; Milton Okun, producer
* *Band on the Run*, Paul McCartney and Wings; Paul McCartney, producer
* *Caribou*, Elton John; Gus Dudgeon, producer
* *Court and Spark*, Joni Mitchell; Joni Mitchell and Henry Lewy, producers
* **Fulfillingness' First Finale**, Stevie Wonder; Stevie Wonder, producer

Best Pop Vocal by a Duo, Group, or Chorus

* Quincy Jones: "Body Heat"
* **Paul McCartney and Wings: "Band on the Run"**
* Steely Dan: "Rikki Don't Lose That Number"
* Stylistics: "You Make Me Feel Brand New"
* Dionne Warwick, the Spinners: "Then Came You"

Best Engineered Recording, Non-Classical

* **Geoff Emerick, *Band on the Run* by Paul McCartney and Wings**
* Rik Pekkonen and Peter Granet, *Southern Comfort* by the Crusaders
* Bill Schnee, *Lincoln Mayorga and Distinguished Colleagues Volume III* by Lincoln Mayorga
* Ken Scott and John Jansen, *Crime of the Century* by Supertramp
* Tommy Vicari and Larry Forkner, *Powerful People* by Gino Vannelli

1976

Best Arrangement Accompanying Vocalists

* Robert Farnon: "Sentimental Journey" by Singers Unlimited
* Clare Fischer: "Green Dolphin Street" by Singers Unlimited
* **Jimmie Haskell and James William Guercio: "If You Leave Me Now" by Chicago**

- Paul McCartney: "Let 'Em In" by Wings
- Claus Ogerman: "Boto (Porpoise)" by Antonio Carlos Jobim

1977

Best Album Package

- **John Berg, *Love Notes* by Ramsey Lewis**
- Glen Christiansen, *Hejira* by Joni Mitchell
- Kosh, *Simple Dreams* by Linda Ronstadt
- Kosh, *Singin'* by Melissa Manchester
- MPL/Hipgnosis, *Wings Over America* by Wings
- Paul Scher, *Ginseng Woman* by Eric Gale
- Paul Scher, *Yardbirds Forever* by the Yardbirds
- Abie Sussman and Bob Defrin, *Color as a Way of Life* by Lou Donaldson

1979

Best Rock Instrumental Performance

- Allman Brothers Band: "Pegasus"
- Dixie Dregs: *Night of the Living Dregs* (album)
- Neil Larsen: "High Gear"
- **Wings: "Rockestra Theme"**
- Frank Zappa: "Rat Tomago"

1980

Best Rock Vocal Performance, Male

- Jackson Browne: "Boulevard"
- **Billy Joel: *Glass Houses* (album)**
- Kenny Loggins: "I'm Alright"
- Paul McCartney: "Coming Up (Live at Glasgow)"
- Bruce Springsteen: "Medley: Devil with the Blue Dress/Good Golly Miss Molly/Jenny Take a Ride"

U.S. Charts

The following are McCartney & Wings' releases and their peak positions on the charts of the three largest American music magazines in the 1970s: *Billboard* (BB), *Cash Box* (CB), and *Record World* (RW). Each magazine's ranking takes into consideration the amount of airplay the single received on radio stations as well as the number of copies the single sold in the magazine's weekly tabulating. In the example of "Let 'Em In," the single peaked at number three in *Billboard*, which meant that when the song peaked, two other singles sold more copies and were heard on the radio more often that week. According to *Cash Box*, however, "Let 'Em In" sold more and was heard more than any other song during the week it was at its peak, which is why it hit number one there. The same can be applied to albums. The trade magazines considered a combination of both record sales and radio airplay in deciding the success of a single each week. If a single was not doing well in both areas, it rarely hit the top ten.

Unfortunately in the case of *Billboard* magazine, it is impossible to fairly compare Wings' chart records with those of today's artists. The magazine has changed its methods of charting songs several times during the rock era. Presently, a song does not have to be released as a single to chart. It can do so on the strength of airplay alone. Also, today a song receiving an enormous amount of airplay but having small sales can still hit number one. This, for example, may have easily made "I've Had Enough," "Venus and Mars Rock Show," and "Getting Closer" top ten hits.

McCARTNEY & WINGS SINGLES: PEAK
RANKINGS ON THE U.S. CHARTS

	BB	CB	RW
"Uncle Albert/Admiral Halsey"	1	1	1
"Give Ireland Back to the Irish"	21	38	36
"Mary Had a Little Lamb"	28	48	38
"Little Woman Love"	—	95	—
"Hi, Hi, Hi"	10	6	7
"My Love"	1	1	1
"Live and Let Die"	2	1	1
"Helen Wheels"	10	5	4
"Jet"	7	5	5
"Band on the Run"	1	1	1
"Junior's Farm"	3	4	5
"Sally G."	17	49	—
"Listen to What the Man Said"	1	1	1
"Letting Go"	39	41	62
"Venus and Mars Rock Show"	12	16	28
"Silly Love Songs"	1	1	1
"Let 'Em In"	3	1	4
"Maybe I'm Amazed"	10	10	26
"Girls' School"	33	31	33
"With a Little Luck"	1	1	1
"I've Had Enough"	25	28	30
"London Town"	39	42	48
"Goodnight Tonight"	5	4	7
"Getting Closer"	20	20	22
"Arrow Through Me"	28	36	27
"Coming Up"	1	—	—
"Coming Up (Live at Glasgow)"	1	2	3

Misc. Releases

	BB	CB	RW
"Walking in the Park with Eloise"	—	—	—
"Seaside Woman"	59	58	92
"Wonderful Christmastime"	—	83	—

McCARTNEY & WINGS ALBUMS: PEAK
RANKINGS ON THE U.S. CHARTS

	BB	CB	RW
Ram	2	2	2
Wild Life	10	6	9
Red Rose Speedway	1	1	1
Band on the Run	1	1	1
Venus and Mars	1	1	1
At the Speed of Sound	1	1	1
Wings over America	1	2	3
London Town	2	2	2
Wings Greatest	29	21	23
Back to the Egg	8	7	7

Misc. Releases

	BB	CB	RW
Concerts for the People of Kampuchea	36	31	31

THE TOP TENS: UNITED STATES

Following are the singles and albums that hit the top ten on one or more of the U.S. charts, and how each fared on the other two charts as well.

Singles

	BB	CB	RW
"Uncle Albert/Admiral Halsey"	1	1	1
"Hi, Hi, Hi"	10	6	7
"My Love"	1	1	1
"Live and Let Die"	2	1	1
"Helen Wheels"	10	5	4
"Jet"	7	5	5
"Band on the Run"	1	1	1

	BB	CB	RW
"Junior's Farm"	3	4	5
"Listen to What the Man Said"	1	1	1
"Silly Love Songs"	1	1	1
"Let 'Em In"	3	1	4
"Maybe I'm Amazed"	10	10	26
"With a Little Luck"	1	1	1
"Goodnight Tonight"	5	4	7
"Coming Up"	1	—	—
"Coming Up (Live at Glasgow)"	1	2	3

Albums

	BB	CB	RW
Ram	2	2	2
Wild Life	10	6	9
Red Rose Speedway	1	1	1
Band on the Run	1	1	1
Venus and Mars	1	1	1
At the Speed of Sound	1	1	1
Wings Over America	1	2	3
London Town	2	2	2
Back to the Egg	8	7	7

THE NUMBER ONES: UNITED STATES

Following are the singles and albums that hit number one on any of the U.S. charts. An *x* means that release hit number one on that magazine's chart. ("My Love," for example, hit number one on all three charts; "Live and Let Die" hit number one in *Cash Box* and *Record World* but only made it to number two in *Billboard*.)

Singles

	BB	CB	RW
1. "Uncle Albert/Admiral Halsey"	x	x	x
2. "My Love"	x	x	x

	BB	CB	RW
3. "Live and Let Die"	(2)	x	x
4. "Band on the Run"	x	x	x
5. "Listen to What the Man Said"	x	x	x
6. "Silly Love Songs"	x	x	x
7. "Let 'Em In"	(3)	x	(4)
8. "With a Little Luck"	x	x	x
9. "Coming Up (Live at Glasgow)"	x	(2)	(3)

Two notes are of interest here: One concerns the success of "Silly Love Songs." In _Billboard_, the song hit number one on two separate occasions, and in _Record World_, the song topped the charts an unprecedented three times over the summer of 1976.

Another note is about the "Coming Up" single. The released A-side was the studio version of "Coming Up" by Paul McCartney (sans Wings). On the _Billboard_ charts, "Coming Up" (studio version) peaked at number one, only to be replaced by the single's B-side, the live version by McCartney and Wings. Although historians overlook this, McCartney is the only artist to have a solo number one single be replaced by not only his own single's B-side, but by a live version of the same song. Also, as _Billboard_ charted only the single's A-side climb up the charts, the live version's replacing of the studio version at the top could arguably be the first instance of a song to debut at number one in the history of the _Billboard_ charts (_Billboard_ did not list the parenthetical "Live at Glasgow" until the single fell to number 2, but the magazine says it considers the live version as the A-side—although that is not what was published on the weekly charts).

Albums

	BB	CB	RW
1. _Red Rose Speedway_	x	x	x
2. _Band on the Run_	x	x	x
3. _Venus and Mars_	x	x	x
4. _At the Speed of Sound_	x	x	x
5. _Wings over America_	x	(2)	(3)

The _Ram_ album peaked at number two on all three charts, being kept from hitting number one by Carole King's _Tapestry_ album, the biggest-selling album of that year. *London Town* also peaked at number two for several weeks on all three charts. The *Saturday Night Fever* soundtrack (which was the biggest-selling album to that date) prevented *London Town* from hitting the top spot.

The three music charts were mostly in agreement on how many total number one recordings that Wings achieved:

	#1 songs	#1 LPs	Total #1 Records
Billboard	7	5	12
Cash Box	8	4	12
Record World	7	4	11

Although popular in the United States, Wings was not quite as successful in Great Britain. The group had only one single hit number one on all three British charts, that being "Mull of Kintyre," and "Let 'Em In" and "Silly Love Songs" each hit the top on one of the three major charts.

As for their albums, *Ram, Band on the Run*, and *Venus and Mars* all reached number one on all three U.K. charts, and *At the Speed of Sound* hit number one in *New Musical Express* only. *Wings Greatest*, however, almost topped the British album charts. In the United States, the album stalled in the low twenties.

THE TOP U.S. HITS

Singles (Ranked in Order from Highest to Lowest)

1. "Silly Love Songs" (Wings 1976)
2. "Coming Up (Live at Glasgow)" (Paul McCartney & Wings 1980)
3. "My Love" (Paul McCartney & Wings 1973)
4. "With a Little Luck" (Wings 1978)
5. "Uncle Albert/Admiral Halsey" (Paul & Linda McCartney 1971)
6. "Band on the Run" (Paul McCartney & Wings 1974)
7. "Live and Let Die" (Wings 1973)
8. "Goodnight Tonight" (Wings 1979)
9. "Let 'Em In" (Wings 1976)
10. "Listen to What the Man Said" (Wings 1975)

11. "Junior's Farm" (Paul McCartney & Wings 1974)
12. "Jet" (Paul McCartney & Wings 1974)
13. "Helen Wheels" (Paul McCartney & Wings 1973)
14. "Hi, Hi, Hi" (Wings 1972)
15. "Maybe I'm Amazed" (Wings 1977)
16. "Venus and Mars Rock Show" (Wings 1975)
17. "Getting Closer" (Wings 1979)
18. "Sally G." (Paul McCartney & Wings 1975)
19. "Give Ireland Back to the Irish" (Wings 1972)
20. "I've Had Enough" (Wings 1978)
21. "Arrow Through Me" (Wings 1979)
22. "Mary Had a Little Lamb" (Wings 1972)
23. "Girls' School" (Wings 1977)
24. "London Town" (Wings 1978)
25. "Letting Go" (Wings 1975)

Of the twenty-four singles Wings officially released (under any varia-
tion of "Wings", not including pseudonym releases), the group had
twenty-seven chartings, including B-sides. *Billboard* magazine for a
while ceased charting separate entries for B-sides and instead combined them with the A-side, a practice the magazine followed from
1969 through the late 1980s. In regard to Wings, their charting B-sides
had either been promoted separately from the A-sides (as was the case
in "Little Woman Love" and "Sally G."), or else radio programmers
themselves promoted the B-side, as was the case with "Girls' School"
and "Coming Up (Live at Glasgow)".

In terms of chart placement in the United States, all of Wings' singles placed on the top one hundred on all three charts, and each single
hit the top forty on at least one of the charts.

Albums (Ranked in Order from Highest to Lowest)

1. *Band on the Run*
2. *At the Speed of Sound*
3. *Venus and Mars*
4. *Red Rose Speedway*
5. *London Town*

6. *Wings over America*
7. *Ram*
8. *Back to the Egg*
9. *Wild Life*
10. *Wings Greatest*

Although *At the Speed of Sound* stayed at number one longer than any other Wings album, the group's biggest seller by far is *Band on the Run*. That album also holds the distinction of being the first album to hit the number one spot in *Billboard* on three separate occasions. It also hit number one in the three main U.S. trade publications on thirteen different occasions, the only time in history that has occurred.

HIT SINGLES BY LABEL

Label/Years	# Records Released	# Records Charted	# Records Gold
Apple singles (1971–1974)	10	12	4
Apple albums (1971–1974)	4	4	4
Capitol singles (1975–1978)	10	10	4
Capitol albums (1975–1978)	5	5	5
Columbia singles (1979–1980)	4	4	2
Columbia albums (1979–1980)	1	1	1

U.K. Charts

Charts included here are the British Market Research Bureau's top one hundred singles and LP charts featured in *Music & Video Week* magazine (M&VW/BMRB; the *Melody Maker* (MM) charts, and the *New Musical Express* (NME) charts, which feature only the top thirty singles and albums. The British charts rely solely on record sales for their listings and do not include radio airplay, unlike the American charts. These lists show where each released peaked on the various charts.

McCARTNEY & WINGS SINGLES: U.K. CHARTS

	M&VW/ BMRB	MM	NME
"Back Seat of My Car"	39	—	—
"Give Ireland Back to the Irish"	16	18	13
"Mary Had a Little Lamb"	9	6	6
"Hi, Hi, Hi"/"C Moon"	5	5	3
"My Love"	9	10	7
"Live and Let Die"	9	8	7
"Helen Wheels"	12	11	12
"Jet"	7	4	6
"Band on the Run"	3	2	3

	M&VW/ BMRB	MM	NME
"Junior's Farm"	16	16	16
"Listen to What the Man Said"	6	6	6
"Letting Go"	41	—	—
"Venus and Mars Rock Show"	—	—	—
"Silly Love Songs"	2	2	1
"Let 'Em In"	2	1	2
"Maybe I'm Amazed"	28	20	27
"Mull of Kintyre"/"Girls' School"	1	1	1
"With a Little Luck"	5	5	7
"I've Had Enough"	42	—	—
"London Town"	60	—	—
"Goodnight Tonight"	5	6	7
"Old Siam, Sir"	35	—	27
"Getting Closer"	60	—	—
"Coming Up" (studio version)	2	2	2

Miscellaneous Singles

"Walking in the Park with Eloise"	—	—	—
"Seaside Woman"	—	—	—
"Wonderful Christmastime"	6	13	16

McCARTNEY & WINGS ALBUMS: U.K. CHARTS

	BMRB	MM	NME
Ram	1	1	1
Wild Life	11	13	11
Red Rose Speedway	5	5	4

	BMRB	MM	NME
Band on the Run	1	1	1
Venus and Mars	1	1	1
At the Speed of Sound	2	2	1
Wings over America	8	8	8
London Town	4	4	4
Wings Greatest	5	5	3
Back to the Egg	6	7	4

Miscellaneous Albums

Concerts for the People of Kampuchea	39	29	—

THE TOP U.K. HITS (RANKED IN ORDER FROM HIGHEST TO LOWEST)

Singles

1. "Mull Of Kintyre"
2. "Let 'Em In"
3. "Silly Love Songs"
4. "Coming Up"
5. "Band on the Run"
6. "C Moon"/"Hi, Hi, Hi"
7. "With a Little Luck"
8. "Jet"
9. "Listen to What the Man Said"
10. "Goodnight Tonight"
11. "Mary Had a Little Lamb"
12. "Live and Let Die"
13. "My Love"
14. "Wonderful Christmastime"
15. "Helen Wheels"
16. "Junior's Farm"
17. "Give Ireland Back to the Irish"

18. "Maybe I'm Amazed"
19. "Old Siam, Sir"
20. "Back Seat of My Car"
21. "Letting Go"
22. "I've Had Enough"
23. "Getting Closer"
24. "London Town"
25. "Venus and Mars Rock Show"

Albums

1. *Band on the Run*
2. *Venus and Mars*
3. *Ram*
4. *At the Speed of Sound*
5. *London Town*
6. *Wings Greatest*
7. *Red Rose Speedway*
8. *Back to the Egg*
9. *Wings Over America*
10. *Wild Life*

U.S. versus U.K.

Interestingly, McCartney earned greater success in the States with Wings than in Britain, just as he had with the Beatles. The following is the listing of Wings' LPs and singles, with information about on which side of the Atlantic they achieved their greatest success. Each record's entry gives the record's chart peak and tells which publication gave each record its highest ranking. The bold numbers show the country and chart in which the release reached its peak position.

There are many notable differences. Of course, the "Mull of Kintyre"/"Girls' School" single—which sat at number one in Britain for nine weeks—failed in the United States, but "Girls' School" did chart there, though it was unable to break into the top thirty. McCartney's solo effort "Wonderful Christmastime" (which was really Wings in disguise but was nonetheless officially released as a Paul solo) peaked at number six in Britain while not even making it onto two of the top one hundred singles charts in America.

Conversely, although "Getting Closer" was a minor hit in the United States (in Wings terms) with a peak position of number twenty, in Britain it only managed to peak forty points lower, at number sixty. Also, "Venus and Mars Rock Show" almost made the top ten in the United States while not charting at all in Britain.

SINGLES (IN ORDER OF RELEASE)

	U.S.			U.K.		
				M&VW/		
	BB	CB	RW	BMRB	MM	NME
"Uncle Albert/Admiral Halsey"	1	1	1	*		
"Back Seat of My Car"	*			39	—	—
"Give Ireland Back to the Irish"	21	38	36	16	18	13
"Mary Had a Little Lamb"	28	48	38	9	6	6
"Hi, Hi, Hi"/"C Moon"	10	6	7	5	5	3
"My Love"	1	1	1	9	10	7
"Live and Let Die"	2	1	1	9	8	7
"Helen Wheels"	10	5	4	12	11	12
"Jet"	7	5	5	7	4	6
"Band on the Run"	1	1	1	3	2	3
"Junior's Farm"/"Sally G."	3	4	5	16	16	16
"Listen to What the Man Said"	1	1	1	6	6	6
"Letting Go"	39	41	62	41	—	—
"Venus and Mars Rock Show"	12	16	28	—	—	—
"Silly Love Songs"	1	1	1	2	2	1
"Let 'Em In"	3	1	4	2	1	2
"Maybe I'm Amazed"	10	10	26	28	20	27
"Mull of Kintyre"/"Girls' School"	33	31	33	1	1	1
"With a Little Luck"	1	1	1	5	5	7
"I've Had Enough"	25	28	30	42	—	—
"London Town"	39	42	48	60	—	—
"Goodnight Tonight"	5	4	7	5	6	7
"Getting Closer"	20	20	22	60	—	—
"Arrow Through Me"	28	36	27	**		
"Old Siam, Sir"	**			35	—	27
"Coming Up (Live at Glasgow)"	1	2	3	2	2	2

—denotes a release that did not chart

* single was not released in this country; "Back Seat of My Car" single was issued in the United Kingdom while "Uncle Albert/Admiral Halsey" was released in the United States

** single was not released in this country; "Old Siam, Sir" single was issued in the United Kingdom while in the United States, "Arrow Through Me" was released instead

*** single did not chart in either country

MISCELLANEOUS SINGLES

	U.S.			U.K.		
	BB	CB	RW	M&VW/ BMRB	MM	NME
"Walking in the Park with Eloise"	***					
"Seaside Woman"	59	58	92	—	—	—
"Wonderful Christmastime"	—	83	—	6	13	16

ALBUMS (IN ORDER OF RELEASE)

	U.S.			U.K.		
	BB	CB	RW	M&VW/ BMRB	MM	NME
Ram	2	2	2	1	1	1
Wild Life	10	6	9	11	13	11
Red Rose Speedway	1	1	1	5	5	5
Band on the Run	1	1	1	1	1	1
Venus and Mars	1	1	1	1	1	1
At the Speed of Sound	1	1	1	2	2	1
Wings Over America	1	2	3	8	8	8
London Town	2	2	2	4	4	4
Wings Greatest	29	21	23	5	5	3
Back to the Egg	8	7	7	6	7	4

MISCELLANEOUS ALBUMS

Concerts for the People of Kampuchea	36	31	31	39	29	—

—denotes a release that did not chart

*** single did not chart in either country

U.S. Record Awards

The following releases were recognized by the RIAA (Recording Industry Association of America) as best-sellers. Originally for albums, a gold record award meant there were $1 million in sales at manufacturer wholesale prices; for singles, one million copies sold resulted in a gold award. This practice was established in 1958.

By 1975, the awards criteria were changed in the album category. An album now needed minimum consumer sales of 500,000 copies, in addition to the manufacturer's $1 million sales to the retailers. In 1976, the RIAA established a platinum award. This was for album sales of one million copies with $2 million in wholesale revenues, or two million singles sold.

In December 1984, the RIAA introduced the multi-platinum award, which heralded such hits as Michael Jackson's *Thriller*, Fleetwood Mac's *Rumours*, and the *Grease* and *Saturday Night Fever* soundtracks. Later in 1989, the RIAA changed its rules once again, and reverted back to the rule of 500,000 singles sold for gold, one million for platinum.

In order to receive an official RIAA award, it is at the discretion of each individual record company to decide if its product is eligible for certification. Companies then apply and are audited by an independent accounting firm to corroborate the required sales. The certification is granted, and the record company purchases the official award plaques through the RIAA. Several of the Beatles and Wings records have not been submitted for multi-platinum certification, primarily

247

because EMI/Capitol has not applied. This is unfortunate for Wings because the band's records continue to sell, as is evident in the twenty-fifth anniversary release of *Band on the Run*, which debuted at number one on *Billboard*'s Pop Catalog charts.

WINGS' U.S. MILLION SELLERS

Singles

"Uncle Albert/Admiral Halsey"
"My Love"
"Live and Let Die"
"Band on the Run"
"Listen to What the Man Said"
"Silly Love Songs"
"Let 'Em In"
"Goodnight Tonight"
"Coming Up (Live at Glasgow)"

Albums

Gold LPs (Long-Play Albums that Sold More than 500,000 Copies in the United States):

Ram
Wild Life
Red Rose Speedway
Band on the Run
Venus and Mars
At the Speed of Sound
Wings over America
London Town
Wings Greatest
Back to the Egg
Wingspan

Platinum LPs (Long-Play Albums that Sold More than One Million Copies in the United States):

Ram
Band on the Run

Venus and Mars
At the Speed of Sound
Wings over America
London Town
Wings Greatest
Back to the Egg
Wingspan

Double Platinum LPs (At Least Two Million Copies Sold in the United States):
Band on the Run
Wingspan

Triple Platinum LP (At Least Three Million Copies Sold in the United States):
Band on the Run

Band on the Run reportedly sold more than six million copies in the United States; *Venus and Mars* and *Wings Greatest* more than two million each, and the three-disc set *Wings over America* sold four million units. *Red Rose Speedway*, which reportedly sold more than one million copies, has yet to be certified platinum. Only *Band on the Run* and the *Wingspan* compilation have been recognized as multi-platinum by the RIAA. Also, it has been said that "With a Little Luck" sold more than one million copies but has yet to be certified a gold single.

Unreleased Songs

Wings recorded more than one hundred songs that were never released to the public. Most of these recordings are locked up in a vault, with only Paul McCartney himself not allowing the legitimate release of the songs. Some of them, however, did find their way into collectors' hands in the form of bootlegged records and CDs. Among the original recordings (not counting extended or live versions of previously recorded material by McCartney and/or Wings) legally unavailable as McCartney & Wings songs are:

"1882," 1972
"After You've Gone," 1977
"All of You," 1974
"Baby Face," 1974
"Baby, You Know It's True," 1974
"Best Friend," 1972 (a.k.a. "Why Do You Treat Me so Bad?")
"Blackpool," 1974
"Boil Crisis," 1977
"Breakfast Blues," 1971 (a.k.a. "Great Cock and Seagull Race")
"Cage," 1978 (from the *Back to the Egg* sessions)
"The Castle of the King of the Birds," 1978
"Complain(t) to the Queen," 1972
"Cornish Water," 1978
"Crawl of the Wild," 1975

"Did We Meet Somewhere Before," 1978 (from the *Back to the Egg* sessions)

"Dr. Pepper," 1974

"Don't You Wanna Dance?" 1977

"Dress Me Up as a Robber," 1977; remade for Paul's *Tug of War* LP

"El Toro Passing," 1977

"Fairy Tale," 1977

"Find a Way Somehow," 1977–78

"Flying Horses," 1978

"Giddy," 1977

"Gotta Sing, Gotta Dance," 1973 (from the *James Paul McCartney* special)

"Great Cock and Seagull Race," 1971 (a.k.a. "Rooster" and "Breakfast Blues")

"Heart that You Broke," 1974 (a country and western ballad from the Nashville sessions)

"Hello," 1977

"Henry's Blues," 1972

"Hey Diddle," from the 1974 Nashville sessions and 1971 *Ram* sessions

"I Can't Write Another Song," 1977

"I'm Gonna Love You Too," 1974

"In My Dreams," 1974

"Jazz Street," 1972

"Karate Chaos," 1975 (from the *Venus and Mars* sessions)

"Let's Love," from the 1974 Nashville sessions

"A Love for You," from the *Ram* sessions and the 1978 *Back to the Egg* sessions

"Love Is Your Road," 1974

"Loving You," 1974

"Luxi," 1973

"Maisie," 1978 (version released on Laurence Juber's LP *Standard Time*)

"Mother's Pride," 1974

"Night Out," 1972 and 1978 *Back to the Egg* sessions

"No No, Not Norfolk," 1977

"No Values," 1979; later remade for a solo Paul album

"Now Hear this Song of Mine," 1971

"Nutwood Scene," 1978

"One Hand Clapping," 1974 Nashville sessions

"One Woman," 1977

"Oobu Joobu," late 1973 or early 1974; later used as theme to Paul's 1995 radio show

"Partners in Crime," 1974

"The Pound is Sinking," 1977; remade for Paul's *Tug of War* LP

"Praying Mantis Hard," 1977

"Proud Mum," from the 1974 Nashville sessions

"Reverse," 1975

"Rode All Night," from the *Ram* sessions

"Running 'Round the Room," 1977

"Ranachan Rock," 1978

"Rupert Song #1," 1978

"Rupert Song #2," 1978

"San Francisco Way," 1977

"Sea," 1974

"Sea Dance," 1975 (from the *Venus and Mars* sessions)

"Sea Melody," 1978

"She Got It Good," 1974

"Sitting at the Piano," 1974

"Standing Very Still," 1977

"Storm," 1978

"Suffragette," 1973; possibly an alternate name for "Jet," but was said to be about an ex-groupie

"Suicide," 1974

"Sunshine in Your Hair," 1974

"Sunshine, Sometime," 1971 (from the *Ram* sessions)

"Super Big Heatwave," 1977

"Sweet Little Bird," 1974

"Thank You Darling," 1972

"Tippi Tippi Toes," 1978

"Too Bad about Sorrows," from the 1978 TV show *The South Bank Show*

"Tragedy," 1972

"Twelve of the Clock," 1977

"Upon a Hill," 1974
"Waiting for the Sun to Shine," 1974
"Walking in the Meadow," 1978
"Waterspout," 1978 (from the *London Town* sessions)
"We're Gonna Move," 1974
"When I Was in Paris," 1975
"When the Wind Is Blowing," 1978
"Women Kind," 1974
"Yea Yea," 1975

Sources

Advertisements: Courtesy of the McMarr collection
Photographs: Courtesy of PJ! Archives
Sheet Music: Courtesy of Marald/Geran
Records and Collectibles: Courtesy of the GCMII collection; LJM ltd.

NOTE: Neither the author nor the publishers of this book condone the manufacturing, distribution, or sale of unauthorized ("bootlegged") recordings. The bootlegging of material belonging to any group or individual is strictly illegal. The bootlegs featured in this book are included solely for the purpose of historical accuracy.

Bibliography

Bailey, Jerry. "Paul & Linda Try the Gentle Life." *The Tennessean*, 18 July 1974, p. 67.

Bailey, Jerry, and Eve Zibart. "McCartney in Nashville for 3 Rs." *The Tennessean*, 7 June 1974, p. 1.

Blake, John. *All You Needed Was Love: The Beatles after the Beatles*. New York: Perigee Books, G. P. Putnam's Sons, 1981.

Bonici, Ray. "Paul McCartney Wings It Alone." *Music Express* 36, April/ May 1982.

Brown, Geoff. "Wings Fly!" *Melody Maker*, 30 November 1974.

Brown, Mick. "Wings in London." *Rolling Stone*, 1979.

Brown, Peter, and Steven Gaines. *The Love You Make: An Insider's Story of the Beatles*. New York: McGraw-Hill, 1983.

Castleman, Harry, and Walter J. Podrazik. *All Together Now*. New York: Ballantine Books, 1975.

Cocks, Jay. "McCartney Comes Back." *Time* 107 no. 23 (31 May 1976), pp. 40–44.

Darnell, Catherine. "Meeting with Paul All Too Brief." *The Tennessean*, 10 May 1997, p. 1D.

DeGraff, Kenneth. Untitled Internet interview regarding "Sally G." song, at edge.net/~tmcm/intervie.html (accessed October 1998).

Du Noyer, Paul, ed. *The Paul McCartney World Tour* Program. London: Emap Metro, 1990.

Elson, Howard. *McCartney: Songwriter*. London: Comet Books, 1986.

Flippo, Chet. *Yesterday: The Unauthorized Biography of Paul McCartney*. New York: Doubleday, 1988.

Fong-Torres, Ben. "Wings Tour Ends Up, Up and Away." *Rolling Stone*, 29 July 1976, pp. 9, 16.

Fricke, David. "One for the Road." *Rolling Stone*, 8 February 1990, p. 42ff.

Friede, Goldie, Robin Titone, and Sue Weiner. *The Beatles A to Z*. New York: Methuen, 1980.

Friedman, Roger. "The Beatle Goes On." *Fame* 3, no. 2 (March 1990), pp. 76–87.

Frost, Deborah. "The Record Interview: Paul McCartney." *Record* 3, no. 11 (September 1984), p. 24ff.

Gambaccini, Paul. "British Rockers Unite in Concerts for Kampuchea." *Rolling Stone*, 21 February 1980, pp. 17–18.

———. "A Conversation with Paul McCartney." *Rolling Stone*, 12 July 1979, p. 39ff.

———. "Paul McCartney's One Man Band." *Rolling Stone*, 26 June 1980, pp. 11, 20.

———. *Paul McCartney: In His Own Words*. New York and London: Quick Fox, 1976.

Garbarini, Vic. "Paul McCartney: Lifting the Veil on the Beatles." *Musician*, n.d.

Gelly, David. *The Facts about a Pop Group, Featuring Wings*. London: G. Whizzard Andre Deutsch, 1976.

Giuliano, Geoffrey. *Blackbird: The Life and Times of Paul McCartney*. New York: Dutton, 1991.

Grove, Martin A. *Paul McCartney: Beatle with Wings!* New York: Manor Books, 1978.

Gunderson, Edna. "Wings Arose to Span a Time after the Beatles." *USA Today*, 11 May 2001, p. 6E.

Hamilton, Alan. *Paul McCartney*. London: Hamish Hamilton, 1983.

Hance, Bill. "McCartney Draws Squeals at Opryland." *The Nashville Banner*, 17 June 1974, p. 17.

Harris, Bruce. "In Defense of Paul McCartney." *Words & Music*, June 1972, pp. 16–22.

Harrop, David. "A Fab Fortune." *People* 20, no. 20 (14 November 1983), pp. 142–144.

Harry, Bill. *The McCartney File*. London: Virgin Books, 1986.

Henke, James. "Can Paul McCartney Get Back?" *Rolling Stone*, 15 June 1989, p. 40ff.

Hipgnosis. *Hands across the Water: Wings Tour USA*. London: Paper Tiger, 1978.

Horide, Rosie. "London Town." *The Beatles Monthly Book* 23 (March 1978), pp. iii–v.

Hyen, Dalma. "The Alarmingly Normal McCartneys." *McCall's*, August 1984, pp. 94–95, 150ff.

"Interview Exclusive: McCartney." *Extra* no. 20 (September 1972).

Jasper, Tony. *Paul McCartney and Wings*. Secaucus, N.J.: Chartwell Books, 1977.

Jensen, James. "Laurence Juber." *Acoustic Music Resource*, at www.acousticmusicresource.com/interviews/juber.html (accessed January 2001).

Lewisohn, Mark. "The Recording of *Band on the Run*." *Band on the Run: 25th Anniversary Edition CD*, Capitol Records (1999), 7243-4-99176-2.

Loder, Kurt. "The Rolling Stone Interview: Paul McCartney." *Rolling Stone*, 11 September 1986, p. 46ff.

Martin, Odile. "Meeting Paul and Linda." *The Beatles Monthly Book*, no. 66, October 1981, p. xv.

McCartney, Paul. *Paul McCartney: Composer/Artist*. London: Pavilion Books, 1981.

"McCartneys Wing Way Back Home." *The Nashville Banner*, 18 July 1974, p. 21.

Mendelsohn, John. *Paul McCartney: A Biography in Words and Pictures*. New York: Sire Chappell, 1977.

Mintz, Elliot. "The Private Life of Paul and Linda McCartney." *Us*, 21 March 1978, pp. 48–51.

O'Donnell, Red. "Beatles' Paul McCartney 'Winging' His Way Here." *The Nashville Banner*, 23 May 1974, p. 1.

Okin, Earl. "A Tribute to Linda McCartney." First published as an open letter to the Song Talk mailing list, at www.halsguide.com/l_mccartney.html (accessed February 2000).

Ono, Yoko. "Linda McCartney Remembered." *Rolling Stone*, 11 June 1998, p. 31.

Orth, Maureen. "Paul Soars." *Newsweek*, 17 May 1976, p. 100.

Pascall, Jeremy. *Paul McCartney & Wings*. Secaucus, N.J.: Chartwell Books, 1977.

"Paul McCartney." *Phonograph Record*. WHCN-FM radio, Connecticut, June 1973.

"Paul McCartney Forms a Band." *Rolling Stone*, 2 September 1971, p. 13.

"Paul McCartney Releases Wide Prairie CD of Linda's Music." 30 October 1998, CalicoSkies website, at members.tripod.com/~calico_skies/ (accessed February 2000).

Read, Mike. Interview with Paul McCartney. Radio One (U.K.), October 1987.

Salewicz, Chris. *McCartney*. New York: St. Martin's Press, 1986.

Sharp, Ken. "The Making of John Lennon & Yoko Ono's *Double Fantasy*," *Goldmine*, 23 March 2001, pp. 14–19.

Stein, Kathleen. "Paul McCartney: Seven Trials Inside 'Band on the Run.'" *Raves*, April 1974, pp. 62–65.

Swingley, Pat. "Linda McCartney: The Woman at Paul's Side." *The Tennessean*, 21 July 1974, p. 1-E.

"Things We Said Today." *Strawberry Fields Forever* (fanzine), ed. Joe Pope, summer 1976.

Tremlett, George. *The Paul McCartney Story*. London: Future, 1975.

Turner, Shelley. "Wings First Flight." *Wings Over Europe* tour program. MPL, 1972.

Vee Gyde, T. "Wings Clippings." *Club Sandwich* 13 (February/March 1979), p. 2.

Wingspan: The Best of Paul McCartney and Wings, VH1, televised May 2001.

Voger, Mark. "Winging It: Drummer Recalls ex-Beatle's 'Other Band.'" *Asbury Park Press, Home News Tribune*. Page X website, at www.injersey.com/pagex/story (accessed December 2001).

Walker, Irene. "McCartney Visit Adds to Contest." *The Tennessean*, 17 June 1974, p. 1.

Welch, Chris. *Paul McCartney: The Definitive Biography*. London: Proteus Books, 1984.

White, Timothy. "A Farewell to the First Solo Era." *Musician*, February 1988, p. 112ff.

———. "Paul McCartney on His Not-So-Silly Love Songs." *Billboard*, 17 March 2001.

Woffinnden, Bob. *The Beatles Apart*. New York and London: Proteus Books, 1981.

Wright, Jeb. "Denny Seiwell of Wings." *Classic Rock Revisited*, May 2001, at www.classicrockrevisited.com/denny_seiwell_of_wings.htm (accessed November 2002).

Index